Cherishing Our Daughters

Also by Evelyn Bassoff, Ph.D.

Mothers and Daughters: Loving and Letting Go

Mothering Ourselves: Help and Healing for Adult Daughters

Between Mothers and Sons: The Making of Loving and Vital Men

Cherishing Our Daughters

How Parents Can Raise Girls to Become Strong and Loving Women

Evelyn Bassoff, Ph.D.

A DUTTON BOOK

DUTTON
Published by the Penguin Group
Penguin Putnam Inc., 375 Hudson Street, New York, New York 10014, U.S.A.
Penguin Books Ltd, 27 Wrights Lane, London W8 5TZ, England
Penguin Books Australia Ltd, Ringwood, Victoria, Australia
Penguin Books Canada Ltd, 10 Alcorn Avenue, Toronto, Ontario, Canada M4V 3B2
Penguin Books (N.Z.) Ltd, 182–190 Wairau Road, Auckland 10, New Zealand

Penguin Books Ltd, Registered Offices:
Harmondsworth, Middlesex, England

First published by Dutton, an imprint of Dutton Signet,
a member of Penguin Putnam Inc.

First Printing, January, 1998
1   3   5   7   9   10   8   6   4   2

Excerpt from Arthur Colman and Libby Colman, *The Father: Mythology and Changing Roles*, © 1988 by Arthur Colman and Libby Colman, published by Chiron Publications. Reprinted by permission of the publisher.
Poem "That I not be a restless ghost" from *Blackberry Winter* by Margaret Mead. © Margaret Mead, 1972. Reprinted by permission of William Morrow & Co., Inc.

 REGISTERED TRADEMARK—MARCA REGISTRADA

LIBRARY OF CONGRESS CATALOGING-IN-PUBLICATION DATA:

Bassoff, Evelyn.
Cherishing our daughters: how to raise a healthy, confident
daughter / by Evelyn Bassoff.
p.   cm.
Includes bibliographical references and index.
ISBN 0-525-94014-6
1. Daughters.   2.Child rearing.   3. Parent and child.   I. Title.
HQ777.B27   1998
306.874—dc21   97-25115
CIP

Printed in the United States of America
Set in Janson
Designed by Jesse Cohen

This book is printed on acid-free paper. ∞

For
Alexia Dorszynski

*It is not the perfect but the imperfect
that is in need of our love.*
—OSCAR WILDE

Contents

᪥

Part Four: Roots and Wings

Part Five: A Daughter's Gifts

Acknowledgments

Many wonderful people helped shape *Cherishing Our Daughters*. For their insights and wisdom, I wish to thank the members of the parents education group: Janice Frazier, Tom Hosmer, Kathy Minter, Charles Minter, and Susan Parks. For their inspiration, I owe much to Louise DeSalvo and Rabbi Deborah Bronstein. For their expert advice, I am indebted to Helen Driver Flanders, Lyn Gullette, Susan Rosewell-Jackson, Merete Leonhardt-Lupa, Ivan Miller, Julie Phillips, Wayne Phillips, Reesa Porter, Jed Shapiro, Kenneth Suslak, Katherine Walker, and Donald Williams.

I would also like to express my gratitude to Jessica Baraka, Geraldine Cassens, Harriet Edelstein, Ben Eilbott, Hannah Eilbott, Dafna Gozany, Art Kaufman, Alice Levine, Judah Levine, Hillary Keyes, Sara Phillips, Mimi Schrader, Pessia Shuker, Emily Suslak, Rich Wildau, and Susan Wildau for enlarging my understanding of relationships between parents and children. And, although I cannot acknowledge my clients by name, I hope they know how very grateful I am for all they teach me. Indeed, their stories are represented throughout this book. In order not to violate my clients' confidentiality, I have disguised their identities by changing the details of their situations.

Heartfelt appreciation goes to my primary editor, Alexia Dorszynski, whose good sense and extraordinary sensibility I have come to depend on during our long professional relationship; to my writing consultant, Ellen Kleiner, who is a master of language and a paragon of generosity; and to my publishers at Dutton, Elaine Koster and Arnold Dolin, whose steady support and warm encouragement have meant so much to me. In addition, I would like to thank senior editor Deb Brody and publicist Tracey Guest for being always helpful and responsive. I would also like to thank Amy Levine for her excellent work as research assistant.

My writing—indeed, everything I do that is worthwhile—is nurtured by those who love me unconditionally. Thank you Bruce, Leah, Jonathan, and Mom for this priceless gift.

PROLOGUE

Cherishing Our Daughters

This book is for parents interested in fostering their daughters' vitality, self-respect, and humanity. Although grounded in down-to-earth stories that mothers, fathers, and daughters have shared with me, it was inspired by a fairy tale.

Briar Rose (in the United States we know her as Sleeping Beauty) is the cherished firstborn of a king and a queen who have longed for many years to become parents. To celebrate their daughter's birth, the royal couple arrange a splendid feast and invite twelve fairies from the kingdom to come and bestow upon the child special gifts that will shape her life. Each of the fairies is kind and generous to the infant princess, and, for this, the king and queen could not be more pleased. As the twelfth fairy is about to make her presentation, however, the thirteenth fairy of the kingdom—enraged at having been left out—disrupts the festivities. Rather than bearing a life-affirming gift, she casts a death-dealing curse: on the princess's fifteenth birthday, she shall prick her finger on the distaff of a spinning wheel and die. No one can undo the vengeful fairy's cruel spell. But the twelfth fairy, who is both wise and clever, is able to mitigate it with her prophecy; as a result, the death sentence at age fifteen becomes a hundred-year sleep that enables Briar Rose's metamorphosis into womanhood.

Just as the thirteenth fairy tries to curtail the life of young Briar Rose, destructive forces in our own "kingdom"—random acts of violence, sexism, bigotry, alcohol and drugs, pressures to be sexual, obsessions with appearance, anti-intellectualism, expectations of immediate gratification, excessive materialism, perfectionism—threaten our daughters' optimal development. As I aim to show, however, we parents can mitigate these dangers and make possible our daughters' passage into healthy womanhood. In other words, we parents can become the wise and clever twelfth fairy.

Jacob and Wilhelm Grimm, who recorded "Briar Rose" two centuries ago, named only some of the gifts that the good fairies give to the beloved child—beauty, virtue, and cleverness—allowing future generations to imagine the others, which I have taken the liberty to do. In conceiving *Cherishing Our Daughters*, I grappled with the questions "What can we give our daughters to help them live successfully and happily in today's world?" and "What do we need to do to become the kind of parents we want our daughters to have—the kind of parents *we* may have longed for?"

Each of the twelve chapters in this book describes a gift. The first ten discuss spiritual gifts we might give our daughters to help them become vital and loving women: the gifts of motherly devotion, fatherly care, loving and letting in, of protectiveness, limits and boundaries, respect, wholeness, and courage; and of roots and wings.

Because parenting our daughter, Leah, for twenty-five years has profoundly changed my husband and me, the last two chapters refer to the spiritual gifts we have received from her as a result of being part of her growth process. Our hunch in sharing these personal experiences is that they express feelings and emotions common to other mothers and fathers. Articulating them, I must say, has reinforced for us the wonder of raising a daughter, which we hope will inspire readers to search their souls to discover what *they* have received from *their* daughters.

In the United States, child rearing and "family values" have become emotionally charged issues—grist for the politicians' mill. I have tried to approach the subject of raising daughters without a political agenda or a particular theoretical bent. I do, however, bring personal biases to this work. One is my belief that we ought to take our responsibilities as parents very, very seriously; it seems to me that especially during the first few years of child rearing, we have an awesome power in facilitating our daughters' potential. Another belief is that we ought not to expect to become "perfect" parents. We will be far better off if we accept and forgive our blunders—which are inevitable—and also try, whenever possible, to learn from them. And by allowing ourselves to be "only human," we teach our daughters to do the same, which in itself is a gift of love.

PART ONE

BEING THERE

I promise you love. Time will not take away that.
—ANNE SEXTON

THE FIRST GIFT:

Mother's Devotion

Amother muses: "She blinks her newborn eyes open and looks at you. With that look you know, you just know, . . . as long as you live, you will never *not* care what happens to this person."[1]

Given half a chance, mothers make an immense contribution to their daughters. They do this by being devoted to them. But maternal devotion is not about the "big things" or about the grand gestures. It simply means "being there"—hour after hour, day by day, year to year—and performing countless *small* acts of love: getting up in the middle of the night to comfort the wailing babe, patiently packing the squirming toddler into her snowsuit, slipping a treat into the first grader's lunch box, schlepping the sixth grader and all her teammates to soccer practice, assuring the teenager with purple hair and pimples that she is lovely inside, stroking the "wings" of the young graduate as she begins to make her way in the world.

Viewed separately, a mother's small acts of devotion may not seem impressive, but, cumulatively, they possess a potent power. The daughter who has been consistently cared for—comforted, encouraged, affirmed—by her mother knows that she is deserving and lovable, and with this knowledge she is forever empowered.

The vast majority of mothers in the world do not need to be taught how to express their maternal devotion; as long as they are provided with some support and adequate living conditions, it comes naturally to them. However, when mothers are overextended and overloaded—as is the case for so many married and single women today—they are robbed of the energy necessary for mother work and mother care. From the letters readers of *Parents* magazine send me for the monthly column I write and from conversations with the new mothers I meet in everyday life, I am consistently reminded that "doing it all" takes an enormous toll; women with babies and young children are a very, very tired lot.

By choice or by circumstance, fewer women than ever before have the "luxury" of being full-time mothers during their children's early years. New mothers are expected (and expect themselves) to hold down a nine-to-five job (or work the night shift) or go to school or start a business or climb the corporate ladder. True, some women who are endowed with extraordinarily high levels of energy and have *plenty* of physical and emotional support successfully combine motherhood and high-powered careers or ambitious creative activities. Most women, however, are not so fortunate, and as a result of carrying the lion's share of child-care and household responsibilities as well as working outside the home, they feel irritable, exhausted, and depressed much of the time. A recent survey reveals that working mothers with young children are nearly three times more likely to suffer work-related injuries than other women.[2] More troubling to many new mothers than their own travails are the guilty feelings that their children are being shortchanged. Of course, many of these problems could be partially solved if fathers shared equally in the caregiving of infants and the very young, but so far that is not the reality. As humor columnist Dave Barry quips, "We modern, sensitive husbands realize that it's very unfair to place the entire child-care burden on our wives, so many of us are starting to assume maybe three percent of it."[3]

The Devaluation of Mothers

Every culture, every generation, has recognized the essential, life-giving, life-affirming role of the mother and has made accommodations for mothers and young children to be together in a calm way—every culture and generation, that is, except our own. Over the last two decades, we North Americans have significantly downplayed the importance of motherhood. In a revolutionary break from past conventions, we have managed to convince parents that it is normal for mothers to return to full-time employment six weeks after giving birth and to leave their infants in the care of a hired helper. The implications of this new way of thinking are clear: young children—even little babies—don't need mother care, at least during "business hours," and women should take in stride the fact that they will be separated from their children all day. Also implied is the notion that regular separations between mothers and babies are actually growth-promoting for both of them. Recently, I had a discussion with an Israeli friend, a physicist, who told me that she had returned full-time to the science laboratory shortly before her daughter (a particularly shy little girl) turned three and that both she and the child wished she had been able to stay home a year or two longer. "In the United States," I explained, "mothers are often parted from their children when they are six weeks old, not three years old," to which my friend gasped, "*Oy*, that can't be!"

Much has been made of the fact that a sizable percentage of stay-at-home new mothers become depressed and, for this reason, ought to find outside employment. Could it be, however, that sleep deprivation along with not having enough physical help and emotional sustenance during the early months and years of child raising are at the root of the depression, and that rest, respites, and the company of supportive adults, rather than more work, are the treatments of choice?

And could it also be that rather than the occupation of full-time mother producing feelings of worthlessness and depression, the experience of being devalued in this role is to blame? Nowadays, we tend to believe that the traditional masculine qualities of ambition, leadership, and achievement are far more valuable than the attributes associated with femininity, such as devotion, nurturing, and caregiving, and that significant contributions are made in the workplace, not in the home.[4] Jungian author Robert A. Johnson goes so far as to say that in our society femininity is the "excluded element"[5]; much like the thirteenth fairy in the tale "Briar Rose," it is the uninvited guest in our productivity-driven lives. Sociologist Jessie Bernard cites an unpublished study in her book *The Future of Motherhood* in which various caregiving roles are rated according to their status. Foster mothers, child-care attendants, nursemaids, and nursery school teachers did not fare as well as undertakers, barbers, or dog trainers and received the same ratings as rest room and parking lot attendants. Bernard concluded that "though we give lip service to the idea that motherhood is worthy, hardly anyone really believes it."[6]

A friend of mine told me the following story: One of her close colleagues, a bright and energetic corporate lawyer, brought her feverish four-year-old daughter, who was too sick to be left at day care, to work with her. The child quietly suffered through a long meeting and, as people were leaving the conference room, asked her mother in a little voice, "Mommy, when we get home, will you tuck me into bed and read me a story?" "No, honey, I won't be able to do that," the mother replied. "I've hired a sitter for you. I have something *important* to do tonight." My friend assures me that her colleague is not an uncaring person; she loves her daughter and wants the best for her. However, as is true for increasing numbers of women, she has been trained to believe that the daily, routine acts of mother care are insignificant and that anyone can provide this type of nurturing as well as (or perhaps better than) she can.

It is not only working mothers who downplay the importance of mother work. In her memoir, *The Motherline*, writer and psychotherapist Naomi Lowinsky, describing her early months as a mother, addresses the feelings of devaluation that countless other new stay-at-home mothers undoubtedly experience: "I felt a deep shame in being 'just' a housewife and mother. I longed for an illustrious identity, a profession I could name, a way to make a contribution, to be seen and appreciated for work well done. Instead, I changed diapers."[7] Certainly, taking care of a baby or young child can be tedious. And during a child's early years it is normal for a mother to feel tired, bored, and frustrated at times. However, feeling *ashamed* of being "just" a mother is surely a unique phenomenon, one that most other women around the world are spared and that our foremothers never experienced. Something is terribly awry in our society when bright and loving women with babies and very young children—Lowinsky's voice is not an isolated one— see little value in mother care. And something is fundamentally wrong when women associate motherhood only with tedium, fatigue, and self-sacrifice, because being a mother is also stirring, amazing, and joyful. The following excerpt is from Marilyn French's novel *The Women's Room*:

> She had seen their birth and the birth of her love for them as miraculous, but it was just as miraculous when they first smiled, sat up, first babbled a sound that resembled, of course, mama. The tedious days were filled with miracles. When a baby first looks at you; when it gets excited at seeing a ray of light and like a dog pawing a gleam, tries to capture it in [its] hand; or when it laughs that deep unconscious gurgle; or when it cries and you pick it up

and it clings sobbing to you, saved from the terrible shadow moving across the room, or a loud clang in the street, or perhaps, already, a bad dream: then you are—happy is not the precise word—filled.[8]

Not long ago, mother care was a woman's only source of prestige and power, her only permissible role of influence. Mother was, as Virginia Woolf wrote, "the angel of the house." In one way, the present devaluation of mother care constitutes a backlash to this past idealization of motherhood, with its narrow view that a woman can be fulfilled *only* by becoming a mother and its insistence that she must take full responsibility for all her children's problems and have no vital interests outside of family life. In another way, the devaluation of mother care springs from our country's ethic of rugged individualism, which emphasizes self-sufficiency over intimate relationships. And in still another way it is related to the absence of a national consciousness regarding the protection and advocacy of children; when a society undervalues its children as ours does, it also undervalues mothers.

Although our efforts to liberate today's mothers from the excessive constraints traditionally placed on mothers of previous decades are justified, we are also in danger of throwing out the baby with the bathwater. Indeed, we seem to have gone from one extreme to another, from investing motherhood with impossible powers to divesting it of all power, from expecting that every normal woman make mothering the central role in her life to suggesting that no normal woman would want to do this, even for a few months, and from overmothering our children to undermothering them. It would be a grave mistake to deny or minimize the effects of this change on society. Undermothered children suffer—there are no exceptions.

When I counsel young married women who plan to have children, I am struck by the fact that many of them underestimate how much children need in the way of consistent and loving care, especially during the first months and years of life. They imagine that having a baby will not disrupt their lives in any significant sense, that they will not be called on to make sacrifices, and that they will easily balance work and motherhood. These misapprehensions worry me. Will these young women think there is something wrong with them if they cannot do it all? Or will they resent their babies once they realize that new motherhood requires extraordinary commitment and selflessness?

It is not only new mothers who may fail to see how much their children need them. Recently, the mother of a troubled teen shared with me her perception that fate, luck, genetics, MTV, birth order, and the astrological sign under which her daughter was born affected the girl more than she ever could. Feeling ineffectual, she had become disengaged as a parent and no longer set or enforced rules for her daughter. As a result, her daughter was acting out and out of control. I have also known women who, seeing themselves as irrelevant, are ready to abandon their daughters altogether. A few months ago, I was called to the hospital bedside of a woman who had attempted suicide. When I asked if she had considered how her death would have affected her fourteen-year-old daughter, she sighed, "Oh, there'd have been tears but it wouldn't have broken her. She's getting ready to leave the nest and really doesn't have use for me anymore." How misguided this poor woman was! I have never known a young woman not to be profoundly affected by early mother loss.

Rediscovering the Worth of Maternal Devotion

The truth of the matter is that being a mother is the most important and most demanding of all vocations. At stake is the life and well-being of another human being. If children are to thrive, mothers must once again realize the importance *and the joy* of being present in their lives, just as the bright, capable women of past generations did. This does not mean that all women give up their personal ambitions and creative aspirations, although these might be realized *before* having children or put off until *after* the children need less in the way of daily care. It does not mean that *all* women forgo outside employment, although, for at least the first year after having a baby, part-time, rather than full-time, employment ought to be considered. It *does*, however, mean that women do everything—*everything*—in their power to ensure that the basic needs of their children are being met; these needs—for consistent, responsible, affectionate, and sensitive care—are inherent, unalterable, and universal. If, for reasons beyond her control, a mother cannot be the primary caregiver and the father is also not available, the parents need to find a stable, warm person (not a series of caregivers who come and go) to whom the child can grow attached. Women always seem to do well trusting their protective instincts, and in today's world, this may mean vigorously standing up to and challenging those, who devalue the role of the mother and disregard the child's needs, whether they are employers, policy makers, politicians, friends, family members, or the court of public opinion.

Allow me a personal story—one in which I take pride. My first job in psychology was as a part-time counselor in an employee-assistance program. On one of my days off, when I was at home with my seven-year-old daughter, Leah, the director of the counseling agency telephoned me, told me that he was understaffed, and demanded that I come to the office right away to see a walk-in client who was in crisis. I refused, explaining that this was my family time and I'd promised my daughter we'd bake cookies together. "Why don't *you* tend to the client in need?" I boldly asked. The next day, when I went to work, I discovered that the director had put a letter in my file, accusing me of insubordination and unethical behavior. Although I was concerned that the letter would jeopardize my career, I was not sorry about my priorities. Years later when this man became a father—and an enthusiastic, loving one at that—he apologized to me for writing the letter: "Back then I couldn't imagine why you were making such a big deal about staying home with your kid to bake cookies. I understand now," he told me. Many policy makers and employers, perhaps because they are childless or disengaged from their own families, fail to achieve such understanding, which can lead to untold miseries for parents, children, and society itself.

Filling the Vessel

In order for mothers to give children the gift of mother care in a spirit of joy and generosity, they need three important things. The first is ample time to be with them, especially during their early months and years. The eminent British psychiatrist D. W. Winnicott once said that "mothering grows naturally out of being a mother."[9] It is the minute-by-minute, hour-by-hour, day-by-day intimacy that allows mothers to become attuned to their children—to develop a sixth sense that allows them to anticipate their needs. "What is it that wakes me seconds before you begin to wimper?" poet and mother Beverly Slapin asks. "It must be the umbilical cord in our minds."[10] Just as babies are meant to be physically close to their mothers and will cry, smile, cling, nurse, and fret to ensure this proximity, mothers are meant to be physically close to their babies. No one can say for certain how a mother's absence from her child affects the mother. We would be unwise to believe that she will suffer no losses, however. One of my clients shared this anecdote:

> Six weeks after Sheila was born, I was back, full-swing, at my corporate job. A wonderful, warm young woman took care of my child. I don't think that Sheila was hurt by my absence. I was the one who missed out by being away from her so much. The notations in her baby book—the first time she laughed out loud, the

summer day she was brave enough to stick her nose under water and blow bubbles, the expression on her face when she tasted frozen yogurt for the first time—are not in my handwriting; they were recorded by her nanny.

Other mothers who spend too little time with their infants may fail to develop strong intimate bonds. In the seventies, some well-respected researchers and theorists speculated that the attachment (or "bonding") between mother and child takes place in the first hours and days, called a "critical period," after the baby's birth. More current research demonstrates that attachment is a gradual process. As mother and child learn to read each other's signals, they become accustomed and attuned to each other.[11] With all her wondrous creations, Mother Nature does not like to be rushed. It was the ancient Greek philosopher Epictetus who wrote "No thing great is created suddenly, any more than a bunch of grapes or a fig. If you tell me that you desire a fig, I answer you that there must be time. Let it first blossom, then bear fruit, then ripen."

The second requirement for mothers is to have some time *away* from her children. It is no secret that mothers without relief are often so worn out by round-the-clock child care that they become depressed, irritable, or hostile. In my work with these women, I often refer to a depleted vessel, one that has nothing to give, cannot overflow with love and care, and cannot dispense riches. In the Victorian era, it was customary for the lady of the house to retire to her room for one hour every afternoon, where she could rest undisturbed. Contemporary mothers also need an hour each day to replenish the soul. And they need friends and family to spell them from the relentless demands of their children.

"I know that a twenty-five-year-old woman is supposed to be liberated from her parents," a woman I counseled explained, "but maybe the rules need to be changed for twenty-five-year-olds with babies. If I had not temporarily moved back to my parents' home after my husband walked out, I don't know how I would have made it. My parents are enormously helpful. And when I feel guilty that I'm imposing on them, they smile and say, 'That's what families are all about—to be there for one another in rough times.' "

Living far from my family when my own children were small, in addition to sharing child care with my husband, I turned to other new mothers for support. In the family housing development where we lived, we women organized a baby-sitting cooperative, which allowed us to have an occasional morning or evening off; in the process of forming the co-op, we also became closer and our toddlers made their first friendships.

The need for support is not limited to the early stage of motherhood. Mothers can also use a shoulder, a sympathetic ear, and words of reassurance or advice as their daughters grow older and frustrate, confuse, and cause worry (as they are sure to do). An old Jewish proverb tells us: "Small children, small problems; big children, big problems." It is too much of a strain to bear our small and big problems alone.

Third, we need to realize that maternal devotion—the ordinary acts of everyday love—is a priceless gift. When I ask adult daughters to tell me what they remember most fondly about their childhood relationships with their mothers, they rarely tell me about "big" things; rather, they remember the "small" ways their mothers expressed their love for them. The adult daughter of a colleague of mine shared this anecdote with me:

> In elementary school, I went through a terrible period when I just couldn't get myself out of bed—especially on those frigid Colorado mornings. My mother bought me not one but *two* alarm clocks, but when they went off, I'd sleep right through them. So she came up with another idea. Each morning at 6:00 A.M. with a cheery "Good morning, honey," she'd appear at my bedside with a cup of hot chocolate spiked with a half-teaspoon

of coffee. Then, while I'd luxuriate under the covers sipping the magical brew, she'd sit at the edge of my bed and chat with me. My mother turned an ordeal—getting up at dawn—into something special for me. By the time I had sipped the last sip of hot chocolate, I was bright-eyed and ready for the day.

In a passage from Hope Edelman's book, *Motherless Daughters*, the author, who was seventeen when her mother died, recounts the small acts she misses most:

> I missed my mother, terribly, when I graduated from college. . . . I missed her when I got my first job promotion and wanted to share the news with someone who'd be proud. I miss her when I'm sick and when I'm lonely, when I can't remember what works best on insect bites, and when nobody else cares how rude the man in the post office was to me.[12]

Thinking back to my childhood, I remember that after my mother would come home, dead tired, from her job in the bakery, she used to starch my petticoats and carefully hang them over umbrellas to dry. And because of this humble act of care, I felt like a special girl.

I hope that the rest of this chapter will remind mothers who may have forgotten, or perhaps never learned, just how valuable they are. Despite the frustrations and disappointments that are part and parcel of the mother-daughter bond, daughters depend on and love their mothers . . . very, very much.

Mother's Body

Maternal devotion is not a simple set of static behaviors. Accommodating itself to the needs of the growing and changing child, it grows and changes over time, although it always begins in the physical relationship. Babies can survive without light, without sound, but without the mothering touch (patting, stroking, holding, carrying, caressing, kissing, rocking) they fail to thrive and can die.[13] In a child's earliest weeks and months, much that is life giving in the world comes from the mother's body; and, when the child needs comfort, no other body is quite as wonderful as mother's. Held in mother's arms, the young child finds security, structure, support, and a shield from excessive external stimuli; at her breast, she finds softness and warmth, and, if she is nursed, sweet-tasting milk. Through the care of the available and interested mother, the young child learns that the world—which mother represents—is basically good, a place in which she can be safe and happy.

It is not possible for adults to remember the mother of early childhood with whom we had such an intense physical relationship. Only in our collective art and literature can we find glimpses of her. Early cultures symbolized Mother as a vessel containing, protecting, and, like a cornucopia, bestowing riches. The ancient Egyptians saw her as Nut, goddess of heaven and sky, who protectively bends over the earth, enveloping all living creatures under a cover of clouds and warmth. The ancient Greeks viewed her as Demeter, provider of food and spiritual sustenance. To other cultures, she is the principle of earth and nature: the flowing water and milk of the sacred herds, the sheltering cave and mountain and house, the fruit-bearing tree, the abundance of vegetative life in forests and steppes, mountains and valleys. For Christians, she is the Madonna who cradles Jesus in her arms. In German fairy tales, she is seen in the fourteen angels who stand watch over Hansel and Gretel as they sleep. From our modern literature, she is a flesh-and-blood mother—Sido, who carries the half-sleeping Colette to her bed: "The two arms were so gentle, so careful to hold me close enough to protect my dangling feet at every doorway."[14]

For the infant and small child, the mother's continuing physical presence—as long as the mother is not harsh or intrusive—is a wonderful thing. If she is *usually* available, empathic, and soothing (for no mother can be perfectly nurturing), she fortifies her child's spiritual being, much as vitamin D, exercise, and sunshine strengthen her body. British psychologist John Bowlby, who spent a lifetime studying attachment, made no bones about claiming that of all the people in the world, mother is almost always the one who can best provide the very young child with what she needs in the way of nurturing. Shortly before his death, having moved away from his father-centered universe, Sigmund Freud described the power of the early tie between mother and child as "unique, without parallel, laid down unalterably for a whole lifetime . . . as the prototype of all later love relations—for both sexes."[15] C. G. Jung described the mother-child relationship as "certainly the deepest and most poignant one we know. . . . It is the absolute experience of our species, an organic truth."[16]

Having experienced her mother's soothing presence, the child will never lose it, even after they are no longer together; for the mother's presence has been alchemically absorbed into the child's body and soul, available to be drawn upon when needed. Whenever I get one of my migraine headaches, I can "feel" my mother's cool hand on my forehead, and the pain subsides. And when I am in a state of distress, I rock my body to and fro, calming myself just as my mother had calmed me in her rocking arms so long ago. For Colette, the French poet of mother-daughter love, the soothing mother of her childhood, Sido, is symbolized in the enclosed garden to which Colette can always return: "a warm, confined enclosure reserved for the cultivation of aubergines and pimentos—where the smell of tomato leaves mingled in July with that of apricots ripening."[17]

Having been sufficiently soothed by the mother of childhood, the adult daughter is able to soothe herself. In bad times, she doesn't have to rush headlong into the arms of a lover to seek the nurture she desperately craves—as Kathie Carlson writes in her book *In Her Image*, "to get from a man what she didn't get from her mother."[18] Similarly, because she has the inner resources to get through her discomfort, she may not need to turn to alcohol to quell the aching within or to binge on food to fill her. Although substance abuse is a complicated disorder with many contributing factors, a striking correspondence exists between the search for the soothing mother and the yearning for alcohol, which warms, desensitizes, and lulls. Similarly, the causes of eating disorders are varied and complex, with some evidence of an association between these illnesses and lack of father love. Still, it is telling that the foods mothers feed babies and young children—cereals, sweets, milk products—are the foods typically associated with binges.

One essential thing that prompts a mother to give of herself freely and spontaneously is her good feelings about her body. If a woman resents the soft, voluptuous, motherly body that comes with new motherhood, she may have difficulty rejoicing in physical intimacy with her infant. For example, negative feelings about one's breasts may interfere with successful breast-feeding. Sadly, many contemporary women in our nation are not comfortable in their bodies, with Caucasian women, far more than African-American women, tending to obsess about perceived imperfections. My colleague Helen Driver Flanders notes that self-demeaning women tend to look at their bodies from the *outside in* and focus on their surface flaws instead of experiencing their bodies from the *inside out* and connecting to their nurturant power and maternal life force. From my own observations, women of other cultures tend not to have the body-image problems that plague us in the United States. On the beaches of southern Europe, for example, women of all ages, sizes, and shapes go topless without seeming the least bit self-conscious. And mothers throughout the world breast-feed their babies in public, an undertaking that only now is being legalized in the United States. Here women have been brainwashed to think of their body parts, particularly their breasts, as mere adornments and sexual lures.

I frequently receive letters from new mothers disgusted with the physical changes wrought by pregnancy, delivery, and breast-feeding; longing for the thin maiden's standard of beauty, they fail to appreciate their new, fuller, mother's body. All too commonly, their husbands, similarly influenced by our culture's obsession with slenderness and youthful appearance, reinforce their wives' insecurities. Whenever I read these letters, I remember the help I had in adjusting to physical changes when I had my daughter and feel sorry that so many other women are not as fortunate. Throughout the pregnancy, my husband was so proud of my growing belly that I could not help being proud of it myself. In fact, one of our photograph albums is filled with pictures he took of me from every angle when I was very pregnant. After giving birth to my daughter, I was lucky enough to be in the care of a wise and empowering physician. When I awkwardly asked him if the prominent red lines on my breasts were normal, he replied with great authority that I was now wearing the "mother's badge of honor" and that I had every reason to be pleased; I remember leaving his office with my head held high and with a silly smile on my face. Over the years, the stretch marks have faded yet, to my delight, not disappeared altogether. Whenever I notice this indelible badge of motherhood, I am reminded of the wonder of having created and nourished two children, and of the miracle my female body is.

For a daughter of any age, mother's body has profound meaning. For the baby, it is the primary source of comfort, security, and structure, and when the mother breast-feeds, it is also a source of nourishment; for the child, adolescent, and adult daughter, it is the pattern for her own physical transformation. One of the best ways that mothers can help daughters accept their bodies is by accepting their own "imperfect" ones instead of fretting over every flaw. "I have never had problems around body image," a client shared with me. "I think this is because my mother didn't have these problems. Mind you, my mother was a big-boned and overweight woman, but this fact did not stop her from getting all 'dolled-up' when she went out. Bedecked in her jewels and dressed in her bright colors, she did not hide that she felt gorgeous, and I, in turn, thought she was the most beautiful in all the world."

For my own part, when I look in the mirror and see the spreading, deepening lines on my face, I imagine my grandmother's wrinkled face, which shone with kindness and joy, and the prospect of looking old becomes less frightening to me.

Some daughters, even as they become adolescents or adults, love to cuddle with mother, to feel the warmth and security of her body. "When I visit my mother, who lives out of state, or she visits me," a woman in her midthirties confided, "we like to sleep in the same bed. Lying next to one another feels comforting." Other daughters require more distance. Yet they, too, often find ways to remain physically connected to mother. A client told me this sweet story:

> When winter break ended and Allison was packing her bags to go back to boarding school, I noticed that tucked in with the silk nightie that she had gotten for Christmas was my pair of old, chewed-up mittens. Whenever I wore them, Allison teased me that they were the ugliest mittens she had ever seen—and she wasn't exaggerating; they look like boxing gloves. At first I couldn't figure out why she was taking them with her to school, especially since she's so fashion conscious. And then it occurred to me that by taking the mittens with her, she was bringing me along to school; wearing them would be like holding hands with mother.

As an adolescent, Leah would sneak into my closet to borrow my favorite clothes. Usually, I did not get annoyed because I understood full well that wearing my outfits was her way of attempting to look grown up and also to be physically close to me. Now that Leah is an adult and living two thousand miles away, I must confess that sometimes I put on one of the shirts or sweaters or the ratty bathrobe she has left behind. Immediately, I am comforted by the sweet skin-to-skin intimacy we once shared.

Mother's Words

Maternal devotion is not only a wordless gift. Scientific studies demonstrate that from within the womb a child "hears" her mother's words and remembers their unique rhythms after birth.[19] They also demonstrate that newborns prefer their mother's voices above all others.[20] Indeed, everything a mother says to her daughter seems to help shape her self-concept and her perceptions of the surrounding environment. Mother is the child's most trusted "interpreter," the one who defines the child's inner and outer worlds by telling her what to approach in the world, what to avoid, whom to like, whom to dislike; she gives her words to name the things around her and the feelings within her; and through her positive and hopeful remarks, she passes on the attitude of optimism, the best antidote to despair.[21] The enduring power of the mother's words is reflected in the adage "What the mother sings to the cradle goes all the way down to the coffin."

The most self-confident, self-assured young women I know were told by their mothers time and again that they were lovely, smart, strong, and capable. Many of the myths and tales of Western civilization allude to an archetypal figure known as the Great Spinner, who spins stories and prophecies that determine the future. The Great Spinner appears, for example, in the guise of the fairies who prophesize Briar Rose's future and in the figure of the old woman at the spinning wheel whom she encounters on her fifteenth birthday. However, the greatest spinner of all comes in the guise of the mother. When I was a little girl, my mother told me that I had a lovely neckline. Objectively viewed, my neckline is surely not extraordinary. Still, to this day, it is what I like best about my appearance.

A few years ago, I had a conversation with a vibrant, engaging young African-American woman who as a child experienced the indignities of poverty and racism. Laverne told me that her mother's unconditional faith in her—in everything she took on—had much to do with her current successes in life. When Laverne was in high school, for example, she heard about a writing contest and, along with hundreds of talented students from more elite schools, decided to enter it. After she excitedly told her mother that the winner of the contest would go to Washington, D.C., to meet the president of the United States, her mother assured her that as long as she put her heart into her writing, she had every chance of producing the winning essay, which is exactly what happened. In its deepest sense, caring is helping another person grow and become all that she might be. It is also encouraging a person to dream, to envision possibilities. This is what the approving, affirming, hopeful mother does.

In a particularly moving passage from *Dreams of Trespass*, Fatima Mernissi, a preeminent sociologist at University Mohammed V in Morocco, describes her girlhood growing up in a harem and the empowering older women who encouraged the children to dream and thereby transform the world:

> "Mothers should tell little girls and boys about the importance of dreams," Aunt Habiba said. "They give a sense of direction. It is not enough to reject this [harem] courtyard—you need to have a vision of the meadows with which you want to replace it." But, how, I asked Aunt Habiba, could you distinguish among all the wishes, the cravings which besieged you, and find the one on which you ought to focus, the important dream which gave you vision?
>
> She said that little children had to be patient, the key dream would emerge and bloom within, and then, from the intense pleasure it gave you, you would know that it was the genuine little treasure which would give you direction and light. She also

said that I should not worry for now, because I belonged to a long line of women with strong dreams.[22]

To assure her daughter of her inherent goodness and her potentiality—to imbue her with strong dreams—a mother needs to feel that she is herself good and that life holds possibilities for her. However, as D. W. Winnicott wrote: "It is as if human beings find it very difficult to believe that they are quite good enough to create within themselves something that is quite good."[23] In my work as a therapist, I observe all too frequently that women who think little of themselves perceive their daughters as inferior. Referring to her sweet and beautiful five-year-old daughter, one such mother said to me: "It figures that if I'm a mediocrity, my daughter will also be a mediocrity. I can see it happening already. The other kids are outshining her." Helping a daughter grow and realize her potential requires a mother first to recognize her own value as a human being. Women who are continually self-deprecating owe it to their daughters and themselves to undergo psychotherapy. With the support of an empathic, dependable, and encouraging therapist, a woman has a very good chance of excising, layer by layer, her self-perception of badness or inferiority and of building up her self-esteem. The woman who learns to value herself is happy to share her life experience and her wisdom. And every daughter wants to learn from her mother. After the eight-year-old daughter of a friend of mine had said something wise beyond her years, my friend asked, "Now where did you ever learn that?" "From you, Mommy," the child replied. "Don't you remember you said that to me when I was little?"

An old English folktale comes to mind:

For ten years, a king sits in his chamber to hear petitions and dispense justice. Each day a holy man in the disguise of a beggar appears and without a word offers him a piece of fruit. Although the king always accepts the trifling gift, he does not give it any thought and merely passes it on to his treasurer, who later tosses it from an upper trellised window into a neglected corner of the treasure house. One day, ten years after the first appearance of the beggar, a tame monkey, who has escaped from the women's apartments in the inner-palace, comes bounding into the king's chamber and jumps onto the throne. Because the king has just received the beggar's fruit, he playfully hands it over to the monkey. When the monkey bites into it, a sparkling jewel drops out and rolls onto the floor. The king's eyes ablaze, he turns to the treasurer and asks what has become of the beggar's many other gifts of fruit. Excusing himself, the treasurer goes into the treasure house and makes his way to the area directly under the trellised window, which he has not visited all these years. There on the floor, amid a mass of fruit in various stages of decomposition, lies a heap of priceless gems.[24]

Very often, the most common gifts—the "throwaways"— contain the most precious jewels. A mother's sayings, her stories, the tidbits of advice and good sense that she passes on to her daughter, perhaps as commonplace as the beggar's pieces of fruit, are as precious as the jewels embedded in them.

My primary editor, Alexia Dorszynski, remarked to me that she never forgets her mother's instructions on buying socks: "She taught me always to buy two pairs of socks the same color so that you still have a pair if the Laundry Gremlin eats one; it's a very little thing, but it connects me to my mother and continues to make me feel cared for all these years later."

The Frazzled Edges of Mother Care

We ought not delude ourselves into believing that the devoted mother is always wise, always sensitive, always thoughtful, always in love with her child, always there for her. Amid the normal vicissitudes of life (financial troubles, health concerns, marriage problems, losses) and the ordinary distresses of the human body (fatigue, headaches, backaches, PMS, anxiety), a mother's devotion is often compromised. I remember one time when Leah, at the age of eight or nine, came to me to have her hair combed before setting out for the party to which we were both invited. We were running late; I was thoroughly annoyed with her for still not having cleaned up her room; she was wearing the soiled red sweater I detested; and I was having a generally rotten day. I pulled the comb through Leah's long, tangled hair. "Ouch, Mommy, you're being rough," she moaned. Deliberately, I pulled the comb through her hair harder still. Not my proudest moment; one of my "human" ones, nevertheless.

Devoted mothers kiss *and* they scold; they are emotionally available *and* they are distracted; they are attuned *and* they are obtuse; they are patient *and* they blow their fuses. As teachers and writers Doris Jasinek and Pamela Bell Ryan quip, "Supermoms and superdads are only on bumper stickers."[25] Mothers tend to be very hard on themselves, however. They think they have failed their daughters if they cannot afford to send them to the "best" schools or provide them with every cultural or educational advantage. They feel guilty for events that are often beyond their control—an unhappy marriage, for example, or divorce, mental or physical illness—that cause their children distress. They worry themselves sick about being too protective or not protective enough, too involved or not involved enough, too strict or not strict enough.

One of the reasons some mothers disengage from a child is the lack of confidence they have in their mothering; they are terribly afraid of making mistakes, and when they do exercise faulty judgment, they often exaggerate its effects. Whether they are married or single, working or stay-at-home, professionals, or even superstars, when it comes to mothering, mothers doubt themselves. Indeed, in all my years of doing therapy, I have yet to meet a woman who says, "I am a very successful mother."

Many more women would perceive themselves as successful

mothers if they learned to accept their faults and lapses. The truth is that as long as a mother is basically empathic and caring, and as long as she is usually interested, available, and willing to learn from her mistakes, she is what Winnicott described as the "good-enough" mother. And to feel loved and cared for, a child needs a parent who is merely good-enough, not one who is always attentive and always good.

Paradoxically, a child's growth and development are fostered by her mother's strengths *and* weaknesses. Indeed, if mothers always had the right answers, would daughters dare to disagree with them and risk making their own decisions? Were mothers always helpful, comforting, understanding, and encouraging, would daughters ever want to grow up and leave them? Frustrated by imperfect mothers, daughters are motivated to become autonomous, self-initiating, and capable. Moreover, imperfect mothers spare their daughters from the worst fate of all: the expectation that they must be perfect children.

Dolly Parton sings a song about a poor woman who, as the winter approaches, makes a coat from odd bits of fabric for her little girl. With its frazzled edges and mismatched patches, it is somewhat ragged-looking, not nearly as fashionable as the coats sold in clothing stores. Yet, despite its flaws, this "coat of many colors"—a metaphor for maternal devotion itself—has been sewn together with love. And, for this reason, the little girl wears it proudly and values it always.

THE SECOND GIFT:

Father's Care

In Colorado, where I live, one of the best-loved trees is the aspen—a graceful tree with thin limbs and heart-shaped leaves that dance in the wind and turn golden in the fall. Although slight in structure, aspens do not need much care to survive; they manage to live through harsh winters and periods of drought and are the first to regenerate after a forest fire. And when environmental conditions are optimal—when the soil is rich and the springtime is long enough to protect new growth—the aspen will do more than produce new branches and leaves: it will actually flower.

If our daughters are to flower, they too need optimal growing conditions: Almost always this means being lovingly cared for by mother *and* father. It is from her mother that a girl learns to be a woman; it is from her father that she learns what to expect from men in the way of love and respect. A great deal of research indicates that a well-fathered daughter will seek love partners who resemble the caring, affirming, available father of childhood and avoid relationships that diminish or compromise her.[1] Indeed, the relationship with father seems to be a dress rehearsal for future heterosexual relationships. Beyond this, it enhances a girl's wholeness; by identifying with father, she hones her masculine side—focus, determination, direction, assertiveness, ambition, adventurousness—which, together with a well-developed feminine side, creates a balanced and flexible personality. By being involved with his daughter, a father is also enhanced. When my male friends and colleagues go on about their daughters, they are absolutely aglow and leave no doubt that they relish their relationships with them.

Some fathers, however, have a hard time making themselves available to their daughters. As is increasingly true for mothers, fathers are rewarded by society for their drive in the world of work, not for their commitment to home and family. In fact, both men and women may look upon those fathers who make parenthood their priority as odd or unmasculine. Despite the inroads of the "fathers' movement," we still typically believe that a man's primary responsibility is making money rather than nurturing and being close to his children. But it goes without saying that a man who works fifty or sixty hours a week (excluding commuting time) is not going to have much left of himself to give his wife and children.

Yet something else, something bigger, holds men back from becoming engaged parents. In my conversations with fathers of daughters, they frequently say that they perceive themselves as the *outsider*. Talking about his relationship with his five-year-old, my friend Peter told me that Deirdre seems to get all she needs from her mother. "As females, they live in the same world," he said, "and I am unquestionably a stranger in it." Peter also explained that, unlike his wife, he often feels at a loss while interacting with Deirdre. He does not believe that his daughter would enjoy the things he likes to do—the things he imagines fathers naturally do with sons, like shooting baskets, watching clips of *The Three Stooges*, roughing it in the wilderness, or roughhousing on the living room floor—and he does not enjoy participating in Deirdre's girl's play: "I can't help feeling foolish playing with paper dolls or dressing up her Barbie or having her put barrettes in *my* hair, which is what she loves to do these days. But I pretend to get into it because I want to be close to her." His wife, who is one of the "movers and shakers" in our community, after overhearing my conversation with Peter remarked that she, too, often was restless while playing with their daughter but that, as a female, her daughter's games and fantasies felt natural and familiar to her.

Whereas the same-sex child promises familiarity, the other-sex child leads the parent into the unknown, triggering insecurities. One single father I interviewed described his experience at JCPenney while his twelve-year-old purchased her first bra: "I was unprepared for this rite of passage and felt quite conspicuous waiting outside the ladies' dressing room while she outfitted herself. I kept thinking that her mother should be here with her, not me. Lingerie departments are not exactly a man's turf."

A married father confided that he feels inept in talking to his two preteen daughters. "My daughters and their mother speak a language that is foreign to me. It is very natural for them to spend lots of time discussing their innermost feelings, and I am not good at this. I am more solution focused. But they are not interested in my logic; they tune me out, and it's only fair to add that I tune them out too."

Because nurturing children has traditionally been the province of mothers—the only turf on which women were allowed to be powerful and competent—some women may become secretly resentful when fathers try to take an active role in their daughters' lives and inadvertently undermine it. In the early years of parenting, for instance, they may relegate the father to status of mother's helper. A young father complained to me that whenever his wife left him with their two preschoolers, she taped to the refrigerator door a detailed list of instructions— what and when to feed them, which games to play, and so on—

and, as a result, he began to make excuses to "get out of *baby-sitting*." As their daughters gets older, some mothers make seemingly harmless remarks—"Your dad just doesn't get it, does he? But we all know what jerks men are"—that whittle away the girl's confidence in her father and the father's confidence in himself. I remember the pained expression that occasionally broke through the forced smile of a close friend as he endured his wife's and his two daughters' relentless "good-natured" digs at him.

Even when their partners are supportive, many men consider themselves to be the secondary parent, *the unessential one.* Male feelings of exclusion and inadequacy typically arise within the first hours of parenthood. For every child, the first love is mother, not father; it is after all from the mother's wondrous body that the child is born and nourished; at the beginning of life at least, baby clearly prefers mother to everyone else in the universe. As a result, fathers may feel hardly necessary. Arthur Colman, a physician, Jungian analyst, and co-author of *The Father*, writes:

> Throughout the pregnancy I had tried to be as involved as possible. . . . As an M.D., I was comfortable in the labor and delivery rooms at the hospital. No one thought of keeping me out—not because I was the father, but because I was a doctor. (This was 1965.) We insisted in advance that we would leave the hospital a few hours after the birth, and again it was my medical degree that earned their cooperation.
>
> When we arrived home, I nurtured Libby and our tiny daughter. I remember feeling profound joy and peace that first night; I was a true father in every sense. Lib was asleep in our bed and Shoshi was in her crib in the living room near me. Then she began to cry, the marvelous ululations of the newborn that reverberate with both life and loss. I wanted to comfort her, ostensibly to let Libby regain her strength after the long labor, but also to take care of her myself. I was bare to the waist because it was a

warm August evening. I took a bottle of sugar water and gently touched the plastic nipple to Shoshi's lips while I cuddled her to my chest. She was quiet for a moment and then began to wail. I tried the bottle and my chest again and again, but with no better effect. My breasts ached. It was probably the fatigue and emotion, but for a moment I was sure that I had milk there for her. I let her lips touch my nipple. She nuzzled slightly and then wailed even louder. Libby was obviously awake by now (she claims to have wakened at the first squeak) and was smiling at me. She held out her arms for our infant and in a moment the crying stopped as Shoshi found a "real" nipple.

It was a hard fantasy to let go, a fantasy in which I could do everything and be everything as a parent. I was depressed for a long while. It was hard to start off second-best. I'm sure it took a lot more courage to stay in there at home than it had to be the father-protector at the hospital. There I had known my way around. At home that night I felt like I had a "disability."[2]

Over time, Colman realized his crucial importance to his daughter. Many other men, feeling "disabled" as parents, do not. As a result, they disengage or disappear as fathers. Why the lingering discomfort? In our parents' and grandparents' generations the role of father was highly defined: his task was to provide material comfort for his wife and children, protect them from external threats, and be a moral presence in the home. No longer is the father's role so clear-cut. In fact, it is in utter disarray. Quite justifiably, the majority of Westerners have rejected outright the concept of the paterfamilias, with its connotations of dominance and authoritarianism. This disdain for patriarchy has led many women and men to believe that a good father is nothing other than a second mother—a *male mother*—and that to be a loving presence in his children's (and wife's) lives, a man must overcome his paternal tendencies and develop a maternal nature.

I, on the other hand, agree with those who believe that

when a man tries to be a "mother," he inevitably comes to feel like a lesser parent and may withdraw from his children as a result. It seems to me that to nurture family life, we must do all we can to help men become not motherly, but fatherly fathers—what Richard Louv calls "fathermen." "I have realized," Louv writes, "that when I'm fathering, I feel more like a man than at any other time in my life."[3]

Father care and mother care take different forms, and children thrive having both of them. The differences, according to Dr. Jerrold Lee Shapiro, a professor at Santa Clara University who for the past decade has been studying fatherhood, are most evident in physical contact, play, discipline, and communication—all of which entail nurturing, tenderness, and caregiving. In an article entitled "Letting Dads Be Dads" that appeared in *Parents* magazine, he writes about his own experience: "My wife is the mother in our family, and she's very good at it. I am not much of a mother, but I still consider myself a good parent to our two children. My approach to raising children is quite different from Susan's—because, if the truth be known, she doesn't know much about how to father. That's where I'm the natural."[4]

When men are encouraged to be fathermen, and not "Mr. Moms," they are empowered—and so are their daughters. I know; I was blessed with such a father.

Father as Trailblazer

Among the American Indian cultures, it is said the father is expected to take his children out into the woods so that they can see "the house beyond the tepee."[5] Describing a family outing to the desert, Richard Louv tells about taking his older child down a familiar path that led to a cliff, where the two dangled their feet over the ledge and watched the ravines far below. "I knew intuitively," Louv writes, "that this moment at the cliff was important."[6]

When I asked twenty-year-old Emily, the daughter of a male colleague, what comes to mind when she imagines the father of her childhood, she answered unhesitatingly: "Sitting on his shoulders and seeing what the world looked like from up there." Listening to Emily, I was flooded with early memories of my own father. I remembered summer days at Jones Beach—reprieves from the punishing heat of New York City—when he took me far, far out into the ocean to jump over the waves while my mother sunbathed on the shore. Knowing that my father was near me, I was unafraid even when the great force of the waves knocked me headfirst into the sand below. I also remembered the time he and I climbed the long, narrow, spiral staircase to the pointed crown of the Statue of Liberty. "We've climbed to the clouds," he told me. My father too had shown his daughter the world "from up there," and I will never forget how beautiful it was.

A female colleague shared these recollections of childhood: "My mother was focused on me. My father, not so much. So when he did focus on me, it carried special weight. He was the one to show me the world—to *engage* me in the world. He took me on peace marches; he took me to the Colorado state mental hospital in Pueblo so I could volunteer—so I could learn how to dance with the 'crazy people'. . . . It's my mother who knows me; it's my father who excites me."

Fathers excite their children from infancy on. Researchers who study parent-infant interactions note that whereas mothers tend to envelop, soothe, and calm the child, fathers are likely to energize the child through their more intrusive and high-keyed interactions.[7] Mother's quieting touch and calming voice help regulate the child's emotional states and serve as a model for eventual self-regulation; we can say that the soothing mother "teaches" the child to soothe herself in times of distress. Father's stimulating touch is also fodder for the child's psychological development; the "jump-starting" father "teaches" the child to initiate activity and leap into life's fray.[8]

His masculine energy fosters the child's drive, assertiveness, and risk taking.

Intuitively, men seem to understand that the aggressive play that goes on between them and their sons—what writer Jeanne Elium describes as "their own language of grunts, farts, burps, chortles, feints, and holds"—has a positive and creative purpose.[9] Yet, all too often they hesitate to interact physically with their daughters whom they may perceive as fragile even after babyhood. Girls, like boys, however, love to play with daddy—to wrestle and tickle and chase. "As a baby, Sara would squeal with joy when her dad lifted her over his head," my friend Julie Phillips remarked, "and when she got older, he'd take hold of her hands and flip her over—and she just loved that." When the young daughters of our friends come to our house, they gravitate like little magnets toward my husband the Wildman, who bounces them on his knee and gives them pony rides on his back.

Recalling my earliest years with my father, I remember how on his days off from work I would eagerly wait outside his bedroom door for him to wake up. Because my father was a baker, he usually had to get up at the crack of dawn, and sleeping late when he did not have to go to work was one of his few luxuries, so I dared not disturb him. As soon as my father roused from his sleep, however, I jumped into bed with him, and our fun began. He would lie flat on his back, bring his knees together, raise them perpendicular to his chest, and let me perch on them while they swayed back and forth. Then quite suddenly when I least expected him to, he'd open his knees, and I, giggling excitedly, would come tumbling down between his legs onto the mattress.

For daughters, the world of the father is usually more dangerous, more enticing, than the warm, soothing world of the mother. A good friend, Art Kaufman, a father of two daughters, shared his favorite "Grace story" with me:

Mindy was out of town so Grace, who was five then, and I decided to order-out a pizza. There's this tavern in Denver called Bonnie Brae that makes the best pizza and that's where I suggested we go. As we were driving there, Grace told me she wanted to go in all by herself to buy the pizza. Well, that wasn't such a hot idea—Bonnie Brae is a bar, a hangout, and usually mobbed . . . no place for a five-year-old. But Grace wanted to have an adventure, and so I said okay, gave her the money, and double-parked right by the door. When she didn't come out after a few minutes, I started to feel a little uncomfortable, waited some more, then went in after her. And there she was—sitting on a barstool, drinking a Shirley Temple, and having a great conversation with the bartender. Seeing me, Grace said that she'd be out when the pizza was ready and that I should leave, which is what I did. A few minutes later, she skipped toward the car—big smile—holding the boxed pizza under her arm as if it were a looseleaf notebook. "I did good," she said, "right?" I opened the box, and of course, from the way she had carried it, the pizza was a gooey mess. We looked at each other and burst out laughing!

Emily, at twenty, remembered that when she was very young she went with her parents to a resort that had a hot tub. Testing the water with her hand, her mother said that it was too hot. Her father disagreed, saying: "Oh, it's fine. Let her go in," and in she went. "My mother was right, the water was too hot," Emily told me, "but I'm so glad I went in."

Of course, the maternal tendency to ensure a child's security and the paternal tendency to encourage her exploration can, and often do, cause marital conflict. In an effort to avoid further conflict, a man may temper his fathering instincts. Chris, a middle-aged man who owns a realty company, told me about an event that occurred while his wife was away for a weekend. At the invitation of a business associate who owned and piloted a small plane, Chris took his eight-year-old daughter flying. When the mother learned about this, she flew into a rage and accused her husband of having endangered their child's life. Fearing his wife's future remonstrations against him, Chris never again dared to be adventurous with his daughter. Rather, he convinced himself that his wife knew what was best for their child and that he needed to leave the parenting decisions to her. Not surprisingly, Chris's present relationship with his daughter, who is now nineteen, is distant, and he has little interest in family life in general.

In the best scenarios, fathers and mothers—whether they are married to each other or not—embrace the idea that they have different yet equally valuable parenting styles: they talk about their differences, listen to and respect each other's concerns, make compromises where possible, agree "to win some and to lose some," and try to work as a team. Having counseled couples for more than fifteen years and being married myself, I am fully aware these are not easy things to do. I distinctly recall the day my husband beckoned our son and daughter, then ages three and six, to climb the long, rickety ladders that connect the cliff dwellings at Mesa Verde National Park in southwestern Colorado. I remember saying to myself, "I'm married to a lunatic," and wringing my hands and closing my eyes until the three of them safely made their way up the ladder. My husband, for his part, can tell stories of maternal lunacy—how, for example, when we were out for the evening at a concert or a play, I would sprint to the pay phone at every intermission, ostensibly to tell the baby-sitter something she needed to know, though really to reassure myself that the children were still okay.

The daughter's need for both mother care and father care is wonderfully described in Maurice Sendak's storybook *Outside over There*. Little Ida faces the scary challenges of growing up, poignantly portrayed as goblins and robbers. To meet these challenges, she wraps herself in her mother's yellow raincoat, knowing it will keep her warm and dry, and climbs out her window toward the unknown—the "outside over there." Whirling past spooky caves inhabited by robbers, she hears in the distance her sailor father's song instructing her how to catch the goblins and spoil their terrible mischief. Just as her mother's coat provides Ida with the needed comfort, her father's song, which she learns to play on her own "wonder horn," helps her to become cunning and courageous.

To be sure, caring fathers not only take their children out into the world, but also teach them how to cope in it. Years ago, I had a conversation with a professor at Ohio University and father of three daughters. At the time, Ben's oldest daughter was entering sixth grade, and her teacher, as everyone in our college town knew, was the meanest person in the school. "Ben," I asked, "are you going to have Madeline transferred to another class?" He answered that he and his wife had agreed not to, explaining this would be the first of many nasty folks that Madeline would inevitably encounter in the years to come. Ben believed that one of his roles as a father was to help Madeline deal with her teacher, which would prepare her for life's other "cold showers." And indeed, after school, Madeline did initiate frequent visits to her father's private study, where the two would huddle and develop cunning classroom strategies.

The Protective Father

Sigmund Freud called the father's protection of his children the "central childhood imperative."[10] When there are monsters lurking under beds and bogeymen hiding in dark closets, a child typically cries out for daddy, not mommy, to come and chase them away. I suspect that the father's big body, rumbling voice, and physical strength offer the child reassurance. These physical attributes also make it easier for fathers to set and enforce limits with their children. My own father was a gentle soul. Nevertheless, when I imagine him, I see his powerful arms, grown muscular from kneading bread and carrying heavy vats of butter, cream, and flour. Whenever I was frightened as a little child, I envisioned them lifting me up and carrying me away from all the danger in the world.

Victoria Secunda, author of *Women and Their Fathers*, writes that "no one 'protects' the way a doting father does. Mothers can hover, but fathers can back up their devotion with a fearsome authority."[11] When my daughter was fifteen, we went camping in the Rockies with three other pairs of mothers and teenage daughters. After setting up our tents, we all decided to take a hike. About two miles away from the campground, the clear sky suddenly became heavy with thunderclouds, and Carla, one of the teenagers, grew frantic. "Oh, no," she wailed, "we're going to be struck by lightning. If only my dad were here, he'd protect us." Although on an intellectual level this bright adolescent understood that her father could no more stop a lightning storm than we women (all experienced hikers) could, at a deeper, more primal level she believed that only he could provide safety from the elements. To Carla, at least in this moment of vulnerability, her father was no mere mortal. He was a god who could counteract the thunderbolts of Zeus.

Many daughters, especially when they are very young, invest their fathers with mythical powers. After all, by believing that father is all-powerful, a child has the necessary illusion of being safe in an unsafe world. Karen Hill Anton, an American writer living in Japan who was raised by a single father, recalls:

> I remember ... the time I accidentally ate the "dead man's meat," or gills of a crab. All of my friends said it would kill me, and I accepted their word, because we all knew that you never were supposed to eat that part. I was afraid to sleep that night, knowing death would claim me as soon as I closed my eyes. But then I realized that if I slept with Daddy I couldn't possibly die. So I crept into his bed and fell asleep with my head nestled on his chest and in the soft hair of his underarm. Surely death could not snatch me from the safety of my father—and it didn't.[12]

The child's image of the father's sheltering chest and the soft hair of his underarm represents the protective father who is both strong and tender. I have known many strong and tender fathers, including my own, and a lovely story about him comes immediately to my mind: When I was in sixth grade, I was assigned an oral report on the traditions of Ireland. Inspired by an illustration of the pretty Irish maiden Molly Malone that I had seen in a book of folk songs, I thought it would be a grand idea to present my report dressed in a costume just like the one she was wearing. Enthusiastically, I set about buying fabric with my allowance, cutting a pattern from large sheets of newsprint, and sewing the pieces by hand. I was, however, an inept seamstress, and the night before the report was due, I had to admit to myself and my parents that my efforts had failed miserably: I had made a mess of things. With a heavy heart, I retreated to my room, fell into bed, and eventually cried myself to sleep. Several hours later, I was awakened by a strange mechanical hum coming from my parents' bedroom. Creeping down the long hallway that connected our rooms, I noticed a light shining through the cracks of the doorway. Timidly, I knocked: "Okay, you can come in," my father answered sweetly. There he sat, hunched over our ancient Singer sewing machine, which had been in disuse as long as I could remember, working the noisy foot pedal and wheel to put the finishing touches on my Irish costume.

I recall another story about a strong and tender man. He was the father of one of my third graders at PS 28 in Manhattan, where I taught during the late sixties. A towering, dark-skinned Jamaican gentleman, Frieda's father worked two jobs to support his family: a day job as a laborer and a night job as a security guard. (I never did figure out when he had time to sleep. Perhaps he didn't.) Even so, whenever Frieda left her lunch box at home—and Frieda was a forgetful little girl—he would come to school with it on his break between jobs. Patiently, he'd wait in the doorway until I happened to see him or until one of the children called out, "There's Frieda's dad!" Then, with apologies for the interruption, he'd walk over to Frieda, exchange a sheepish grin with her, gently stroke her hair or give her a peck on the cheek, and hand her the lunch box.

Richard Louv writes that "a father may or may not nurture his children differently than a mother because of his gender. But the fact that he does nurture, and the reflection of this nurturing in his children, is more important than the culture teaches any of us."[13] For one thing, fathers who nurture their children seem to deepen the level of compassion they will have as adults. A twenty-six-year study that tracked young children into adulthood reveals that the father's involvement in his children's daily lives is the strongest parent-related factor in the development of empathy. Psychologist Richard Koestner and his associates Carol Franz and Joel Weinberger, of McGill University in Montreal, found that fathers who spend time alone with their children more than twice a week, giving them baths, meals, and other intimate care, reared the most empathic adults.[14]

Considerable evidence indicates that contrary to popular assumptions, feelings and emotion are transmitted from one generation to the next not solely across the mother line but by way of the father line as well. Karen Anton notes that when she wrote to her father from abroad, informing him that she had given birth to her first child, he promptly answered, "Now, Karen, you must begin to cultivate patience," something about which he knew a great deal. "Nursing [baby Nanao]," she goes on to say, "I found myself singing a song my father had sung to us at bedtime when we were very little. I hadn't heard that song for twenty years, and I'd never heard anyone other than my father sing it, but it seemed to be waiting in my throat for my baby."[15]

The "Other"

"Je suis un autre," the French poet Arthur Rimbaud wrote. "I am an other." For every young girl, father is the mysterious *other*, the one who leads her toward the unfamiliar and teaches her things that her mother may not know about. During the latency years, before a girl enters puberty and begins to focus on clothes, makeup, and boys, she is usually eager to share her father's passions, whether these are sailing the seas, skiing the slopes, or surfing through cyberspace. These years can be remarkably satisfying for father and daughter alike. By teaching and mentoring his daughter, the father realizes his positive authority; in being taken seriously by her father, the daughter comes to value her own intelligence and competence.

I have always loved learning. As a young girl, my mother, who grew up believing that women should not outshine men, often told me that if I became "too smart," boys would never be interested in me. My father, thankfully, gave me just the opposite message. He seemed to delight in the fact that I was mentally quick and expected me to excel in school. On one of my frequent visits to the bakery where he worked, he put my cousin Bobby, the owner's son, and me through a test. He placed two large, identical trays of sponge cake, cut into numerous small squares, in front of us and asked who could count the squares more quickly. As Bobby, two years my senior, counted by twos, which took forever, I multiplied the number of squares on one side by the number on the other side and came up with the right answer in a flash. "She's only in third grade and already good with numbers," I heard my father brag to one of the other bakers. Being smart, I inferred from his sweet and approving smile, was not as dangerous as my mother had warned.

I am reminded of a story a former client shared with me. In her midthirties, Sandra left her job as a police officer to go to graduate school for a degree in botany. The textbook she purchased for her first class seemed oddly familiar, but she could not understand why. Then Sandra remembered. She recalled sitting on her father's lap as a little girl and leafing through a book of flowers and fauna with him—one of their few tender times together. Although her father, a gruff man who allowed no intimacy, took little pleasure from life, he had a passion for botany. The book they shared back then, Sandra realized to her amazement, was an early edition of the textbook assigned to her in botany class. This discovery allowed Sandra to acknowledge—many years after her father's death—that the man she hardly knew as a child nevertheless affects her profoundly.

Sandra's story recalls a similar one. Sophia, one of my daughter's friends, never met her father. If Sophia's mother was bitter that her child's father would have nothing to do with ether of them, she did not—to her great credit—ever convey this fact to Sophia. Rather, she described the man's wonderful qualities, especially his thirst for travel and adventure. From these descriptions Sophia "invented" a positive father with whom she could identify. Sometimes she fantasized about accompanying him on voyages around the world, which inspired her to draw maps and read about faraway places. Three years ago, Sophia and I had a special date; we met in London and went to a play together. With the Eurail pass her mother had given her as a college graduation present, Sophia was traveling abroad on her own, following in the footsteps of the adventurer-father she had created.

Father Care in Adolescence

Father care is necessary at every stage of a daughter's life, especially during adolescence. This is the time when, compelled by some powerful force from within, a girl begins to separate psychologically from her mother, to assert her differences, and lay claim to her own unique life. Because the mother-daughter bond is so intense and their identities so closely aligned, the daughter's efforts to separate are usually threatening to both of them. Frequently, the only way a girl can make the break from mother is to convince herself that there is nothing admirable about the woman and that the best course of action is to become her polar opposite—which, of course, creates antagonism in their relationship. "I don't want to look like you. I want to look like *me*," my daughter, at about age fifteen, tearfully told me after an old family friend, whom I had not seen in twenty years, briefly mistook her for the young me.

During adolescence, a time of tensions and tears, the girl clings to her peers; they become a living security blanket, replacing the intimate mother of childhood whom she must give up. She also turns to her father. Although fathers and teenage daughters do at times rub each other the wrong way and also need to break away from each other, friction between them is less irritating than that between mothers and daughters. The teenage girl does not have to struggle to *disidentify* from father—to disown the similarities between them in order to affirm her "selfness"—because she has always felt inherently different from him. Her close tie with father, in other words, does not pose as great a threat to her autonomy as does the tie with mother. Around father, she can relax and more easily accept guidance, support, and advice; he is one of her safe harbors. He is also someone who can help her smooth the troubled waters in her relationship with her mother. As Charles, a participant in a parents group that I lead, pointed out, "I realize that when my wife and daughter are caught in a power struggle and I butt in, I would make matters worse by undermining my wife's authority. What I try to do instead is point out to both of them how they are pushing each other's buttons. And this is often all it takes to stop the mutual provocation."

The adolescent girl's longing for the father is vividly illustrated in a dream recorded in the memoir *Fierce Attachments* by Vivian Gornick, whose own father died when she was an adolescent:

> One night when I was fifteen I dreamed that the entire apartment was empty, stripped of furniture and brilliantly whitewashed, the rooms glistening with sun and the whiteness of the walls. A long rope extended the length of the apartment, winding at waist-level through the rooms. I followed the rope from my room to the front door. There in the doorway stood my dead father, gray-faced, surrounded by mist and darkness, the rope tied around the middle of his body. I laid my hands on the rope and began to pull, but try as I might I could not lift him across the threshhold. Suddenly my mother appeared. She laid her hands over mine and began to pull also. I tried to shake her off, enraged at her inter-ference, but she would not desist, and I did so want to pull him in I said to myself, "All right, I'll even let her have him, if we can just get him back inside."[16]

Many fathers disengage from their adolescent daughters, and for numerous reasons. If a father has never felt important to his daughter, he may consider himself especially ill-prepared to be there for her as she confronts the Sturm und Drang of adolescence. Or he may be turned off by her new interests: her exquisite attention to every detail of her appearance, her need to conform to peer standards, her romances, her music. Or he may experience her wish for emotional intimacy with him as threatening, especially if he prefers to avoid close relationships. Or he may feel increasingly uncomfortable—perhaps nervous about his own erotic thoughts—as her little girl's body trans-forms into a more womanly one; withdrawing is a perfect way to avoid confronting the reality of the daughter's maturation, which can be so threatening.

The sad irony is that this disengagement occurs precisely when a daughter needs her father more than ever. Better than anyone else in the world, he can affirm her loveliness as a woman. "Thinking back to the gifts I got on special occasions, I remember one best," my colleague Lyn Gullette told me. "It was a vial of perfume my father gave me when I was seventeen. The gift represented his respectful way of acknowledging my womanhood, the fact that I was dating and had become appealing to men." An old school friend who by conventional standards was not particularly attractive but never lacked for beaus remarked to me, "When I used to ask my dad if I was too fat—and the truth is that I was overweight as a teenager—he'd give me a hug and tell me I was beautiful." Knowing that her father finds her attractive and acceptable, a young woman assumes that the other men in her life will also, and this assumption promotes self-confidence, which in turn enhances desirability. A male friend of mine, who is quite the bon vivant, once told me that "for a man, the greatest turn-on is not a woman's physical endowments but her self-confidence."

Just as undermothered daughters may engage in self-destructive behavior such as addictions and compulsive sex in misguided attempts to feel soothed, underfathered daughters may destructively act out their distress in order to feel loved. Margo Maine, director of the Eating Disorders Program at the Institute of Living in Hartford, Connecticut, points out that daughters *literally* hunger for their fathers; she links anorexia, yo-yo dieting, and other female food disorders with under-fathering. "[Daughters] will," she writes, "choose physical hunger by dieting or abusing their bodies, desperately hoping for [father's] attention rather than face the pain of his neglect. They will bring this father hunger to all their other relationships as they seek approval, acceptance, and love."[17] Paul Lewis, president of a parenting education program in San Diego called Family University, agrees, stating, "I'm convinced by the available research, and after working with thousands of families, that when fathers withdraw from their adolescent daughters because of discomfort with their daughter's sexuality it sets the stage for the daughter's sexual experimentation or promiscuity: the daughters are looking for closeness that has been withdrawn by their fathers."[18]

To be sure, young women need to be validated by their fathers in a nonseductive way that does not provoke sexual competitions with their mothers. When I counsel married couples with teenage girls, I often remind husbands that while captivated by their daughters' physical loveliness they ought not to disregard their wives. When a man overvalues his daughter and undervalues his wife, the adolescent will become confused and frightened. Just as a young boy struggling through the Oedipal stage does not really want to steal mother away from father (after all, he wouldn't know what to do with her), the adolescent girl, aware of her own desirability and stirred by new feelings of desire, becomes overwhemed if she believes that in father's eyes she is sexually superior to mother. Such victories are self-defeating because the weight of illegitimate power crushes the child.

Through the ages, women who have learned that their value derives primarily from their physical appearance and sexual allure have downplayed their other attributes. When a father recognizes his daughter's physical allure *as well as* her intellect, talents, interests, and concern for others, he encourages her to be both a womanly woman *and* a vital, loving human being. In a culture such as ours, in which looks are overvalued, a father can help his adolescent daughter immeasurably by taking her seriously *as a person*. Indeed, numerous studies have shown that a father's interest in his daughter helps her develop a strong sense of identity and positive self-esteem.[19] However, although young women thrive within a close relationship with father, it ought not to be overly close. The father who insists on having discussions about sexual matters, is always noticing her, and presses for details about her life violates the young woman's needs for privacy. Every growing girl longs for a protected space, in which no eyes peer out at her, so that she may grow and flower in peace.

Human Ordinariness

Just as a father's belief that he is unimportant in his daughter's life can contribute to his disengaging from it, his awareness that he is important can trigger anxieties: "Do I have what it takes to be the kind of father my daughter deserves?" "Will I meet her needs ... or disappoint her?" For both men and women in our achievement-driven culture, human ordinariness is not well tolerated; we expect and are expected to be *extraordinary*. Sadly, the pressure to be extraordinary as parents robs us of much of the pleasure we might otherwise have in relating to our children. Constant worries about whether we are measuring up drain away the enjoyment we would otherwise experience.

For fathers, there is a lesson to be learned in L. Frank Baum's story *The Wizard of Oz*. Appearing in various guises, both beautiful and scary, the wizard first tries to impress Dorothy and her friends with his sorcery. As "the Great and Terrible Oz," he promises that he can fix all their problems and in his beautiful balloon transport Dorothy from the Emerald City, the land of illusions, to Kansas, her real home. Of course, in the end, he fails at his wizardly mission, whereupon both he and Dorothy must come to terms with his *ordinariness*. And so they do. Even though the wizard cannot keep his promise to Dorothy, she forgives him. She knows that although he may not be a very good wizard, he is a good man because he tries his best. In the same way, daughters do not need their fathers to be wizards, just ordinary good parents.

"My father sewed the buttons on my skirt," Phyllis Yasutake, an actress and mother of six, remembers. "My father clipped my nails. My father sat in on my band concerts at Franklin High and fell asleep in the front row. And he snored loud, and I'd say, 'That's good, he's here.' "[20]

The Sweetest Smell

My friend and colleague Katharine Walker shares a story that reminds us how enduring the gift of father care is, even when its wrappings are plain. According to Katharine, her father was a hard man, dry and prickly, much like the New Mexican terrain in which they lived. Aside from disciplinary measures, there was little relationship between young Katharine and her father. One day, however, he took her by the hand and they went walking in a meadow filled with wildflowers. As she described it:

> I was a little girl, just past the knees of my tall father. The meadow grasses in which we were walking topped above his ankles, but there were tall as my legs.
>
> It was a sunny day. Warm. The colors were those seen only in New Mexico. The meadow was silver-green and shimmered in the passing breeze. The reigning ponderosa pines were dark green and majestic. And the soil and rocks were a deep earthen red.
>
> As we walked along on our adventure (it was a special treat to be taken on an errand so far from the house), my father pointed out plants and flowers to me. Then we came to one tall plant with a pretty pink blossom on top. My father told me to be careful about touching the leaves and stem, for they had stickers. I knew about stickers because I was familiar with both roses and cacti. My father was carrying some burlap. He put the burlap between me and the stickers and told me to smell the thistle blossom. It had a beautifully sweet scent.
>
> It is the best and sweetest smell I have ever known.

THE THIRD GIFT:

Loving and Letting In

I n many cultures around the world, after the birth of a child, the new mother, father, and baby enjoy societally sanctioned days or weeks of relative seclusion, which allow them to grow close as a family. After this period has passed, the baby is "reborn" into the wider society of people who will love her. In the Sudan, for example, family members and friends of the new parents feast on a ceremonial lamb and dance late into the night to celebrate the baby's membership in the community. The Mbuti pygmies of Zaire form a circle of those closest to the parents and pass the infant from one to another for holding, kissing, and comforting. And women of the Andaman Islands in Indochina not only cuddle one another's babies but, during times of lactation, suckle them.

Among some tribal cultures, the newborn is linked for life with one nurturing person other than the mother or father. The Thonga baby of South Africa is assured of a special relationship with her father's sister, in whose arms she is placed during her naming ceremony. The Dinka baby of the Sudan develops a lasting and intimate relationship with the midwife who assisted in her birth. Similarly, for the Gabbra baby of Kenya, the midwife becomes a dependable mother figure; as the child grows older, she will visit the midwife, who will lavish the girl with tokens of affection.[1]

How much happier our American children would be if they, too, knew from the start that when mommy or daddy was busy or out of sorts, there were other arms to hold them, other ears to listen to them, and other laps to provide them safe refuge. And how much more relaxed we parents would be knowing we could count on loving support as we raised our children. The African proverb "It takes an entire village to raise a child" is catching on in the United States, where men and women are learning firsthand that child rearing requires many hands and hearts and that it is permissible to reach outside the immediate family for help and guidance. But given the realities of contemporary American society, how *do* we let loving, nurturing people into our lives and those of our children? How *can* we build family-friendly "villages" when almost everyone around us seems self-absorbed or just too plain busy?

Where Have All the Grandparents Gone?

Throughout history, grandparents, functioning as teachers, consultants, and nurturers, have served as sources of family support. Yet most grandparents in the United States today play only a peripheral role in their grandchildren's lives, sometimes because they don't want to be too involved but more often because we parents don't want them to be. In fact, psychiatrist, author, and grandparent activist Arthur Kornhaber asks whether the notion of the extended family has slipped so far from our collective consciousness that each new generation is left alone to reinvent the nurturing of our children. The answer—sad but true—appears to be yes. But why has our society come to dismiss this essential role of grandmothers and grandfathers?

One explanation for the disempowerment of grandparents is the problem of "ageism" that plagues our society. We Americans are infatuated with youth and often dread becoming old. Many of us feel uncomfortable around aging parents; if they are no longer healthy, their physical losses may frighten or even repel us, in part because our parents remind us of our own aging process. We may also believe that we have little to learn from our elders, that facts gleaned from the most up-to-date research carry more value than the wisdom that grows from experience. "When I want to know what the safest sleeping position is for our newborn or how to help my two-year-old through night terrors or if my wife and I should send our six-year-old daughter to public or private school, I will read articles on the subject or turn to the professionals," a bright and involved father of three pointed out to me. "I won't ask my mother or father because I don't think they'll give me educated answers. They're just not on the cutting edge of knowledge."

An additional explanation may be that when grandparents live far from their adult children and grandchildren, as is typical in our society, family bonds weaken; literally as well as figuratively, generations that are separated by miles are *out of touch* with each other. Occasional visits simply do not feed the feelings of intimacy the way daily or weekly interactions do. Telephone, fax, and E-mail communications cannot really replace reassuring hugs, expressions of empathy, and the taste of grandma's chicken soup or the pleasure of playing chess with grandpa.

The most serious threat to strong cross-generational relationships are the festering resentments that many adult children bear toward their parents. Time and again, I hear from clients that they cannot feign respect for a mother or father who has treated them disrespectfully, or that they cannot trust their children to be in the company of a grandparent who is likely to do or say damaging things to them. As one client put it, "I would love to have a wise mother to support me when I am confused and overwhelmed. I would love my children to have a good granny they could turn to for a dose of old-fashioned common sense or for a loving hug. But my mother was and continues to be an abusive woman, and I must protect myself and my children from her by keeping us at a safe distance." Surely, my client's decision to limit ties severely or even sever them altogether with a person who poses a physical or psychological threat is the right—although inevitably painful—one. I have worked with other clients, however, whose reasons for keeping their children away from the grandparents were not so clear-cut or justifiable.

For good and for bad, we are far likelier than men and women in authoritarian societies to confront our elders, set stern limits with them, or to disengage from them completely. We believe we have a "right" to run our lives with minimal interference from our parents and our in-laws—*especially* our in-laws. "I do not think of myself as a cowardly man," a college professor who was raised in Beijing recently told me, "but I would never have dared to set the rules with my wife's parents that my American-born daughter sets with her in-laws. In the society in which I was raised, we were socialized to think less about satisfying our personal needs and more about honoring the wishes of our elders."

If the letters I receive from subscribers to *Parents* are any indication, the cross-generational relationship that creates the most tension for parents with babies or young children is the one between daughter-in-law and mother-in-law. Despite the prevalence of male mother-in-law jokes, I have yet to receive a letter from a new father complaining about his wife's father or mother, and I have heard only a few gripes from new mothers unhappy with their fathers-in-law. Mostly I hear from new mothers who bitterly resent their mothers-in-law. Studies conducted by University of Minnesota sociology professor Lucy Rose Fischer likewise indicate that although new mothers usually welcome their own mothers' advice—in fact, daughters who were not particularly close to their mothers in earlier years commonly develop warm feelings toward them after giving birth—they devalue the advice or information about babies that their mothers-in-law provide. As Fischer summarizes, "When the daughters have children, it is mothers-in-law, rather than mothers, who tend to be seen as subverting the daughter's right to manage her own child."[2] Should the new mother eventually divorce her husband, the role of the paternal grandmother is likely to be further diminished; indeed, custodial mothers may look upon her as persona non grata.

Earlier generations of young women were no doubt just as suspicious of their mothers-in-law as their contemporary counterparts are, and probably there were just as many power plays then as now. Today's young women, however, tend to feel more justified in shutting out the in-laws, since respect for one's elders is no longer as compelling a moral imperative as it once was. No wonder many paternal grandparents feel stymied as they try to bond with their grandchildren. As Mimi, a pediatric nurse and the mother of five, has told me:

When my son and daughter-in-law gave birth to my first grandchild, I was bursting with good advice for them. I had so much to give them—baby care, after all, was my area of expertise. Not only did I bring up my own brood, but I have ministered to the needs of hundreds of new mothers and their babies over the years as a career nurse. My son, however, made it clear to me that I was not to impose my views on them. He strongly implied that my giving advice made his wife feel dominated, and that he needed to protect her from my domination. I felt like a Santa Claus, laden with gifts, who is barred from coming down the chimney and sent back out into the cold.

The new father is frequently put in the uncomfortable position of mediating between his wife, who asks that he protect her against his "opinionated" mother, and his mother, who demands a central role in her grandchild's life. In a solid marriage, a husband's first allegiance is toward his wife, not his mother, yet in power struggles such as the one Mimi described, the entire family loses out when grandma's wisdom and expertise are utterly discounted. Benjamin Spock speaks eloquently for grandparents when he writes, "Most grandparents try hard not to interfere. On the other hand, they have had experience, they feel they've developed judgment, they love their grandchildren dearly, and they can't help having opinions."[3] The missing ingredient in Mimi's family, as in so many others, seems to be mutual goodwill, which entails a sincere effort on the parts of the new mother and the new paternal grandmother (with the new father's encouragement) to talk together openly, to understand and respect each other's needs, hopes, and desires, and to make accommodations for each other. The capacity to tolerate relationships that are thorny is also necessary if mothers-in-law and daughters-in-law are to maintain harmony. "I don't really like my mother-in-law, let alone love her," a friend revealed, "but she loves my daughter and my daughter loves her, and that's reason enough for us to try to get along together."

Between Grandparents and Grandchildren

The truth is that while we may have all manner of difficulty with our parents or parents-in-law, our children may adore them. Indeed, a parent with many deficiencies may become a grandparent with many assets. My mother-in-law confided to me a few years ago that as an adolescent she *hated* her father, whose ferocious temper had intensified after her mother died and he was left to care for four children. The "ogre" she described was the same man my husband had idolized as a child—

the passionate grandpa who pickled his homegrown tomatoes and enjoyed nothing more than seeing his grandson relish their strong taste. This was also the nurturing great-grandpa my adult daughter remembers as the man who squeezed oranges by hand on his eightieth birthday so that she, a toddler at the time, could have her first glass of *real* juice.

"When I was a little girl," a maternal aunt told me more than once, "Mutti would leave me in the care of indifferent housekeepers while traipsing off to Paris by herself to have a good time on weekends. I still don't understand how she could have been such a self-centered and thoughtless mother." This was the same woman who became my primary caregiver when I was two years old and both my parents were working full-time outside the home. My aunt's *irresponsible Mutti* became *my darling Grandma*—a woman who delighted me with make-believe stories of talking animals and guardian angels; who presented me with yellow daffodils in the dead of winter; who tucked me into bed, then brought me a cup (a delicate china cup) of hot tea with lemon and cubed sugar after we arrived home soaked to the skin from a summer downpour; who discovered a huge turtle in New York City's Fort Tryon Park, captured it, and lugged it home so that I, an only child, would have a pet; who was never too busy to play Monopoly; and the only one in the family who shared my excitement when I poured milk into my bowl of Rice Krispies each morning and listened for the sounds of "snap, crackle, and pop."

When grandchildren and grandparents have the opportunity to be together, a special, intensely intimate relationship can develop. Perhaps this is because older people—unlike many young and middle-aged adults who are stressed out by the relentless demands of work and home—are able to fully attend to the present moment and are often eager to take notice of small wonders (such as a bowl of "talking" cereal).

The grandparent-grandchild relationship has different possibilities than the parent-child one. Jimmy Carter writes that because grandparents are usually free to love, guide, and befriend children without having to take full responsibility for them, they can often reach out to them "past pride and fear of failure."[4] This sentiment is elaborated by Arthur Kornhaber:

> For [grandparents] a grandchild no longer represents their hopes and dreams as their own child did. For them the grandchild represents joy, renewal, and happiness. This is the secret they see in one another's eyes. While parents must temper their affection with lessons and discipline, either granting or withholding their love depending on the behavior of their children, grandparents can most often offer love with no strings attached.[5]

By the same token, children are less apt to engage in power struggles with grandparents than with parents. Children need to separate psychologically from their parents, which means defining themselves as "other" and laying claim to their unique lives. The separation process takes on special urgency during adolescence, and for a girl the tension is particularly evident in the relationship with her mother—the person with whom she is most identified and, precisely for this reason, from whom she must now differentiate in order to see herself as "her own person." It is safer for a teenage girl to identify with her grandmother than with her mother because she is less bound up with grandma. Indeed, the worst insult for most adolescents is to be told that they are just like their mothers in looks or manners. On the other hand, they are likely to welcome such comparisons with their grandmothers. As one young woman shared with Kornhaber:

> I took ballet lessons when I was a little girl, and my grandmother was the one who chauffered me. She had been a dancer in her youth in Russia, and before my first lesson, when I was eight years old, she taught me how to do the right hairstyle, with

looped braids caught up in colored ribbons. I practiced and practiced until I got it smooth and perfect. My teacher was so impressed. Then, over the years, my grandmother taught me how to make a bun and a twist, the more grown-up styles. She showed me pictures of herself as a girl with exactly the same hairstyles. I loved that, especially since I look so much like her.[6]

Grandparents can play various enhancing roles in their granddaughters' lives. They are the family historians who, through story and anecdote, link the child to her past, and they are the role models who demonstrate, through example, how to live fully and how to age and die with grace. They are also teachers, mentors, and nurturers. Shortly before her death, my mother-in-law bequeathed two items to my daughter. One was her diamond wedding ring; the other, a chipped white enamel pot in which she used to make soup for the family—a spouted pot she had inherited from her mother sixty years before. I knew that my mother-in-law had thought long and hard about the things she wanted to leave Leah, her cherished and only granddaughter. "A diamond is forever," and so is the maternal love, the warmth and vitality, that went into the pot that held the soup that nourished and nurtured children and husbands and aunts and grandparents for a hundred years. In addition to these material gifts, my mother-in-law bequeathed much good advice—or more accurately, wisdom. She taught my daughter that misfortunes were also worthwhile experiences, that it is far more gratifying to give than to receive, and (in response to the question "Grandma, is it okay if I invite a friend?") that there is *always* room for one more at the dinner table.

Kornhaber points to a "secret" role that grandparents often play—that of crony. Just as a girl will turn to a compassionate father when she needs to find some space away from mother, she will turn to a kind grandparent when she needs to get away from both her parents. As an old saying reminds us: "Why do grandparents and grandchildren get along so well? They have the same 'enemy': the parents." A sophisticated twelve-year-old I know recently quipped: "My mom and dad are health-food freaks: no sugar, no processed foods, no preservatives dare touch our plates. But when I go to Grandpa's house for the night, I know that he'll have a quart of tutti-frutti ice cream just for me. 'What your parents don't know won't hurt them,' he says with a mischievous twinkle in his eye, and then we both dig in." To my parents' dismay and to my delight, when I was very young, my Viennese grandfather taught me the bawdy lyrics of the drinking songs he had sung as a young man, and he also taught me some choice German and Yiddish curse words. Being coconspirators can empower both the grandparent and the grandchild; as long as the parents' authority isn't seriously undermined, having a little bit of fun at their expense is a harmless form of rebellion—and all girls need to rebel every now and then.

Perhaps the greatest gift that grandparents give their grandchildren is unconditional love. According to Cornell psychology professor Urie Bronfenbrenner, every child needs to be loved "irrationally," at least some of the time. When a child has someone in her life who waxes eloquent about her, who sees only the good in her, *who is absolutely crazy about her*—and a doting grandparent is often this someone—she cannot help knowing that she is a precious and special person. Louise DeSalvo, a Hunter College English professor and author with whom I regularly correspond, recently spent a significant part of a letter describing her pleasure and amazement as she watched her six-month-old grandchild eat Cheerios. In Louise's estimation, her grandchild's discovery that by pounding a mound of Cheerios with a wet palm you could get a bunch to stick to your hand and could then lick them off one by one was a feat of enormous consequence. "Of course every baby in the world who gets offered Cheerios figures out a great method for eating them," she conceded. "Still, I think [my grandchild] has invented something totally new."

Years ago when I was taking a postgraduate course on child development, my professor pointed out that while treating troubled children and adolescents, he was more hopeful about outcomes if his young patients had a strong relationship with at least one grandparent. For whatever reason, he contended, these children seem to like themselves better and to feel more secure than those without ties to the older generation. I suspect the reason is the grandparent's "crazy love."

Despite daunting physical distances and exorbitant airfares as well as family tensions or other formidable obstacles, relationships between grandchildren and grandparents can be sustained if the will to do so is strong. The parents of my childhood friend Barbara, determined to provide their daughter and son-in-law with the help they would need, concocted a radical plan. After learning that Barbara was pregnant with twins, they decided that living three thousand miles away from her would not do. And so, without conferring with their daughter or son-in-law (who they suspected would talk them out of their "foolish" plan), the grandparents-to-be packed their belongings into a U-Haul, trekked across the country, and within weeks of Barbara's due date, called from a neighborhood gas station to announce: "We're here! For good." At the time my friend, who had moved far from her hometown explicitly to get away from her doting parents, was appalled. "I thought I would die when I got that phone call," she told me. Now that her twins are twenty, however, Barbara acknowledges that her parents' help with them when they were young was invaluable and made it possible for her to keep her job as a school principal. Over the years, she also came to treasure her parents much more than she had as a younger woman, when she was trying to assert her independence from them. What she and her parents came to have in common was a love and concern for the growing children, which generated warm and generous feelings among them all.

Sometimes parents are the ones to initiate close ties with their children's grandparents. One of my dearest friends has been divorced from her daughters' father since they were toddlers; even so, she finds a way for them to visit her ex-husband's parents each Christmas. My friend is determined to maintain strong relationships with her in-laws so that her daughters can have a viable extended family. As she says with pride, "We've made the trip from Boston to Boise by plane, by train, and, when we're really hard up for money, by bus—but we always get there."

Helping Hands and Generous Hearts

Embedded in the term "extended family" are two concepts. *Extend* means both to enlarge and to reach out. It may no longer work for many relatives to live under one roof, as often occurred in times past, but, wherever we reside, we can still reach out to one another for mutual support, succor, and sustenance. Within the last few years, sociologists are reporting, American families have begun to place greater emphasis on family traditions and to go out of their way to be together for holidays. This renewed longing to be with our families suggests that we are ready to depend on each other again. "Call it a clan, call it a network, call it a tribe, call it a family," writer Jane Howard remarks. "Whatever you call it, whoever you are, you need one."[7] What we and our children need are people who are there for us, not just this week but also next week, next month, next year, and in the years to come. *Consistent caring* of this sort can be provided by loyal friends and devoted family members, such as aunts, uncles, and older siblings.

The reknowned psychologist Erik Erikson explained that the developmental task for all healthy adults is to become "generative"—to contribute in significant ways to the well-being of the next generation—lest they feel stagnant and incomplete. Today many adults are choosing not to have children of their own, and this frees them up to nurture the children of their siblings or close friends. I am presently counseling two women,

Judith and Fran, both childless by choice, who are wonderful examples of generative women.

For weeks Judith, a never-married architect, regaled me with stories about her ten-year-old niece, Zoe, who would soon be visiting with her for a week, as she does each year. In preparation for this year's visit, Judith asked me endless questions about the psychology of ten-year-olds so that she could better understand Zoe. Ordinarily clients talk about their needs during therapy sessions, but not Judith—she wanted only to talk about Zoe's needs. Judith's commitment to her niece reminded me of my paternal aunt's commitment to me when I was young and how much I was enhanced by it. The childless wife of a prominent surgeon in Chicago, Aunt Risa ensured that I would have the cultural and educational experiences my working-class parents could not provide. When I visited her, she took me to art museums and the ballet, bought me pastels and a sketch pad (meticulously keeping every one of my drawings in leather binders, as if they were destined to become great contributions to posterity), introduced me to such exotic foods as Turkish halvah, and drove to the suburbs to show me how wealthy folks lived. For my eleventh birthday, Aunt Risa bought me the full set of the *Encyclopedia Britannica*, which continued to open doors for me for years.

My client Fran is married and an attorney by profession. When one of her oldest and closest friends was in the midst of a divorce and unable to function, Fran stepped in without hesitation to support the children. With their mother and father at each other's throats and the household in chaos, Fran provided the two school-age girls with their only source of sanity and serenity. She listened to their problems, validated their scared and confused feelings, and from time to time allowed them to spend a few days with her so that they could escape from the tension and tears in their own home.

It is perfectly natural for children of all ages to confide in, look up to, emulate, and even develop crushes on the special people who take an interest in them. For some parents, however, this sort of adoration can create feelings of exclusion, jealousy, or envy. Working parents who turn over their babies and young children to nannies and other surrogates may experience these feelings to an extreme degree. When clients tell me that they resent a special person in their daughter's life, I usually say something like this: "Jealousy and envy are normal human feelings. They don't indicate that you are a bad person or a bad parent. Still, try to gather up all your courage and all your will not to *act* on these feelings lest they harm the child you love." I usually find that, committed to serving their child's best interest, most parents are willing to follow this advice.

When Leah as an adolescent found it difficult to talk about personal matters with me, she sought out adult female confidantes and became especially attached to two of her acting teachers, Melody and Betty. Whenever I began feeling envious of these women for being an intimate part of my daughter's life in a way that I was not, I forced myself to recognize the great service they were performing for her. Mature and wise, they counseled her in matters of love and sex, sensitively preparing her for womanhood. I recall one incident in particular: It was my turn to pick up Leah and her friends from acting class and drive them home. Arriving a bit early, I took a seat at the back of the darkened auditorium, where a rehearsal was in progress. Unobserved, I watched Melody confidently guide my inexperienced daughter through a tender kissing scene with a young, similarly inexperienced male actor.

During the early teenage years—when being different from one's peers feels like a curse—Leah was embarrassed that her family was "highbrow." She made no secret of the fact that she detested the classical music we played at home and found it perverse that we spent our money on artwork. Then Leah made a discovery: She found out that Betty loved classical music and art. Enlightened, she ended her condemnations of our "weird" lifestyle—another reason I owed Betty a debt of gratitude.

My friend Ellen calls the bighearted friends, neighbors, teachers, coaches, therapists, and other nonfamilial carers who bless a child's life "angel-friends." Every nuclear family, it seems to me, can use a few angel-friends.

The Blended Family

We do not always have the luxury of picking and choosing the people who take part in our daughters' lives; moreover, we may genuinely dislike some of them. In addition to the volume of letters I receive from aggrieved women who get along poorly with their mothers-in-law, I receive an impressive number from parents (especially mothers) and stepparents (especially stepmothers) complaining about one another. We have no term for the complicated relationship that exists between a divorced parent and the man or woman who has married the parent's former mate and is now the child's stepparent. Still, the feelings engendered by this nameless relationship are real enough; at the very least there will be jealousy, envy, resentment, competition, or mistrust.

Understandably, most men and women do not like the idea that this new spouse of their "ex" is now a significant part of their child's life. I recall a father—a proud alumnus of Harvard—who described how hurt and betrayed he felt when his teenage daughter appeared wearing a sweatshirt emblazoned with the name of her stepfather's alma mater—Yale. And I remember a mother who confided that she choked back tears when her school-age daughter exclaimed, "I'm so excited! Daddy's new wife is teaching me to crochet," something the mother had promised to do but had never gotten around to. Worries about the child's physical and emotional well-being are equally common: "Will my former husband's spouse re-member to buckle my daughter into her car seat?" "I hate it that my ex-wife's husband smokes around the kids, but what can I do?" "My daughter feels unwanted when she is at her dad and stepmother's house. I am terribly upset that they don't treat her well enough."

Of all the profound losses that a divorced person experi-ences—the loss of a marriage partner, the loss of a family meant to stay together, the loss of self-esteem that results from failing in a marriage, and, often, the loss of financial well-being—perhaps the one most feared by parents is that of the child's loyalty. A recently divorced client speaks for many, I am sure, when she says, "I suppose I can accept that my husband has found a wife to replace me. But what I would never accept is that my children would love her more than they love me."

The bad feelings that the natural parent and stepparent harbor for each other cannot help but affect the child. It is dif-ficult enough for a child to bond with a stepparent—especially for an older girl to bond with her stepmother—but it is nearly impossible if she anticipates that it will hurt her real parent. The truth is that children are extraordinarily loyal to their par-ents and would rather suffer than see them suffer. But a suffer-ing child committed to sustaining hostile relations with her stepparent serves no one. The child is likely to become racked with pain, and life within the blended family is doomed to misery.

As hard as it may be—and it is often excruciatingly hard—parents need to do what they can to help their child develop amicable relations with the stepparent. Similarly, it behooves the stepparent to work toward a friendly relationship; for by circumstance if not by choice, he or she will be a vital presence in the "village" in which the child grows and develops. What is needed is a more encompassing vision. The correspondence that follows is a blueprint for a healing dialogue between par-ent and stepparent that benefits the child:

Dear Stepparent,

Because you have married my daughter's father (mother), you will undoubtedly play an important part in her life. In advance, I would like to thank you for all the times that you will attend to her needs because you are there with her and I am not. When you married my daughter's father (mother), you probably didn't relish the idea that they are a *package deal*. And understandably so. I think that the role of stepparent may be the most difficult of all family roles, especially when one's stepchild is still reeling from the effects of divorce between her parents.

Because I love my daughter with all my heart, I hope she will make a positive adjustment to her new family, and of course, this means feeling comfortable with you. Toward this end, I will do my best to promote a good relationship between the two of you. Although I do not expect that you and I will become friends, I am hopeful that we can accommodate each other whenever possible. Feel free to contact me directly if there is an issue regarding my daughter.

Sincerely yours,

A Caring Parent

Dear Parent,

Thank you for your recognition and cooperation. For my part, I would like to reassure you that I will take responsible care of your daughter when she is in my charge. I, too, am aware of the difficulties of being a stepparent and, if I had my druthers would not *choose* this role for myself. At the same time, I know it can't be easy for you to turn your daughter over to me, as I am someone you hardly know. On the days she is with me and your former spouse, you must miss her a lot and maybe worry too. I empathize with your losses.

I cannot and will not try to take your place, of course. No one can replace a parent. However, I gratefully accept your offer to help your daughter and me develop a positive relationship. In every child's heart, there is room for a kind adult friend, and perhaps eventually I can be this friend.

I think you and I are in basic agreement. As adults, we must at times learn to set aside our own interests and put those of the child first. I will certainly contact you about your daughter should the need arise.

Yours truly,
A Caring Stepparent

We speak so often of loving and *letting go*. A very wise mother of two daughters once remarked upon hearing this phrase that it was every bit as important to strive for loving and *letting in*. She explained that letting in good and caring people seemed critical to her children's well-being at every stage of their development. Had I asked this insightful woman how we might go about letting in not only those who are close to us (trusted family members and friends) but those who are not (a difficult mother-in-law or a former spouse's new partner, for instance), I suspect she would have answered, "With a generous heart and a tolerant spirit."

PART TWO

PROTECTIVE LOVE

Child, I weep when you are born. In joy and disbelief . . . I am overwhelmed with love and fear. How will I care for you? How will I keep you safe?

—JULIE OLSEN EDWARDS

THE FOURTH GIFT:

Protectiveness

One of the most formidable tasks of parenthood is walking the fine line between being underprotective and over-protective. To do this, we must learn both to watch our children with vigilance and to look away when our glance becomes too intrusive; we must learn to intervene when they are endangered and to teach them strategies of safety so that they can protect themselves. Feminist philosopher Sara Ruddick says it well: "Children are not so fragile as goldfish . . . nor will they flourish if they are perpetually watched and guarded. On the other hand, they are not like roaches and weeds, hardy survivors regardless of what is done to them."[1]

Mother Nature does her best to ensure that human babies, her most helpless and immature creatures, will be adequately protected. Just as she "programs" babies to let out piercing cries when they feel threatened, she also prepares mothers to be exquisitely alert to these signals of distress, and to rush toward their infants and take them in their arms. Mother Nature also equips fathers to be fiercely protective; with their strong bodies and aggressive energy, they are primed to protect mother and baby from physical threats.

Even after their offspring are past the stage of babyhood, mothers and fathers will instinctively safeguard them. Given the number of potentially dangerous objects all around us—the pot of soup simmering on a hot burner, the bright yellow granules in the box of dishwasher detergent, the nervous dog that belongs to the neighbor, the cigarette butt left in the ashtray— and given the unlimited curiosity of very young children, it is a wonder (and a tribute to their parents) that the vast majority of them grow up in one piece. Ruddick notes that in the service of protection, caregiving parents develop a cognitive style she calls "scrutinizing."[2] With alert, action-ready glances, they are on the lookout for potential dangers in the environment *before* they materialize. Scrutinizing requires an enormous amount of mental energy, which may partly account for the fatigue that plagues parents of young children.

Anxious Parents

Unfortunately, scrutinizing can easily turn into worrying: "Oh, my God, what happened to the loose vitamins I left on the table. Did Katie eat them?" "That new kid in the play group had a weird rash on his arm; maybe he exposed Becky to some horrible disease!" "What if Vicki is kidnapped on her way to school?" I have observed that among married couples with children, one parent often becomes the designated worrier. Indeed, this was the role I assumed in my family.

To outsiders, the lengths to which we designated worriers go in order to safeguard our children may seem absurd. And although we ourselves are aware of the strangeness of our behaviors, we tend to have a terrible time curbing them. Janice, a participant in the group for parents and daughters that I facilitate, confessed that before putting her preadolescent child on the bus to summer camp, she cornered the bus driver and insisted that he tell her his life story. "I wanted to make sure he wasn't a child molester," she sheepishly explained. Similarly, author Margaret Drabble confides, "I used to be a reasonably careless and adventurous person before I had children: now I am morbidly obsessed by seat belts and constantly afraid that low-flying aircraft will drop on my children's school."[3] Author Judith Viorst provides this autobiographical anecdote:

> I once (I know this sounds ludicrous) was positive that as long as I was right there, my sons couldn't choke to death on a piece of meat. Why? Because I knew that I would keep nagging them to take smaller bites and chew carefully. And because I also knew that if worse really came to worst, I would seize a knife and perform a tracheotomy. Like many mothers, I saw myself—and in some ways see myself still—as their guardian angel, their shield of invulnerability. And although I have had to let my sons explore more and more of this perilous world alone, I am haunted by the anxiety that they always will be at far greater risk without me.[4]

Viorst goes on to say that mothers are not the only ones who see themselves as all-protective. She recounts the story of a father who, when his son first learned to crawl, would get down on the floor and crawl behind him so that if an overhead light fixture suddenly fell from the ceiling he could catch it before it landed on the child's head.

During my early years of being a mother, I was constantly on the lookout for threats to my daughter's well-being. As an enthusiastic champion of Adelle Davis and the health food movement of the early seventies, for instance, I was convinced that any foods not a hundred percent natural would do Leah's growing body harm. Hence, upon discovering that an elderly neighbor she often visited was treating her to Chuckles, I pounced on the bewildered gentleman, gave him a tongue-lashing, and made him promise that he would no longer "corrupt" her with his offers of artificially flavored candy.

Eventually we parents learn—and learn again—that, despite our overwhelming love, we cannot protect our children absolutely. As they venture into the world, we realize that our arms are simply not long enough to wrap around them and protect them from life's jabs and blows. In my own case, I discovered that my protective mother love was not potent enough to shoo away viruses. Or prevent a car accident. Or deter the mugger who assaulted Leah one bright spring day in the tranquil French village of Pau. And despite my war against Chuckles, my daughter developed perhaps the world's sweetest tooth, which, over my tiresome protests, she faithfully indulged.

When bad things happen to our children, it does us little good to nurse our guilty feelings and tell ourselves that if only we had done this or not done that the crisis could have been averted. In fact, I have noticed that when parents expend energy blaming themselves, they become so absorbed in remorse that they cannot give their children what they really need: comfort, encouragement, and strategies for coping with the misfortune. Rather than berating ourselves for not being fully protective, we would be far better off remembering that life is full of chance. This does not mean we should become passive and abdicate our supervising responsibilities. It means, rather, we should try to temper our protectiveness with humility. Only then will we be able to respect the limitations of our protective power and accept that we cannot control the world.[5]

How Much Protection is Enough?

Having struggled for years to keep my own tendencies toward overprotection in check, I was faced with a particularly difficult decision during Leah's junior year at Carleton College. She was set to study in Paris for a semester when the Persian Gulf War suddenly broke out. To my mind, this was not the time for an American to travel to Europe. Although the college administrators were also concerned about terrorism, they decided not to cancel the foreign-study program and instead urged students to decide for themselves whether or not to follow through with their plans. Several students who had originally intended to study abroad backed down. Despite my pleas to my daughter to follow suit, she would not, and it soon became clear that the only way I could stop her from going was to forbid it outright. My husband, less nervous about Leah's plans than I was—remember, I am the designated worrier in our family!—opted to leave the decision to me. Every protective bone in my body moved me to keep Leah in the States. At the same time, I recognized how much the semester would enrich her; this was her chance to become fluent in French, to make friends with people culturally different from her, to be far away from the comforts of home, to figure it out and fend for herself. What was I to do? After much soul-searching, I decided to let Leah go. To rob her of her sense of adventure, zest for new experiences, and confidence in her growing competence seemed more threatening to her well-being than terrorist activities.

Charles, a participant in my parents group, often points out that parents cannot limit their children to risk-free experiences, that helping our children live life to the fullest means allowing them to take some *calculated risks*, just as we do when we are adventurous. As I am writing this page, pondering the differences between calculated risks and high risks, my daughter is somewhere in Guatemala, traveling alone. Before she left for this latest adventure, I provided her with a hefty list of cautions. Then I gave her my blessings for a wonderful trip. Perhaps cautions and blessings are the best we have to offer our children as they venture forth.

Reporting on a chance encounter with a young girl, syndicated columnist Ellen Goodman underscores the hazards of insulating children from the world:

CASCO BAY, Maine: Just this morning, a small girl I don't know stopped me on my walk to point out an injured swallowtail. We talked for a minute about the fragility of a butterfly's wings and then went our separate ways.

It was a passing event but one that might have never happened on a city street. In cities, suburbs, even small towns, children are now carefully taught to be afraid of people they don't know. Their wariness is worn like a shield. A stranger becomes reluctant to penetrate that defense. . . .

I'm not surprised that we have become so protective of children. . . . As our children spend more time out of our care, we worry more. As we know fewer people in our communities, there are by definition more outsiders.

But at some point in time, we must also begin to acknowledge the risks of protectiveness. Risks that come when children are taught to be afraid. Risks that come to a diverse society when kids grow up suspicious of "others."

Without even knowing it and with the best intentions, we can stunt our children with our deep longing to keep them safe.[6]

Of course, we would be remiss if we failed to warn our children about dangerous situations and dangerous people. Ava Siegler, director of the Institute for Child, Adolescent & Family Studies in New York City, asserts that the protective parent's most powerful weapon is "plain talk" about the hard facts of modern life: AIDS, drug abuse, rape, and more. She notes that parents, out of their own fear, sometimes mistake silence for protection. "Parents say they don't want to spoil their child's innocence," says Siegler, "or they tell me, 'What they don't know won't hurt them,' and I say it is exactly what your children don't know that *will* hurt them."[7] To be sure, such candid talk ought to be delivered with sensitivity to children's needs, one of which is *hope*. Hence, in discussing modern-day dangers with young children, we can remind them that Mommy and Daddy are there to see that no harm comes to them. We can ease the anxieties of older children by pointing out that most problems have solutions, or at least partial ones, and by teaching them self-protective strategies. I am indebted to the self-defense teacher who taught my daughter to scream her way out of dangerous situations. And scream she did when she was assaulted in France, scaring off her assailant before he had a chance to rape her.

Instead of pointing out to our daughters only what is unsafe—and thereby painting the world as a shadowy, foreboding place—we need to emphasize what is safe and approachable. For instance, we might say to a young child, "It's not safe to pet stray dogs, but it's fine to play with Queenie because she loves children." Or, "You must never go anywhere with a person you don't know well, but it's perfectly all right to smile back at and say 'Hi' to the homeless people we pass on the street." As a young child beset with fears and anxieties, I was fortunate to have a grandmother who portrayed the world as welcoming and wondrous. One time when I confided to her that I was afraid of the night, she suggested that we take a stroll after dark. "You are right," she replied, "a little girl like you should not wander alone at night, but if we go out together and stay on the busy streets, nothing bad will happen to us, and we will see that the night is lovely." On our adventure, we chatted with passers-by walking their dogs; we identified Venus and the Big Dipper; and we made up funny stories about the man in the moon. As an adult, I still harbor fears and anxieties about many things, but the night is not one of them.

Psychiatric social worker Katharine Walker, who counsels many children, once told me how she responds to young clients who have been victims of atrocity or traumatized by the media coverage of murders, abductions, war crimes, terrorist attacks, and the like. "Sure, it's true that there are some very bad people out there," she tells them "and it's also true that most of the people you'll run into are very good." Our times are so rife with nationalism, sexism, ethnocentricity, and religious bigotry that the "us's" of all sorts are becoming irrationally suspicious of the "them's" of every variety. Now, more than ever before, it is crucial to remind our children that in any subgroup the decent people far outnumber its thieves, murderers, and other scoundrels.

Helping Our Daughters Stay Safe

When I was a young woman living in New York City, I was mugged at knifepoint. My assailants followed me into my apartment building—being a polite person, I graciously held the front door open for them—and later attacked me on a stair landing. From the moment I set eyes on the two men, I had a funny feeling that they were up to no good and knew I should not have let them into the building. And, in fact, later when I tearfully asked the police officer to whom I reported the crime how to avoid muggings in the future, he said, "Always listen to your funny feelings and never hesitate to act on them. Even if you think you're overreacting and being ridiculous, call the cops or scream for help or just get the hell out of the threatening situation." To be sure, times arise when danger catches us unaware, and we can do nothing to avert it. Most often, however, our sixth sense seems to protect us from harm; it is the closest thing we have to a guardian angel. Passing on this bit of wisdom to our daughters is one of the best ways to ensure their safety.

A twenty-year-old client used these words to explain why she, unlike several of her friends, had never been sexually violated:

> From the time I was in elementary school until I left home, my parents told me, "Wherever you are, if you sense that things are not quite right, chances are they're not. Call us. We'll come and get you." Whenever I took them up on their offer—usually at high school parties that had gotten out of hand because of drugs and alcohol—they didn't make me feel ashamed or that I'd done something wrong. They'd just remind me that it was always a good thing to trust my intuitions.

The seventeen-year-old daughter of a friend told me that what has kept her safe is the word *no*. Kirstin explained that in a self-assertiveness class, her mother learned the art of saying no and passed on this art to her when she was only seven years old. Together the two would role-play situations such as fending off a bully on the playground or a drug dealer in the school yard and practice saying no in a way that could be heard. "I'm a master no-sayer," Kirstin proudly confided. "In most societies, girls are taught to be compliant, to say yes so that they won't hurt anyone's feelings. They are trained to do things against their will and against their better instincts. But I have no compunction to say no: 'No, don't touch me,' or 'No, I don't want to sleep with you,' or 'No, I never take a ride with someone who's been drinking,' or just 'No is no—and I don't have to give you a reason for it.' " Interestingly, in a survey taken in the mid-1980s, in which 1,000 thirteen- through sixteen-year-old sexually active girls were asked to select from more than twenty sex-related topics those they would like help with, the majority of respondents wanted more information on how to say no to sex without hurting boys' feelings.[8]

The New Sexual Revolution

In industrialized societies, adolescence is normally a vulnerable time for girls. Today's girls are maturing faster than their mothers did and considerably faster than their grandmothers did. The average age for the first menstruation is twelve and a half, although it is no longer unusual for a girl to begin menstruating at nine. We have no definitive explanations for the earlier onset of puberty. Some researchers attribute it to better nutrition, others to the growth hormones added to the beef and chicken we consume, and still others to increased exposure to natural and artificial light.

As their little-girl bodies mature into nubile ones, adolescent girls are both tempted and pressured to become sexual

despite the fact that they may not be ready for sexual intercourse. It is no secret that early sexual activity can create psychological problems for girls—feelings of being exploited and
objectified as well as feelings of losing control and being swallowed up. I remember a fifteen-year-old I counseled after her
parents divorced. My young client, like many of the other
popular girls in her class, was sexually active. When I asked her
if she enjoyed having sex, she answered with a sweetly sad expression, "No, it's something I just get through. When I have
sex with my boyfriend, I don't think about what's happening to
me; I try to keep my mind on nice things, like taking my puppy
for a walk."

Early sexual activity can also lead to serious medical problems such as HIV infection and to pregnancy, both of which
are occurring in ever-greater numbers. Because the immature
cervix is more susceptible to sexually transmitted diseases, the
younger children are when they engage in sex, the more likely
they are to become infected. Indeed, one in four sexually active
girls contracts a sexually transmitted disease each year.[9] Often
these "silent" diseases are not diagnosed at their onset, setting
women up for infertility and medical complications years
later.[10]

Many of us parents are hard put when it comes to setting
standards and rules for our daughters' sexual behavior. Those
of us who came of age in the late sixties or early seventies, when
the reigning spirit was to "make love, not war" and the avail-
ability of the birth-control pill gave us the green light for pre-
marital sex, may be reluctant to discourage our teenagers from
sexual activity for fear of appearing hypocritical. Moreover,
parents of all ages, taken in by today's "let's get *real*" ideology,
are convinced that we cannot stop our daughters from having
sexual experiences and that our objective should be instead to
encourage them to have "safer sex."

However, if we listen to our teenage daughters carefully,

we may discover that they do not feel ready for sex. What they need from us during their adolescence are support, supervision, and sensible standards for sexual conduct so that they will be able to have healthy relationships when the time is right. In order to guide our daughters, we may need some guidance ourselves; trusted family members and friends, therapists, health-care professionals, and other parents with teenagers or adult children can help us look beyond our own experience to do what's right for our daughters.

A close friend shared the following story. Her seventeen-year-old daughter came to her with a troubling dream. Arielle dreamed that she had asked her mother's permission to marry, and her mother said: "Why, I'm pleased as can be that you'll be married soon. Now, let's get you all ready for the wedding." My friend did not at first understand why the dream disturbed her daughter. "Don't you get it, Mom?" Arielle asked. "I really didn't want your permission. I'm much too young to get married." In real life, my friend was not encouraging her teenager to marry in the near future. She was, however, intimating that it was natural for teenagers to be sexually active, necessary for them to use contraception, and time for mother and daughter to go to the women's clinic and see about birth-control methods. After we talked, my friend came to realize that marriage in Arielle's dream was a euphemism for sexual intercourse—something for which she felt emotionally unprepared. Arielle did not want her mother to take her for birth control; on the contrary, she wanted her mother to protect her against temptations to be sexual, which in her surroundings were difficult to overcome. Open and empathic, my friend took her daughter's cue, setting stricter curfews and no longer allowing her to be alone in the house with her boyfriend for long periods of time.[11]

Being strict may not make us popular with our daughters, but it is what they need from us during adolescence. A story from my own youth comes to mind. When I was sixteen, I had a date with a boy named Ralph who was cocky, sexually experienced, and of the mind that he was entitled to anything he wanted. After Ralph came to my home to pick me up, we joined some other friends at a bowling alley. We were not there for very long, however, when I heard a voice booming over the PA system, "Evelyn Silten, there's a phone call for you. Come to the front desk immediately." I rushed to the phone. It was my father. Without a shred of hesitancy, he told me that he and my mother agreed that the young man I was with seemed ill-mannered and untrustworthy, and that I was to come home immediately. They would pay for the cab when I arrived. I pleaded with my father not to embarrass me by treating me like a child, but he did not give in, and I did as I was told. For days after this mortifying event, I would not speak to or look at my father. And of course, I never let him know I was secretly relieved that he had gotten me out of a situation that was over my head. The truth of the matter was that because Ralph was good-looking and sexy, and because I ached to have a boyfriend, I might very well have said yes to him when I should have said no.

As I grew older, my father became less controlling and intrusive. I recall an incident when I was nineteen. One morning after I had stayed out very late on a date (with the young man who would become my husband a year later), my mother approached me anxiously asking, "Where were you? What did you do with your boyfriend? Why didn't you come home sooner?" Believing that I was a responsible young woman and fully understanding my need for my mother *not to know* about my sexual adventures, my father intervened: "If you ask her these questions, you will only be forcing her to lie." From that time on, my mother respected my privacy by not asking too much, for which I was grateful.

Protecting and respecting our children entails knowing when to supervise and when to look away. Such discrimination is not always easy, of course, and we parents, being human and fallible creatures, are bound to err in one direction or the other from time to time. It is reasonable to assume, however, that until our daughters outgrow the impulsiveness of early and mid-adolescence and until they develop the strength of their own convictions, our responsibility is to protect them from sexual temptations and pressures. Psychotherapist Mary Pipher in her book *Reviving Ophelia* puts it well: "The decision to have sex should be a North Star decision, that is, one that's in keeping with a sense of oneself, one's values, and long-term goals."[12]

The Protective Hedge

Protecting our daughters during their transition from childhood to womanhood is an age-old problem with age-old solutions. The quintessential story of the adolescent girl's sexual unfolding is "Briar Rose," as recorded by the Brothers Grimm. In addition to describing the mysterious inner world of the pubescent girl, it provides insights and directives for parents, reminding us, too, that happy endings are possible. In the prologue to this book, I provided a synopsis of the tale. Let us return to "Briar Rose" now and discover more of its meanings.

The story goes like this:

Once upon a time there lived a king and queen who for many years longed for a child. One morning as the queen was bathing in a pond, a frog whispered in her ear, "Your wish has been fulfilled. Before the year's end, you shall bring a daughter into the world."

Sure enough, the frog's prophecy came true. The queen had a lovely baby girl, and the king, overwhelmed with joy, prepared a feast to celebrate the royal birth. Included on his guest list were relatives, friends, acquaintances, and also twelve fairies. Actually, there were thirteen fairies in the kingdom, but because the king and queen had only twelve golden plates for them to eat from one fairy was not invited.

The feast was held in great splendor, and as it was drawing to an end, the fairies presented the child with gifts that would prepare her to live a blessed life. After eleven of the fairies had presented their gifts, a dark cloud suddenly obscured the child's bright future. Seemingly out of nowhere, the thirteenth fairy appeared. Seething with rage for having been excluded from the festivities, she sought revenge and called out in a shrill voice, "The princess shall prick herself on the distaff of a spinning wheel in her fifteenth year and shall fall down dead."

At these prophetic words, everyone gasped in terror. Only the twelfth fairy, whose wish was still unspoken, seemed unperturbed. Although she could not cancel the curse, she could soften it. Stepping forward, she made her pronouncement: "It shall be not death but a deep sleep lasting a hundred years into which the princess will fall." Despite the good fairy's assurance, the king was determined to do everything in his power to protect his child from any misfortune, and then and there he commanded the destruction of every spinning wheel, every spindle, every distaff in the whole kingdom.

One by one, the promises of the fairies came true. The young princess grew up virtuous, beautiful, and clever. Now it happened that on their daughter's fifteenth birthday the king and queen were away from home and the princess was left alone in the castle. Intoxicated by a spirit of adventure, she wandered happily about the castle, room by room, until she came to an old tower. Climbing the tower's narrow, winding staircase to the very top, she discovered a little door with a rusty key protruding from its lock. When she turned the key, the door flew open and there sat an old woman at a spinning wheel, deftly spinning her flax. Never having seen a spinning wheel before, the princess was intrigued. Reaching out to touch the spindle, which whirled around the distaff so merrily, she pricked her finger. And as the twelfth fairy had promised, the princess fell immediately into a deep sleep.

At this very moment the king and queen, having just returned home from their sojourn, also fell into a deep sleep, as did their courtiers, the cook and the scullion, the horses in the stable, the dogs in the yard, the doves on the roof, the flies on the wall. The fire flickering on the hearth grew dim, the wind died down, the leaves on the trees in front of the castle became perfectly still.

But 'round the castle, a hedge of briar roses began to grow. Years passed. The hedge grew so tall and thick that it hid the castle from view. The townsfolk in the surrounding kingdoms spoke in hushed tones of a lovely princess named Briar Rose who lay sleeping behind the wall of thorns. And from time to time, the most daring of the young men would set out to force their way through the hedge into the castle to encounter the sleeping beauty. But the thorns, like claws, caught them in a lethal grip and would not let them go, and so the suitors died a miserable death.

A hundred years passed. At long last, the day came when Briar Rose, according to the promise of the twelfth fairy, was to wake up. And on this very day, undaunted by the tragic tales he had heard about the doomed suitors of ages past, a young prince set out to discover for himself the lovely Princess Briar Rose. When the prince caught sight of the briar hedge that surrounded the castle, he was amazed to see that it was all in blossom. As he came closer, the beautiful pink and red flowers—of their own accord—opened and made way for him to pass through unharmed. Guided by some mysterious force, he headed toward the old tower, climbed its narrow winding staircase, and came upon the room in which the sleeping princess lay. As he bent down to kiss her tenderly on the mouth, she awakened and met his gaze with friendly eyes.

At this very moment the king and queen, the courtiers, the cook and the scullion, the horses and hounds, the birds and insects also roused themselves from their long sleep. After a hundred years, life had returned to the castle. Soon after the king and queen prepared a grand wedding. And, as fate would have it, Princess Briar Rose and her prince lived together happily for a long, long time.[13]

What meanings can we draw from this fairy tale? The first is that even the most cherished child cannot be kept perfectly safe. Indeed, in one way the curse of the bad fairy represents the inevitable misfortunes that beset every child's life. Although we parents can mitigate the dangers that confront our daughters, we cannot eliminate them. Nor can we stop time and lock our daughters in eternal childhood to preserve their innocence, which is what the king tries to do by banning the spinning wheels.

The bad fairy's curse can also be interpreted literally: the colloquial term for a woman's monthly bleeding is "the curse." When the Brothers Grimm recorded "Briar Rose," girls normally began their periods around age fifteen, and the thirteenth fairy's decree that in her fifteenth year Princess Briar Rose would prick her finger on the distaff (a female symbol) of the spinning wheel and die reflects the pessimistic belief that the first menstruation, marking the "death" of childhood, is a dire event.[14] The twelfth fairy, however, alters this grim prophecy. "It shall not be death but a deep sleep lasting a hundred years into which the princess shall fall," she promises. At its deepest level, the story of the princess Briar Rose is about changing the curse into a blessing—about transforming every girl's anticipation of womanhood from an experience of affliction, exploitation, loss, and death to one of joy, enhancement, generativity, and renewal.

Some feminist thinkers assert that the story of Briar Rose denigrates women; they look upon the hundred-year sleep that Briar Rose falls into as a metaphor for a woman's unhealthy passivity—the comatose existence that is expected to last until she is rescued by a man's sexual overtures. But can we not view the hundred-year sleep as a symbol of the time of quiet growth and maturation that the pubescent girl requires to nurture her inner life through fantasizing, dreaming, problem solving, and learning? Every society has its proclivities, and our Western one promotes activity and productivity to the exclusion of passivity and receptivity. From the time our children are very young, they are hurried along from one activity to the next, leaving them with hardly any time to muse, daydream, observe, or contemplate. A balanced life requires, on the other hand, both the capacity to do and the capacity to be, both an energy directed outward and an energy directed inward—toward the self, toward self-understanding. And can we also not interpret the hundred-year sleep as the waiting period between the onset of menstruation and sexual union? Like her parents, the king and queen, who waited years to have a child, Briar Rose learns to wait patiently for her true love. With our encouragement, our daughters can also learn to cultivate patience, a critical antidote to the allure of immediate gratification promoted in our culture.

The term "Briar Rose" refers not only to the name of the princess but also to the hedge of thorny roses that grows so tall and thick that no one can penetrate it for a hundred years.[15] Throughout a daughter's growing years, from infancy to young adulthood, the loving mother and father serve as her hedge of thorny roses, protecting her as best they can from anything that might do her harm. In effect, the vegetation surrounding the castle performs a dual function. It keeps out harmful influences and, like the blossoming hedge that allows the young prince to enter the castle, lets in enhancing ones.

On a recent plane trip, I conversed with the young woman seated next to me, who illustrated this twofold function in contemporary terms. What immediately impressed me about Miriam was that she appeared to be comfortable with herself; nothing about her presence seemed stilted or false. Upon learning that I write books about parents and children, she was eager to tell me about her happy childhood. She explained that during her middle-school years, she felt as if her mother and her mother's closest friends had formed "a protective circle" around her within which she was able to grow strong and confident. At ages ten and eleven, Miriam's schoolmates were beginning to obsess about their looks, their weight, and their chances of "getting" a boyfriend. This group of older women, former flower children of the sixties whom she loved and respected, poohpoohed the idea of her dieting or buying clothes with the "in" label or groveling for male approval. In conversation after conversation, they drummed into her that what really mattered was not looking like the cover girl on a fashion magazine or having a steady boyfriend, but learning, being creative, caring about the world, and actively participating in it. My young acquaintance went on to tell me that from one of her mother's friends she learned to play the guitar, from another she learned about theater, and from a third she learned to love poetry. In her words, "I was so busy doing wonderful things during my adolescence that I didn't have the time to get caught up in the destructive craziness going on all around me and could tune out all the sick messages that proliferate in our culture."

To be sure, our daughters are exposed constantly to sexist and sexually exploitative TV programs, movies, and music, pounded by messages convincing them that their happiness depends on being thin and beautiful, and consistently overstimulated by images of loveless or violent sexuality. Nonetheless, although "protective hedges" cannot keep out all these harmful influences from our daughters' lives, the positive values and expectations that we cultivate in our "enclosed gardens" can counter them to a significant degree.

"Briar Rose" ends with the harmonious meeting of the prince and the princess—the fateful kiss, revival of the castle community, and wedding celebration. Finally, the story teaches us that *after* awakening to her own selfhood a young woman is ready for sexual intimacy. According to reknowned psychologist Bruno Bettelheim, "Briar Rose" emphasizes that a traumatic event—such as a girl's bleeding at the beginning of puberty, and later, in intercourse—can have the happiest consequences.[16]

Fairies and the Soul

And what can we learn from the fairies who visit Briar Rose? Fairies symbolize the transformation of the human soul, personifying the stages in development of the spiritual life. The nature of fairies is paradoxical: they fulfill humble tasks yet possess extraordinary powers. Their powers, however, are not magical but are the revelations of latent possibilities; the riches they dispense are their gifts of wisdom.

As our daughters grow into adulthood, our protective functions necessarily diminish: We know that we cannot prevent the growth pains that accompany their lives or spare them from life's hardness. However, by demonstrating our faith in our daughters' choices, we—like good fairies—will encourage them to realize their innate possibilities and to become all they might be.

Limits and Boundaries

All good-enough parents establish rules and restrictions to keep their children from being overwhelmed, getting hurt, and violating others. For many of us, however, setting and enforcing limits is fraught with self-doubt. It's hard to convince ourselves that saying no to our daughters can be as loving as saying yes. Or to accept that no matter how reasonable we try to be, power struggles between us are inevitable. Or to revise our rules continually to accommodate our growing daughters' changing needs for protection and freedom. When I asked the members of my parents group, "What happens to you when you try to discipline your daughters?" they all talked about having uncomfortable feelings: "I feel mean," "I feel like a dictator," "I feel guilty," "I feel foolish," "I feel weak and wishy-washy," "I feel paralyzed," "I feel like an old fuddy-duddy," "I quake all over; it's almost like having dry heaves inside."

Recollections

All healthy children test parental limits while searching for safe boundaries. Remembering my early years as a parent, I can say that my daughter's responses to having limits were no less complicated than my reactions to setting and enforcing them. Leah's first bed was a lace-covered cradle that a great aunt and uncle had crafted from a wicker basket. Leah, however, much preferred my arms to the lovely cradle and cried bitterly the first time I put her in it. Although I wanted to pick her up immediately and soothe her, both my husband and my mother convinced me that she would fall asleep within a few minutes if I simply let her be. Sure enough, Leah settled down before long. When I returned to the nursery to peek at my sleeping baby, though, I noticed that she was not where I had put her. Barely a week old, she had managed to inch her way to the upper edge of the mattress. With her head crammed against the cradle's wicker frame, she looked most uncomfortable. Careful not to awaken her, I gently moved her to the middle of the mattress and tiptoed out of the room. Returning a few minutes later, I observed that, like a potted plant incessantly turning its flower-head toward the sun, Leah had squirmed to the edge of the mattress once again. In those first spacey days of motherhood, I was not in a state to intellectualize about the meaning of my daughter's behavior. Looking back, however, I can see that the walls of the cradle, like my holding arms and the swaddling blankets in which I wrapped her, allowed her to feel contained and secure.

As Leah got older, she began to explore boundaries that extended beyond the cradle, the room, the house, the backyard. She was about five years old when she decided to run away from home: We had had an argument, and I heard her storm out the front door. A few minutes later, I went to look for her. I found her sitting by the corner of the block clutching a small red-and-white vinyl suitcase. "I was very angry at you," she said in her most serious voice, "and I wanted to run away, but I'm not allowed to cross the street by myself. That's why I didn't get very far." I held out my hand. With great relief she took it, and we walked back to the house together.

For Leah and me, her elementary school years were for the most part harmonious. She accepted rules and structure both at home and in school. One of her favorite pastimes was playing "teacher" with her little brother and having him follow *her* rules—and she was quite bossy! When Leah reached puberty, however, she seemed to experience the walls around her (our house rules, schedules, and curfews) as bothersome constraints on her freedom and found ingenious ways—procrastination, evasion, small lies—to chip away at them.

Recently, while I was sorting through boxes of old letters and cards, I came across a letter Leah had written at the beginning of tenth grade. In it she tried to convince her father and me that we should allow her to stay out late on weekday nights with her new high school friends, insisting that her social life would not interfere with "getting good grades" and imploring us to trust her judgment completely. The tone of the letter was unwavering until the last line: "I am a little confused about where I am as far as maturity and making the right decisions go." In the midst of declaring her independence, Leah was reminding us of her dependency. It is the tension between the teenager's wish for autonomy and her desire for parental supervision—the ambivalent and mixed messages—that can make early adolescence such a bewildering time for teens *and for us mothers and fathers.*

By her senior year in high school, the wrangling over limits abated. I was generally able to trust Leah's good judgment, which undoubtedly helped her trust herself. Then, sometime during her college years, it became obvious to both of us that she no longer needed my rules and restrictions. Indeed, she had transformed herself from a girl into a woman. Now Leah is twenty-five, living in New York City, fully self-supporting, and, I assume, crossing streets by herself. She confidently makes her own decisions and is guided by her own principles; very occasionally, she asks for my advice. She has developed, in the jargon of psychology, an "internal locus of control," the mark of healthy independence and self-confidence.

Kathy, one member of my parents group, describes the metamorphosis from childhood into adulthood more vividly. She says that over the years a child, bit by bit, "swallows" her parents' external walls—their rules, routines, rituals, morals, ethics, and values—and builds on them to form new structures of her own. Tom, another member of the group, portrays the child's passage into adulthood and freedom in the following lovely way:

> Imagine two parents gently holding their child's hand while she explores her new surroundings—the home they have built for her. The child runs her fingers along the walls that they have put up to protect her against the elements and the other overwhelming forces. After she is familiar with the walls and contents of one room, they lead her to the next room and the next, including the attic, the basement, even the closets. They explain what is in each of these rooms, the obstacles she can expect to encounter, and the ways she can get around them. Eventually they go beyond the household walls toward the surrounding grounds, which they also explore together. The child discovers many gates, and, all the while, the parents are present—behind her, on either side, or in front of her— and they respond to her explorations with enthusiasm and help her focus on the path ahead. When the child opens with her own key the last gate, the parents step aside and the child, now transformed into an adult, passes through it alone.

Wanting and Hating Limits

What I learned from my daughter as well as from the many young women clients I have counseled is that along the route

toward adulthood the growing child feels increasingly ambivalent toward her limit-setting parents. On the one hand, she resents her parents' dominance; after all, it is belittling to live
under the sway of their power. Hence, she challenges them in
myriad ways, testing their limits, pushing their buttons, and
trying to disassemble their walls. At the same time, she wants
her parents to be strong and firm so that they can reliably protect her and help her maintain her stability and focus. Most of
all, she desperately needs them to keep on loving and caring for
her, even while her defiance provokes their frustration and
anger. Because a girl's core being is tied up with having warm
and close bonds, acting out against her parents stirs up fears
that she is jeopardizing her relationship with them. (A boy also
depends on his parents' loving care, but he is less likely to fret
about being on the "outs" with mother or father from time to
time.[1]) All in all, the opposing forces at play in a girl's psyche
are confusing to her; childhood, we would do well to remember, is not a carefree condition.

In *The Thousand and One Nights*, Princess Scheherazade
tells the story of "The Fisherman and the Jinny," which addresses the child's resentments about containment. In this
story, a fisherman casts his net into the sea four times. On his
first three efforts, he comes up with nothing but debris. On
his fourth try, however, he pulls up a copper jar, and as he
opens it a giant jinny emerges. The jinny threatens to kill the
fisherman because, having been contained in the tiny jar for
many years, the jinny is full of rage. A young girl can easily
identify with the rageful jinny for she, too, often feels confined. Simultaneously, she can identify with the fisherman.
Although things at first look grim for the fisherman, his
cleverness proves more awesome than the jinny's power. By
doubting aloud that the jinny could ever fit into such a small
jar and thereby inducing it to return to the jar to prove its
prowess, the fisherman outwits the jinny. A little girl often ex-

periences her mother and father as overpowering giants and fantasizes about outwitting them and getting the better of them, just as the fisherman triumphs over the jinny.[2]

Of course, fantasizing is one thing; overpowering one's parents is quite another. When I was very young, I lived in an apartment with my parents, maternal grandmother, and paternal grandfather. My grumpy old grandfather spent most of each day sitting on an overstuffed armchair. Whenever I asked him if I could sit there, he denied me this luxury. Then, one day, I lied that someone was at the door to see him, and when he went to check who it was, I "stole" his chair. At first, Grandpa's cushy chair seemed wonderful to me, but within a minute or two I felt bad that I had tricked him into abdicating it. Moreover, I quickly realized that this chair was too big for me, or more accurately, that I was too small for it.

I have counseled many women who during childhood found it necessary to reverse roles with their parents. Because these parents were immature, overwhelmed, or out-of-control due to emotional or mental instability, substance abuse, or sexually promiscuity, these children wound up "supervising" them. Joan, for example, had to coax her mother, who had fallen apart after a divorce and remained depressed for years, to eat and to take her medications. "As soon as school let out, I would rush home to make sure Mama was okay. I simply accepted that my role was to be my mother's caretaker," she recalls. Little by little, Joan lost her childhood. She became afraid to experiment (the prerogative of youth) and make mistakes because no one would be there to supervise *her* and ensure that *she* would not get hurt.

Without parental walls—or with only flimsy ones—children know neither what is expected of them nor what they can expect from others, which produces free-floating anxiety. Dana, a client whom I am presently seeing, explains that her well-meaning but misguided parents set no rules for her.

They simply expected that I would be a good little girl. From the time I was very small, they trusted me and implied that I didn't need to be told what to do. The trouble was that without their rules or guidelines to follow I never knew whether I was doing the right thing or not. I worried a lot that I might be doing something bad. And when I wasn't perfect, I thought it was the end of the world. I was very hard on myself. To be asked to be so responsible at such an early age was a very big pressure.

At age thirty-two, Dana has not yet developed the capacity to let go and have fun. Having grown up with a mother and father who refused to limit her in any way, she was forced to become her own critical parent, creating an exacting and inflexible internalized parent who continues to tyrannize her.

When a youngster's parents relinquish their regulatory roles, the child may act out. Some girls develop severe emotional or physical problems to coerce their parents into taking charge. On occasion this strategy works. When one adolescent daughter I know discovered that her father, a recovering alcoholic, was drinking again, she swallowed fifty aspirin and landed in the emergency room. Duly alarmed by his daughter's near-fatal act, the father realized that she needed a dependable and stable parent to guide her, and at that point, he decided to get help for his drinking problem.

When Walls Become Prisons

Traditionally, parents have restricted their daughters far more than their sons; the custom of keeping girls chaste while encouraging boys to "sow their wild oats" has resulted in a loss of freedom and absence of adventure for girls and women. Moreover, when parental walls have no windows and gates that open to the outside world, the children locked within feel claustrophobic; they cannot breathe and have no growing space. Relying completely on their parents' external controls,

daughters have too few opportunities to develop an internal locus of control—a trusted inner voice. Hence, they become dependent on others to tell them what to do and what to think
and, conversely, fail to develop the confidence to make decisions and gradually take charge of their lives, which includes
the permission to make mistakes.

Especially during the adolescent years, when the wish for
independence is intense and urgent, children need to be able to
"wheel and deal" with their parents around limits and rules in
order to feel that they are clever and effective. Good-enough
parents, reluctant to cave in to a daughter's unreasonable demands or overlook her safety, will *negotiate* with her and try to
arrive at an acceptable middle course. Authoritarian parents, on
the other hand, able to see only in black and white, will be
blind to the gray zones of compromise. Relinquishing even a
modicum of control threatens them to such an extent that give-
and-take with their teenagers is simply out of the question.

"In my home," a former client confided, "there was a rule
for everything and a punishment for every rule broken. I was
always in trouble." As Susan, a member of my parents group,
pointed out, "An enclosure with many, many walls is no longer
a good protective place; it is a maze."

Viewing Walls As Stumbling Blocks

The sparring that goes on between parents and children
around the issue of limits necessarily creates tensions. Many
parents, unable to tolerate these tensions, see limit setting as
the most onerous aspect of being a parent. We parents lug with
us baggage from the past. The ways our parents raised us bear
heavily on the conscious and unconscious decisions we make
with our children. Newspaper columnist Ellen Goodman says
this beautifully: "Every generation finds it hard sometimes to
hear what our children need, to feel what they are missing, because our own childhood is still ringing in our ears."[3] Hence,

having grown up in a home with too few or weakly constructed walls may prompt us to create a very structured family life. The opposite is also true: having grown up with walls so thick and impenetrable that childhood felt like a prison sentence may induce us to raise our own children with rickety walls or without any walls at all.

We are also influenced by the spirit of the times. Whereas, as a rule, our parents' and grandparents' respected authority and valued obedience, our generation typically resents following orders and is justifiably suspicious of those in power. For many of us who came of age in the sixties and seventies, when "being up against the wall" was the worst place to find yourself and when the guiding principle was to "mistrust authority," assuming an authoritative role with our children simply feels *wrong*. As the middle-aged father of a rambunctious two-year-old told me, "I don't want to be the daddy who is always saying no. I don't want to be the daddy who brings on tears and tantrums. I want to be the daddy who says yes and makes my daughter happy."

Until very recently, when we could no longer deny that human greed and waste had taken their toll on our planet, we Americans believed that the good life knew no limits and that our wants and desires warranted immediate gratification. As one of my clients remarked, "If we wanted it, we thought we needed it; and if we needed it, we thought we deserved it; and if we deserved it, we were entitled to get it any way we could!" Setting and enforcing limits with our children, however, acknowledges to ourselves as well as to them that there is an *end*, an *enough*, a *"no,"* a *"that's all there is,"* a *"sorry, can't do."* In setting limits, we are dispelling the myth of limitless possibility and cornucopian abundance. Simultaneously, we teach our children to tolerate frustration, to make do when necessary, and to be inventive.

I once counseled a newly divorced woman who, after having had an upper-middle-class married lifestyle, was now scraping by on very little money. Because she could not afford to buy a car, designer-label clothes, or any number of other luxury items for her college-age daughter, she thought she was harming her. Only after months of close observation could this woman see that her limited funds were actually strengthening her daughter, who was learning to dress creatively and get by without a car of her own. Similarly, I have noticed that when young children are not overindulged with toys or constantly entertained by videos and television programs, they are forced to use their imaginations and develop their inner resources. As my colleague Kenneth Suslak, a child psychologist in Boulder, Colorado, summarized, "Establishing limits in a family is really a loving act—a way of caring for our children *and* for ourselves."

Psychologists who study the effects of parental behavior on children have focused on two broad dimensions: affection and strictness. Affectionate parents tend to be accepting, responsive, and attuned to their children's needs. Strict parents tend to be demanding and in charge. Different combinations of these dimensions produce different kinds of children. Teenagers whose parents are neither affectionate nor strict—who are disengaged—are likely to develop severe emotional problems that may lead to delinquency and chemical abuse. Teens whose parents are unaffectionate and strict—dictatorial—are often socially inadequate and lacking in confidence. Teens whose parents are affectionate and lax—indulgent—tend to be impulsive, irresponsible, and overly dependent. The best adjustment is associated with children whose parents are engaged—both affectionate and strict; these teens generally are socially responsible, independent, and self-confident.[4]

Respecting Boundaries

Saying no can be an affirmative act. The two-year-old who says no to the mother—"No, I'm not sleepy!" "No, I don't want to get dressed!"—recognizes the boundaries between her mother and herself and is becoming a separate individual with wishes and opinions of her own. Similarly, the parent who says no to her child of two, twelve, or twenty demonstrates that people who love each other often do not have the same feelings and desires. Sonya, a young friend who has shared many family stories with me, illustrates mothers' and daughters' mutual need for boundaries:

> Until I was well into my teens, I took my mother's things without asking—clothes, jewelry, makeup, what have you. I think I bugged the hell out of my mother, but she was unable to be clear enough or strong enough to ask me to stop. Oh, she'd yell sometimes, but I didn't take her seriously because she didn't take herself seriously. Then, at one point, she began to change. She began to watch out for herself, to say with authority, "No, you can't take that; that's mine" or "Yes, you can borrow this, but you must put it right back when you're through with it." I felt total relief. When Mom began to respect her boundaries, I understood that I could have boundaries too. I began to take care of my things, knowing that they were *mine*. I also made all these special little places for my treasures. When Mom began acting like a separate person who deserved respect, I began feeling like a separate person too.

Soon afterward, I had occasion to speak to Sonya's mother, Diane. Her own submissive mother, Diane said, had joylessly served her husband and their six children and had never made her own wishes known. In turn, she taught Diane that being a woman meant putting up with anything and everything—a destructive notion that existential French philosopher Simone DeBeauvoir called the "chain of female misery." Diane's father, by contrast, was harshly authoritarian, insisting that others do his bidding, whether they wanted to or not. Diane explained that from her mother she learned that women had no business setting limits, and from her father she learned that limits were "arbitrary, nasty, and mean-spirited." Only after years of psychotherapy did Diane finally recognize that she had rights as a human being and was justified in asking her children to respect these rights.

As a a psychologist, I have often observed that the issue of absent or diffuse boundaries affects many more women than men and that women who are not sure of their boundaries become confused about establishing limits for their children. Emma, for example, remembers that as a youngster her assumed role in life was to please her mother, an infantile and narcissistic woman. On the few occasions that Emma refused to meet her mother's needs, the woman would pout, become wet-eyed, or even break down and cry, which made Emma feel like "a very bad person." After Emma left home, she became involved with a series of men who used her sexually, and lest she "hurt their feelings" or "be selfish," she complied with their wishes. Later, as a single mother, she indulged her son. Whenever he wanted a new toy, she bought him one, when he refused to go to sleep, she let him stay up with her or spend the night in her bed. Emma first came to therapy for help in learning to discipline her child. It soon became clear, however, that before Emma could become an effective parent, she needed to define her own needs, wishes, and ambitions, instead of experiencing herself as a tool in service to others.

When Leah was thirteen, she and I went to see the French film *Rouge Baiser* [*The Red Kiss*], which traces the romantic adventures of a passionate and somewhat self-centered teenage girl. As the story opens, the mother is pinning together a party dress, which the girl can't wait to wear to her next formal affair. After putting the finishing touches on the stunning garment, the woman announces—to her daughter's astonishment—that she wants this dress for *herself*. And indeed, she looks beautiful in the dress. After the movie, I asked Leah if she thought the mother was being mean. "No," she answered thoughtfully, "the mother had probably made plenty of dresses for her daughter and deserved to have this one for herself." She added, "And now that the mother wasn't being a martyr, the daughter wouldn't have to feel guilty."

During the earliest phases of motherhood, the experience of giving myself completely to my child was so profound that even as she got older I was not always certain to which one of us *my* body and *my* "being" belonged. The movie mother in *Rouge Baiser* became a role model of sorts. And so, when Leah wore my favorite dress to a high school dance, badly soiled it, and did not bother to apologize, I became furious at her. Yes, I, too, could deny my daughter from time to time; yes, there could be a boundary between us; and yes, not all of me or all that I possessed was hers. In establishing boundaries for myself, I was also doing something crucially important for my daughter—allowing her to feel separate from me.

The Right to Be Angry

Recently, I had a discussion with the father of a ten-year-old girl; he was having trouble setting limits for her. Arnie told me that his own childhood had been chaotic, punctuated by shrill arguments between his father and mother. For him the home front was a battlefront "with grenades flying every which way." After Arnie married and became a father, he vowed he would create a peaceful atmosphere in his own home. Rather than confronting and working through each conflict that arises, he tries to nip it in the bud—"to fix it so that everybody will be happy again." By giving in to his daughter's demands, he tries to ensure that she will not become agitated or, worse still, angry *at him*.

In truth, our daughters do need to learn to protest, just as surely as they need to learn to walk and talk. And we need to learn to tolerate their occasional expressions of anger, indignation, and outrage. Why? Because girls who are free to say what they think and feel have the best chance of growing up forth-right, honest, and outspoken, instead of manipulative, indirect, and timid. Traditionally, girls and women have been forbidden from expressing their bawdiness, competitiveness, anger, and other aggressive instincts; they are instead coaxed to be always pleasant, pleasing, and compliant. As a result, they are cut off from their own vitality and genuineness.

Much of my work with female clients entails helping them accept and vent their "un-nice" feelings instead of "stuffing" them, which leads to all manner of psychosomatic and other emotional problems. Adopting new patterns of behavior, I have observed, becomes increasingly difficult the older a woman is. In fact, what is learned in adult therapy with great effort can be learned in childhood with ease. We parents need only accept that our daughters will be angry at us from time to time. When they bang against the walls we erect to protect, contain, and control them, we can help them accept their feelings as normal. We can say something like "It's only natural that you're feeling furious at me because I won't let you _____, but I have to do what I think is best for you and me." In this way, we teach our daughters two things: they have a right to feel angry and their angry feelings will not destroy us emotionally or diminish our love for them.

Although our daughters have a right to be angry, they do not have a right to be violent or abusive. Many parent survivors of emotional or physical abuse, unable to distinguish between anger and abuse, have a hard time drawing the line for their children. The distinction, however, is quite clear-cut. Anger is an expression of intense displeasure and agitation—a response to feeling violated, invalidated, or impinged upon. The angry child may defensively lash out with fists or with hurtful words that temporarily sting, such as "I hate you, Mommy and Daddy," though it is obvious that her intent is neither malicious nor sadistic. Abuse, on the other hand, is deliberately injurious, insulting, and demeaning. The abusive child may threaten violence or spew out humiliating obscenities designed to strip away the parent's dignity; in extreme cases, she may try to inflict physical harm. A child's abusive behavior not only wounds the parent; it also wounds the child. Every daughter identifies with her mother and father and wants to look up to them. In trusting that her mother and father are good and strong, she can trust in her own goodness and strength, but in bringing her parents down, she loses her positive role models and is left with a terrible, empty, orphaned feeling.

For their daughter's good as well as their own, parents need to do all they can to see that she does not cross over the line that separates anger from abuse. If, for example, she becomes verbally abusive, the abused parent is right to cut her short by looking her in the eye and saying, "Your language is absolutely unacceptable, and I won't have it." The other parent is also right to intervene by telling her, "I find it offensive when you speak to your father [mother] this way. This is not permissible behavior in our family." Indeed, a child learns to "honor thy mother and father" only with the mother's and father's guidance.

Sonya told me how her mother, Diane, stopped her in her tracks the one time she acted abusively toward her:

> I was in junior high. A lot of my friends said really rude things to their parents and thought nothing of it. I can't remember exactly what my mother did to irritate me, only that I lost control and called her a bunch of bad names. When I was done with my little outburst, she glared at me and said, "Why, you little bitch, how dare you!" I felt so awful when my mother called *me* a bitch, so demeaned, that I burst into tears. Then the two of us talked for a long time about treating human beings with respect. We shared with each other how terrible it felt to be cursed at or called an ugly name, and we agreed that we would never be verbally abusive with each other again—a promise we have kept.

Being called a little bitch stunned Sonya. However, it was not the name calling but the loving talk that turned the nasty scene into a positive experience for both mother and daughter. All of us have breaking points and at times blurt out cruel words; we also have the capacity to apologize and to learn from our mistakes.

Parents who were physically or verbally abused as children are often afraid of repeating patterns of abuse with their own children. They anticipate that any annoyance or frustration with their children will explode into a devastating rage. Fearful of losing control, they may withdraw from their children or adopt an overly permissive or rigid parenting style. Often their spouses are also afraid that the abuse will be repeated, so they watch the other parent with eagle eyes. Under such scrutiny, this parent is bound to feel increasingly defensive, uncomfortable, and insecure.

According to Martha Farrell Erickson, coordinator of the University of Minnesota's Project STEEP, a study of high-risk parents and infants, it is true that nearly all child abusers were abused or badly neglected as children. It is also true, however, that abused children need not become abusing parents.[5] Indeed, over the years I have worked with many clients who as children were badly mistreated but who have become some of the most sensitive, empathic, and inspiring parents I have ever known. For men and women who suffered abuse as children, the best protection against abusing their own children comes from sharing the pain and shame of the past with a trusted spouse, friend, or therapist. If there is to be a healing from childhood abuse, the silent "child" must learn to talk; the stoic must learn to weep. It is when abused people become indignant at the outrages committed against them as children that they are most likely to break the cycle of abuse.

Human Ordinariness

It is easy for a frazzled adult engaged in a battle of wills with a sassy child or teenager to act in an utterly foolish or incompetent manner. An old priest was once asked what he had learned about human nature after fifty years in the confessional. He answered that no one fully outgrows feeling like an incompetent child. My husband, for instance, once became so exasperated by Leah's provocations that he cracked a raw egg over her head. A friend responded to her seven-year-old daughter's refusal to practice her Suzuki lessons by jumping up and down on the child's costly violin and breaking it in two. A colleague warned her three-year-old, "Stop that right now *or else*," and was forced to retreat when the child smirked, "Or else *what*, Mommy?" A family therapist became so mad at her fourteen-year-old that she yelled, "You're grounded for a year and I mean it!" and then had to dredge up face-saving ways of reducing the ridiculously long sentence.

Several parents I know have, out of frustration and anger, said deeply hurtful things to their children. As one young mother puts it: "I know that when disciplining, a parent should make a distinction between the child's action and the child's person. I know that the right thing to say is, 'You're a very good girl, but what you *did* just now was not nice at all.' And yet, when my five-year-old took a swat at her baby brother, I screamed out, 'You're a mean and nasty girl!' As soon as the words came tumbling out of my mouth, I realized how degrading and shaming they were."

In trying to set limits for my own children, I have made many mistakes. I will not forget the time that Leah, at sixteen, pleaded to drive with a group of friends to Estes Park, a mountain town an hour's drive away from our home in Boulder, to see their acting teacher perform in a play and then stay in her cabin for the weekend. Because it was beginning to snow, I decided that a trip into the mountains would be unsafe and told

Leah that she could not go. Leah became hysterical: "How can you do this to me? This means so much to me. All of my friends' mothers are letting them go. It's just a little snowfall. Why are you always so overprotective? Why are you acting like a prison warden?" Leah received a flurry of phone calls from her friends, who sympathized with her sad plight and agreed that her mother was being totally unreasonable; still, I would not relent. After my daughter's friends took off on their adventure and Leah resigned herself to being stuck at home with me, I began to feel unsure of the stand that I had taken: Maybe I was overreacting and should have allowed her to take the drive. . . . Perhaps the other mothers were right and I was wrong. . . . Why didn't I call the highway patrol to check on road conditions before forbidding Leah from going? As my self-doubts grew, I knew that only worsening weather could prove my decision right and help me feel less guilty. Longingly, I looked out the window, hoping for the biggest Colorado blizzard of the century. Instead, I noticed the sky clearing. The weekend, as my daughter would let me know more than once, turned out to be sunny and mild.

A story about my father's temporary fall from grace also comes to mind. I must have been about eight years old. My mother had bought me a pair of scratchy denim overalls with an appliqué of Howdy Doody on the bib. Convinced that Howdy Doody was for babies and that my schoolmates would laugh at me if I wore these outlandish overalls, I decided to cut a small hole in them, hoping it would soon grow into a big rip and make them unwearable. At dinnertime, my father noticed the hole and asked if I was responsible for it. I told him that I certainly was not. Although my father was an inordinately gentle and restrained man, I suppose he believed that it was a father's duty to spank a child for lying. And so he took me over his knee, pulled down my pants, and smacked me. I could not stand being humiliated in this way, and in an effort to gain back a semblance of pride, I laughed and told my father I had not felt a thing. Taunted, he decided to give me a smack that I *would* feel. Again, I laughed and insisted I had not felt a thing, although in truth my backside was smarting. Our power play continued. Each time I sassed him, he hit me harder until the pain was so bad I could no longer hold back my tears. Having experienced firsthand the abusive power of the Nazis when they imprisoned him years before, my father deplored all forms of humiliation; yet in this instance he could not stop himself from humiliating his own child. Many years later, my mother told me that my father, realizing a stern reprimand would have been enough to teach me a lesson about lying, had felt deeply ashamed of himself for breaking me down. His behavior had degraded him even more than it had degraded me.

The reality is that building good walls is difficult work. In the process, we may become foolish, intemperate, unreasonable, or even vindictive on occasion. Yet, as long as our acts of unkindness are rare and not a part of a pattern of hostility, they are unlikely to do any lasting damage to our children. Instead of being overly hard on ourselves when we act badly, we would do well to have a little self-compassion, to laugh at ourselves if we can, and to remember how human and fallible we are. Almost osmotically, our children will learn to accept their human flaws as well.

It is also true that even well-built walls may not always contain our children. When they consistently rebel against our rules, we are likely to feel totally ineffective. And we may fear that they are hopeless causes. Rather than lose heart and abdicate our roles as parents, however, we need to remind ourselves that perserverance pays off.

A family therapist shared the following anecdote with me. A few years ago, she was working with a married couple and their teenage daughter, who was acting out terribly and causing myriad problems for them. Therapy was not effective and did not last long. At its conclusion, the daughter was as wild as ever and the parents were thoroughly frazzled. Years later, the therapist encountered the daughter, who by then was in her twenties. To the therapist's surprise, she was extremely likable, competent, and self-assured. In the course of their conversation, the therapist asked the young woman if her parents had done anything to get her on track.

"Absolutely not," she answered. "Nothing they did worked. My parents couldn't enforce any limits on me. They were useless. Everything they tried backfired."

"Then why did you turn out so well?" the therapist continued.

"Because they never stopped trying," the young woman replied.

PART THREE

NURTURING THE SPIRIT

Help us to be the always-hopeful gardeners of the spirit who know that without darkness nothing comes to birth, as without light nothing flowers.

—MAY SARTON

THE SIXTH GIFT:

Respect

Adults know intuitively that respect is essential to their lives, but they may not grasp that it is essential to children as well. We find it natural to love children, to adore them, to take precious care of them . . . but to *respect* them? And yet, for children of every age, being respected by those who know them best—especially their parents—allows them to respect themselves: to feel from deep inside that they are glad to be who they are and that they *are* somebody. Dr. Seuss knew whereof he spoke: "A person's a person, no matter how small."

Even if we were not respected by our own parents, we can learn to respect our daughters; indeed, the practice of respect is a conscious endeavor built on awareness, understanding, and tolerance. The dictionary tells us that respect means to feel or show honor or esteem, to notice with attention, and to avoid intruding upon. The word *respect* derives from the Latin root *spectare*, meaning to see, to look at—as do the words *spectator* (an observer), *spectacles* (the eyeglasses that make vision clear), and *spectacle* (a marvel)—and from the prefix *re*, meaning again and anew. To respect, then, is *to look and look again in order to see clearly what is before us and marvel at it.* In Yiddish, this is called *kvelling*—the trembling awe that parents experience when they behold their sons and daughters in all their unique, marvelous, ever-changing complexity.

As our children grow, we have many opportunities to respect them, to *kvell* over them. We are amazed by our child's first words and growing mastery of language; her relentless efforts to crawl, pull herself up, stand on her own two feet, then walk unaided; her delight in drawing pictures and singing songs; her courage in climbing trees and turning somersaults; her responsiveness to people, animals, places, and ideas; her miraculous transformation from girlhood to womanhood; and her expanding capacity to love and to work.

From the first days of life, every child yearns to have her experiences acknowledged and, as psychiatrist and author Heinz Kohut describes, "to be looked upon with joy and basic approval by a delighted parent."[1] When, for example, the baby crawls out of mother's lap toward the box of toys at the far end of the room, she will look back to ensure that mother is still there. She will also check to see that mother is sharing the suspense, scariness, and wonder of her adventure. The exuberance in mother's voice, the glimmer in her eyes, the movements of her body all affirm the child's experience, allowing the child to feel *real.* They also give her the green light to continue her exploration—to stretch, reach, and progress. Martin Buber, the existential philosopher and theologian, used the lovely phrase "confirming the other" to describe the act of validating not only the other's being but her *becoming.*[2]

When parents respect their daughter's competence and convey this respect through words and body language, they promote the best in her. This fact was brought home to me during a conversation with my dearest childhood friend, Geri. Against formidable odds, including poverty, fatherlessness, and an imperious mother, Geri grew up to become a nationally acclaimed neuropsychologist. "How do you account for your professional success?" I recently asked her, and she answered without hesitation, "My mother, who we both know was a very difficult woman and hardly a model parent, was really responsible for my self-confidence. She was convinced that I could do anything I set my mind to, and I simply trusted her judgment." In contrast, a brilliant young woman I am working with has a history of academic self-sabotage; she hands in papers late and habitually leaves herself too little time to study for exams. As long as she can remember, her mother's message was, "You'll never make it. No one in our family succeeds. So why even try?" She, too, trusted her mother's judgment.

Some parents believe that they should hide or temper pride in their children lest they get swelled heads. When pride is withheld, however, the child loses out. A struggling young artist friend of mine, who moved from her home state two years ago, confided how wonderful she felt when she returned to her parents' house and saw that the oil painting she had sent them was magnificently framed and hanging above the mantelpiece in the living room. "My parents have exquisite taste, and I know they must notice the technical flaws in my painting. Yet, they showed their respect for me as a young artist by displaying the oil so prominently." In a similar vein, an adolescent client who is a member of an amateur acting troupe told me that whenever she performs in a play, her father is in the audience, "right up front—first row, center," smiling at her, applauding her, and giving her courage.

Of course, beholding and affirming our children entails recognizing the hurtful and troubling aspects of their lives as well. For example, when faced with a crying child who has been benched most of the sports season not because she doesn't work hard at practice but because the coach favors the other players, the respectful mother does not talk her out of her distress. Instead, she lets her know that the hurt and angry feelings are justified. When approached by a teenager who feels horrible because the boy she likes doesn't notice her, the respectful father does not make fun of her adolescent woes but rather takes her unhappiness seriously. A child whose emotional experience is validated comes to trust her perceptions, whereas a child whose innermost feelings are consistently discounted by the adults around her comes to doubt herself. Hearing her parents say, "You have no reason to be sad (angry, upset, frustrated, scared)" or "You're overreacting!" or "You certainly have strange ideas," she becomes ridden by self-doubts and questions, such as "How *do* I know my feelings and thoughts aren't crazy ones? How dare I trust myself?"

I have sometimes wondered why we have a biblical commandment admonishing children to respect their parents but none admonishing parents to respect their children; the need for respect, after all, lies at the core of well-being for every person. My friend Art Kaufman illustrates this point in a telling anecdote he shared with me about his daughter Grace:

> Like any young child, my daughter may wimper or cry if things don't go her way or if she can't have what she wants, but the only times I've seen her *weep* are when she feels disrespected. If I thoughtlessly belittle or mock what Grace is thinking or feeling, her hurt and outrage seem boundless.

"Only if we become sensitive to the fine and subtle ways in which a child may suffer humiliation," Swiss psychoanalyst Alice Miller writes, "can we hope to develop the respect for him that a child needs."[3]

Just as humiliating a child does violence to her soul, so does using a child to fill one's own needs for comfort, companionship, or self-aggrandizement. Indeed, respectful love is never possessive, never appropriating. Rather, it is an honoring of the boundaries that separate one person from another and a recognition of the other's otherness. Whenever a child experiences herself as a commodity, a tool, an object, a thing, a possession, or an extension of another person, she suffers self-degradation. I remember sobbing inconsolably at a family gathering when I was a child of four or five after an uncle "playfully" chased me, grabbed me, and hungrily kissed me on the mouth although I had tried to push him away. From then on, I cowered at the sight of him.

Even well-intentioned adults may inadvertently compromise children's self-confidence by insisting they follow a scripted role rather than simply be who they are. Typically, girls are cast as caregivers, comfort givers, or mediators. A middle-aged client of mine, while mourning the loss of her father, also grieved for the mutually respectful relationship they never had. "My father knew me only as a nurturer," she explained, "the one who took care of the house and younger siblings, the one who did what my sick mother was not able to do. My father never really knew me as a person. I felt valued for what I *did* to improve his life, but never for who I *was*." Girls who are particularly attractive may be seen as merely beautiful objects. A redheaded, green-eyed college student in therapy with me bemoaned the fact that her father, dazzled by her appearance, never really saw *her*. "How can my dad respect me if he doesn't even want to know me as more than a pretty face?" she asked. This father had apparently become caught in the snares of our culture's obsession with appearance, what Mary Pipher, therapist and author of *Reviving Ophelia*, calls "lookism."

Paradoxically, while seeing their children for all they are, we must not insist on seeing too much by probing into matters they wish to keep to themselves. The gift of respect is, in part, deliberately choosing not to know when knowing would become intrusive. A friend of mine who is particularly sensitive to the feelings of others attached a lock to the inside of his daughter's bedroom door after she turned eleven. "When I was a teenager, my mother once barged into my room to collect my dirty laundry," he explained. "There I was stark naked, admiring my bulging parts in a full-length mirror. I would never want to accidentally intrude on my daughter and embarrass her like that. With a locked door, she can have the privacy she needs." We, too, can show respect by avoiding the temptation to "overhear" our daughters' telephone conversations and by refusing to read their diaries or letters they receive from their friends.

Privacy becomes increasingly important during adolescence. Sprawled on the floor listening to music or daydreaming on the living room couch or sleeping in on a Saturday morning or writing in her diary, a teenager will reach deep down into her soul—which is unlike any other soul on earth—to discover its innermost truths. Respecting these forays into self-discovery helps us acknowledge that we cannot know who our daughters will become. The most we can do is honor the journey and the junctures at which our children's individuality comes to expression—whether in the form of a bookworm, a social butterfly, an activist, a vegetarian, a dreamer, a lesbian, a leader, a follower, a fundamentalist, or an atheist. With characteristic insight, Jungian psychologist Irene Claremont de Castillejo writes, "We do *not* know the destiny to which another has been born. We do not know where he is to rebel, which mistakes he is to make. Perhaps some idiosyncrasy or some failure to fit into society may be that child's particular contribution to the world, which should not be cured but fostered."[4]

In his book *The Seven Spiritual Laws of Success*, Deepak Chopra refers to the Sanskrit Law of Dharma. According to this law, each person has a unique talent and is obligated to discover and cultivate it. Chopra taught his own children beginning at age four to meditate on their possibilities. "I never want you to worry about making a living when you grow up," he said. "I don't want you to focus on doing well in school. I don't want you to focus on getting the best grades or going to the best colleges. . . . What I really want you to focus on is asking yourself how you can serve humanity, and asking yourself what your unique talents are. Because you have a unique talent that no one else has, and you have a special way of expressing that talent, and no one else has it."[5] According to Chopra, it was precisely because his children were focused on their divine purpose in life rather than on the external signs of success that they ended up going to the best schools, getting the best grades, and becoming financially self-sufficient.

Should our daughters choose paths different from our own, our sense of loss may be great. If our daughter rejects our religion, we may feel terribly sad that we can no longer worship together or be guided by the same beliefs. If she chooses not to read books or newspapers and we are well educated, we may feel resentful that we cannot engage her on an intellectual level. If she is gay and we are heterosexual, we may find ourselves grieving for our dashed dreams—seeing her marry a nice young man and living her life free of insults and discrimination. As hard as it can be to witness our daughters embarking on pathways so unlike our own, we must try to let them become themselves.

I once counseled a nineteen-year-old college student who wore a nose ring, combat boots, dangling rhinestone earrings, and waist-length hair dyed magenta. Her father, a conservative businessman from Utah, and her mother, the local Junior League president, did not hesitate to express outrage at her appearance and to tell her that, dressing as she did, she embarrassed them at public functions. After a period of estrangement, this young woman and her parents worked hard to reestablish ties. During a counseling session, I listened as my client passionately defended her decision to dress in her own style and look like no one else. She described how liberating it was to have transformed herself from a "plain girl" into a "living work of art" who captured the attention of passersby. It was only after my client saw her parents trying to accept her as she was that she began to consider their sensibilities. At a counseling session, she told me: "My parents have really been great. The next time they invite me to one of their social events, I think I will tone down my dress a little—maybe not wear my nose ring—so that I don't stand out so much. That would please them, don't you think?"

Barriers to Respect

What stands in the way of respecting our children? If we grew up with parents and other family members who habitually disregarded our feelings, we may automatically repeat these behaviors. Respecting our children requires learning to respect ourselves by transforming the harshly critical inner voice that guides us to a kinder, more forgiving one. I once had as a client a woman who was so disrespectful toward her young adult daughter that my stomach became tied up in knots whenever my client described their interactions. Although at the start of therapy my temptation was to point out how hurtful her disparaging words were, she was so defensive that I decided instead to focus exclusively on the humiliations she had experienced in her childhood family and to take every opportunity to help her see her own good qualities. Over a year of therapy, as my client began to appreciate herself more, her relationship with her daughter dramatically changed for the better.

For some of us the need to be always in control stands in the way of showing respect for our children. Rather than honoring and confirming our daughters' individuality, we may undermine it, ostensibly for their own good. Behind our overcontrol is often our fear that if our daughters do not do things the way we think best, they may be physically or emotionally damaged or pay some other heavy price.

Psychoanalyst Daniel Stern, noted researcher in infant development, includes this vivid account of a controlling mother in his book *The Interpersonal World of the Infant*:

> Molly's mother . . . had to design, initiate, direct, and terminate all agendas. She determined which toy Molly should play with,

how Molly was to play with it ("Shake it up and down—don't roll it on the floor"), when Molly was done playing with it, and what to do next ("Oh, here is Dressy Bessy. Look!"). The mother overcontrolled the interaction to such an extent that it was often hard to trace the natural crescendo and decrescendo of Molly's own interest and excitement. . . . Molly found an adaptation. She gradually became more compliant. Instead of actively avoiding or opposing these intrusions, she became one of those enigmatic starers into space. . . . This general dampening of her affectivity continued . . . and was still apparent at three years.[6]

As a consequence of her mother's intrusiveness, Molly is now on her way to developing a false self—one that complies with others' wishes to such an extent that it has lost its vitality. Allowed to continue in this mode, she may join the legions of adults who, not trusting or even recognizing their wants and needs, lack focus, direction, and confidence.

The adverse effects of parental overcontrol of an older daughter are illuminated in an article by psychologist Richard Geist, who specializes in the treatment of eating disorders.[7] Geist presents Penny, a twenty-year-old anorexic patient who recalls that when she dressed up for special occasions, she was discouraged from combining everything "so it felt like me." Whenever Penny asked her mother how she looked, her mother would find something wrong, saying: "You'd look fine if it weren't for your hair; let me fix it" or "Yes, dear, you look nice, but that necklace ruins the whole thing. I'll get you another." As Geist explains it, Penny's mother, rather than allowing her daughter to weave makeup, jewelery, clothes, and hairstyle into her unique fashion statement, substituted a hairstyle or necklace of her own choosing. In the process, she splintered her daughter's efforts to feel whole, right, and real.

More than a century ago, the Danish philosopher Søren Kierkegaard pointed out that relinquishing the willingness to be oneself causes the most common form of despair and that choosing to be anyone other than oneself leads to the deepest form of despair. "To be that self which one truly is," said Kierkegaard, "is indeed the opposite of despair."[8]

As a new mother, I was fortunate to be guided by a wise and funny pediatrician who was a strong advocate of young children's individuality. Expressing my concern that two-year-old Leah was not taking in enough calories—she liked fruit, but rejected starchy foods—I asked him whether I should mix her foods together and mask the taste of rice or a baked potato with applesauce so that such starches would be acceptable to her. "Definitely not," he boomed. "Leah needs to learn what she likes and what she dislikes. If you mush her foods together, how will she be able to figure this out? She'll end up with mushy ideas about everything, instead of definite ones!"

In addition to Dr. Rappaport's tutelage, I had a neighborhood friend who became a wonderful role model for me. Like the good doctor, she believed that parents ought to take every opportunity to empower their daughters by giving them manageable choices. By observing Janet with her two daughters, I learned that young children have a right not only to choose what foods they want to eat but also the clothes they wear. One of my favorite early photographs of Leah is evidence not only of her budding flair for fashion but of my letting go *some* control: she is wearing plaid overalls, a striped polo shirt, and a string of pearls her great-grandmother had given her!

Probably as a result of both my Germanic upbringing and my nature, I did not evolve into an easygoing mother like Janet, although I certainly tried to. Basically, I am a pretty uptight person and had to struggle against tendencies toward overcontrol during my children's growing-up years. Biting my tongue was the short-term strategy I employed whenever I was overtaken by the urge to give my daughter excessive advice or to manipulate her into doing things *my* way. Ensuring that I had a full life of my own—a vibrant marriage, strong friendships, and meaningful work—was the long-term strategy that helped me back off from Leah and give her the freedom to think and do for herself.

Selfishness, as playwright Oscar Wilde once wrote, is "not living as one wishes to live" but rather "asking others to live as one wishes to live." Had I not gradually diverted a good portion of my energy from my family to the outside world, I would surely have become the classic selfish mother who, lacking a rich existence of her own, turns her children into her lifework.

Another parental behavior that subverts the giving of respect is the tendency to project our wishes, fears, hopes, and dreams onto the child instead of seeing her objectively. We may, for instance, expect our daughters to follow in our footsteps:

"My mother studied piano at Juilliard," a client told me. "She wanted to believe that I had inherited her talents, and although we were not well off, she paid for private music lessons for me. I had no talent whatsoever for playing the flute, violin, piano, or cello, and no interest for that matter, but she would not see this, and as a result, I suffered through those god-awful lessons for years, when I would much rather have been training as a runner." While attempting to foster her daughter's nonexistent talents as a musician, this mother failed to recognize and encourage her true talents as an athlete; she was so intent on creating the child of her fantasies—actually, a replica of herself—that the real child got lost.

Contrary to insisting that our daughters become replicas of ourselves, we may manipulate them into developing in themselves what remains undeveloped in us. An acquaintance of mine from a working-class background, seeing herself as culturally inferior to the other wives in the university town we lived in, was determined to give her two daughters all the "advantages" she missed having as a child, such as violin lessons, ballet lessons, art lessons, and French lessons. Denise was so intent on shaping her girls into refined and supereducated young women that, despite their protestations, she failed to see how miserable the regimen of self-improvement classes made them. I suspect this family would have been much happier if Denise, instead of her daughters, had enrolled in the music, dance, art, and language classes.

Projection sometimes occurs in the form of idealization, in which we refuse to believe that our children are less than perfect. This tendency is especially evident among parents who have waited a long time to have a child. It is also common among enthusiastic fathers who, bowled over by their little girls' charm and coyness, look upon them not as human beings but rather as young goddesses. And it occurs among parents who look upon their "perfect" child as proof of *their* goodness, brilliance, charm, and beauty. Idealizing, which is seeing what we want to see rather than what is really in front of us, needs to be distinguished from *kvelling*, which is responding with awe to our child *as she is*. The idealized child, while often enjoying being treated so regally, also worries that she does not deserve this special treatment. She wonders, If people ever discover the *true* me, will they still love and value me? If I expose my faults to them, will I disappoint them terribly? Feeling *ashamed* that her true self does not measure up to her parents' expectations, she may try to create a more acceptable self—what British psychoanalyst D. W. Winnicott called the "false self"—by becoming whatever she imagines they would want her to be. Underlying the belief that our children are perfect is the yearning to see ourselves as perfect parents. Good-enough mothers and fathers and good-enough children, we need to remember, will do just fine.

Susan Wildau, a close friend and the mother of three lovely middle-aged adults, told me that when her children were young she made a conscious effort to see them through clear, unshielded eyes, rather than don rose-colored glasses. "I tried not to criticize my children. And I also tried not to idealize them. I thought it important to recognize their shortcomings as well as their strengths," she remarked, "because only then could I do what was necessary to help them with their problems." This is what Sara Ruddick, the author of *Maternal Thinking*, calls "attentive love" and "loving attention"—"a kind of knowing that takes truthfulness as its aim but makes truth serve lovingly the person known."[9]

The Art of Listening

In his book *On Becoming a Person*, Carl Rogers, the originator of client-centered psychotherapy, describes the art of listening. Although his instruction was originally intended for therapists, we parents who wish to communicate in a respectful fashion with our children will find much to learn in it:

> Our first reaction to most of the statements which we hear from other people is an immediate evaluation, or judgment, rather than an understanding of it. When someone expresses some feeling or attitude or belief, our tendency is almost immediately to feel "That's right"; or "That's stupid"; "That's abnormal"; "That's unreasonable"; "That's incorrect"; "That's not nice." Very rarely do we permit ourselves to *understand* precisely what the meaning of his statement is to him. I believe this is because understanding is risky. If I let myself really understand another person, I might be changed by that understanding. And we all fear change. So I say, it is not an easy thing to permit oneself to understand an individual, to enter thoroughly and completely and empathically into his frame of reference.[10]

The process of understanding that Rogers describes requires listening that is attentive, receptive, and nonjudgmental. Good listeners convey the message that they are interested in hearing what the other person has to say and are willing to take time to listen. They do not interrupt; they do not contradict or debate; they do not cut the person short by launching into a discussion about themselves. They *do*, however, ask questions for clarification ("I'm not sure I understand. Could you give me another example or say it another way?"). They also check with the other person to make sure they are on track ("It sounds to me like you're saying _____. Is this right? If not—if I'm misunderstanding you—please correct me."). Good listeners are also humble; they are able to let go of their authority and engage the other person as an equal. Many adults who want to listen to their very young children bring themselves down to their level by kneeling or squatting or sitting on the floor.

And how does the speaker respond when respectfully listened to? Rogers explains:

> In the first place, as he finds someone else listening acceptantly to his feelings, he little by little becomes able to listen to himself—to realize that he *is* angry, to recognize when he is frightened, even to realize when he is feeling courageous. As he becomes more open to what is going on in him he becomes able to listen to feelings which he has always denied and repressed. He can listen to feelings which have seemed to him so terrible, or so disorganizing, or so abnormal, or so shameful, that he has never been able to recognize their existence in him. While he is learning to listen to himself he also becomes more acceptant of himself . . . and therefore ready to move forward in the process of becoming.[11]

Sharing Rogers's sentiments, Nel Noddings, in her book *Caring*, maintains that children who are respectfully listened to become more responsible for their conduct. Noddings provides an example that many of us parents can relate to:

> Suppose that a child of, say, eight years comes home from school angry. He storms into the kitchen and throws his books on the floor. His mother, startled, says, "What happened, honey?" (She resists the temptation to say something to the effect that "in this house we do not throw things.") The child says that his teacher is "impossible," "completely unfair," "mean," "stupid," and so on.

His mother sympathizes and probes gently for what happened. Gradually, under the quiet influence of a receptive listener, the child calms down. As his mother sympathizes, he may even relax enough to say, "Well, it wasn't that bad," in answer to his mother's sympathetic outrage. Then the two may smile at each other and explore rational solutions; they can speculate about faults, mistakes, and intentions. They can plot a course of action for the future. The child, accepted and supported, can begin to examine his own role in the incident and, perhaps, even suggest how he may have behaved differently.[12]

It is one thing to listen respectfully while our children share feelings and ideas that do not threaten our self-esteem. It is far more difficult to sympathize with statements that attack us in some way. The hard work of respect is illustrated by a father who, too tired to play with his toddler, *permits himself to understand* that she is angry at him for being inattentive to her. And by an adoptive mother who permits herself to understand that her little girl yearns for her birth mother. And by a single mother who permits herself to understand that her youngster would rather live with her dad for a while. And by a highly educated father who permits himself to understand that his adolescent daughter does not want to go to college.

Ingeborg Blixen, the mother of the famed Danish writer Isak Dinesen, provides an extraordinary example of parental respect under difficult circumstances. Upon learning that her daughter, recently divorced and facing the bankruptcy of her beloved Kenyan coffee plantation, had been considering suicide as an alternative to returning to her mother's house, she wrote the following in a letter to her son:

> You know that for the whole of my life with you I have tried my best to understand you, and you may be sure that I understand what Tanne [Isak] is going through now. For I have always known that the environment I offered her was not suited to her

character and talents—this has caused me great pain, but it has not been possible for me to change it so much that it would make her happy. . . .

I will be able to give Tanne complete freedom to do what she thinks is best for herself—I will not hold her back if she thinks life is too hard for her, I will not for one moment put her under an obligation to "be something" to me in these years. The sole consideration for me is that she should live according to her nature—I neither can nor will demand anything else of her. . . .

Tanne has often caused me anxiety, probably more than any of my other children, but she has filled my life with so much love, so much festivity, I have been—and am—so proud of her, that whatever she may come to do I will always love and bless her.[13]

To respect our children, we must—hard as it may be—develop the strength to allow their separateness—to let them be who they are and to follow their own paths, even those we would not have chosen for them, even those that lead them far away from us.

Teaching Respect for Others

All children are by nature empathic. Within the first days of life, babies cry in response to the cries of other babies; as early as age two they try to intervene when others are suffering; and by age three they develop a sense of respecting rather than belittling others, of supporting and protecting rather than exploiting or dominating them. For children's innate capacity for kindness to grow, however, they require two conditions: to feel secure and loved and to observe the adults closest to them treating others in a caring, respectful manner.[14] The way we relate to people shapes our children's relationships with others.

In the early fifties, my mother, father, and I took a road trip from New York City to Miami Beach. From the backseat of our Oldsmobile, I stared out the side window for hours, never feeling bored; indeed, for a city child like me, the sight of flowering meadows and grazing cows was magical. However, the farther south we drove, the more quickly the pretty little towns we passed gave way to rows of shacks inhabited by blacks. Seeing the inequities in living conditions between the blacks and the whites, I felt sad and angry. My mother, I knew, was also upset. As we passed a group of pathetically thin black children dressed in rags, she turned to look at me, tears welling in her eyes.

On the third and last day of our drive, which had become unmercifully hot, we stopped at an air-conditioned Woolworth for lunch. While my parents were ordering sandwiches, I wandered around the store and came upon two water fountains a few feet apart. A wad of cotton wool hung over one; a chocolate bar over the other. I decided to drink from the fountain with the chocolate bar. Before I could even take a sip, however, a huge white man lunged at me and started screaming that I was at the wrong fountain. Hearing the commotion, my father rushed over and led me away without saying a word, although I knew he was furious at the man. We left Woolworth without having lunch.

Back on the road, we soon came to an intersection. My father stopped to yield to another car, but the driver of the other car, an elderly black man, nervously signaled for us to go first. My father would not budge. "Why don't you go, Daddy? Why are we just sitting here?" I asked, worried that there might be trouble. In his quiet voice, my father answered, "Because the other driver has the right of way. It doesn't matter that he has dark skin, and I don't care that we're in the South. *He* has the right of way." After what seemed like a very long time, the driver slowly crossed the intersection.

My parents' basic sense of fairness in human relationships left an indelible impression on me. I grew up believing that all people deserve to be treated respectfully and equally; when they were not, I was deeply offended, just as my mother and father had been. Over the past few years, I have come to believe that only by teaching our children to value members of other races, nationalities, socioeconomic groups, religions, cultures, and sexual orientations can we anticipate a promising future. We human beings are interdependent, and if our species is to endure in a civilized form, we must learn to be respectful of one another.

We can help our children cultivate an attitude of respect by exposing them to, instead of insulating them from, people who are different from them. By having a gay teacher, the child from a straight family learns that homosexuals are simply people who choose life partners of the same gender as themselves. An upper-middle-class child who befriends a child from a welfare family sees how very hard life is for poor folks. A physically healthy child who plays with a youngster with severe disabilities learns about human resilience and the inborn capacity to overcome the most daunting challenges. A Christian child who attends her schoolmate's bat mitzvah or observes a Ram Navami ceremony discovers that there is more than one way to practice religion. I, for one, am ever grateful to my Jewish grandmother, who regularly took me to the beautiful Roman Catholic church in our neighborhood so that I could marvel at its stained glass windows, the paintings and sculptures of the Virgin and Child, the flickering candles dripping sweet-smelling wax, and the heavenly music of the high mass.

Human nature compels us to be both attracted to and suspicious of the unknown. It doesn't, however, cause us to dehumanize the stranger, the foreigner: only the messages we pass on do that. When my husband was in college, he went to Europe for the summer and met a young woman who lived in a tiny Swedish village. Never having known a Jew before and having learned from her elders that horns grew from the heads of Jewish men, she was surprised to find nothing but dark hair protruding from his scalp. The truth is that as soon as we get to know the stranger and to converse with the foreigner, we learn—as did the young Swede—that we are all simply *human*.

And we realize that because of our individual differences, we together form the wonderfully diverse human family.

If we adults make the effort to value the differences in people, our children will learn by our example to become tolerant adults. If we speak up and let it be known that we are offended whenever we hear someone make a joke or a nasty remark about a person of color, a Jew, a Muslim, a Christian, a homosexual, a person with a physical or mental disability, or anyone else who is different from the majority, our children will gain the courage to do the same.

Getting Along in an Imperfect World

Treated respectfully, the great majority of people on earth respond in kind. A small minority of human beings, however, have been so psychologically traumatized that they cannot or will not relate to others in a respectful manner. Girls growing up with respectful parents, I have observed, tend naturally to stay away from such destructive folks. Accustomed to being treated fairly, they are outraged when degraded. In addition, self-respecting girls, like self-respecting women, give off such powerful verbal and nonverbal cues against abuse of any sort that they often repel potentially exploitive individuals before a relationship can even get off the ground. Tragically, the opposite is true of girls who do not respect themselves; they become vulnerable prey for abusers.

Several years ago, a Buddhist client defined "trust" for me. I, in turn, passed on her interpretation to my own daughter, in the hope that she would benefit from it as much as I had. Trust, according to my client, is not a naive belief in the goodness and integrity of others; it is instead an accurate understanding of the world we live in. Hence, you trust that a rock is hard and that banging against it will result in injury; you trust that fire is hot and will burn your skin; you trust that a bee stings you if you stick your hand in its nest. *And you trust that people who put*

*you down or take advantage of you or treat you like an object instead
of a human being are not fit company, and that it is best to keep a respectful distance from them.*

As parents, we can reinforce our daughters' self-protective
instincts and thereby help them become self-respecting women.
From the time they are very young, we can teach them to recognize exploitative or disrespectful behavior in others through
discussions about real-life experiences—how the substitute
teacher was demeaning or the "best friend" acted mean, for instance—and, together, we can interpret the actions of the characters they come across in stories, books, movies, and TV
shows. Children who are taught to identify deceitful, controlling, selfish, entitled, or manipulative motives are in far better
positions to protect themselves against being taken advantage
of than are naive children, who "don't know what hit" them
when they are being used. We can also explain that if an adult
or another child is rude to them, they are absolutely right to
feel angry at that person and to put an immediate end to the of-
fending behavior, and we can offer our daughters different
strategies for carrying this out—by confronting the person directly, reporting the person to an authority such as a teacher, or
walking away from the situation. We can also teach our daughters that just because someone is rude to them, they do not
have to be rude back; a person can be firm and strong without
resorting to insults or profanities. A young mother shared with
me how her four-year-old disarmed a bully on the playground
by simply saying to him, "I won't play with you until you start
being nice to me."

Our daughters will learn how to maintain their respect-
ability from our behavior as much as from our instruction. And
so we, too, need to learn to effectively protect ourselves from
those who would devalue us. Describing her education as a parent, author Joyce Maynard reminds us, with a touch of humor,
that in the process of being good to our children we may learn
to be good to ourselves: "Like every parent, I want nothing so

much as my children's well-being," she writes. "I want it so badly I may actually succeed in turning myself into a contented and well-adjusted person, if only for my children's sake."[15] A wonderful prophecy for the rest of us.

THE SEVENTH GIFT:

Wholeness

When I was a graduate student, I became fascinated with
Gestalt psychology, the study of our sensory perceptions and the impulse to complete what is unfinished. I remember a class assignment in which we were asked to describe
geometric shapes that had been flashed in front of us. Our
brains played tricks on us; when a shape was incomplete—a
broken circle, for example—we reconstructed it in our mind's
eye by closing the gap and supplying the "missing connection."
As I came to learn, both from my studies and my life experience, the tendency toward wholeness is not limited to sensory
processes. It drives much of human behavior. Within each of us
is the longing to be whole—to lead balanced lives, be well
rounded, and develop and integrate all aspects of ourselves.

A century ago Sigmund Freud provided what may still be
the best guideline for conducting a whole and healthy life,
namely balancing the ability to love (to grow with another in an
intimate relationship) with the ability to work (to be productive
and make a contribution to humanity). The question is, how do

we develop this dual ability in ourselves and foster it in our children?

Sadly, many of us lead one-sided lives in which loving precludes achieving or achieving precludes loving. To a large degree, societal expectations dictate which part of our personality will be developed and which will remain undeveloped. Girls in my generation and those previous often channeled their energies into relationship at the expense of career. From parents and other adults, we learned that popularity hinged on being pretty and sweet, not brainy and assertive, and that being openly intelligent, passionate about ideas, competitive, and ambitious would alienate us from our peers. A client in her early forties confided that while taking exams in high school, she deliberately replaced her correct answers with incorrect ones to avoid coming out with "too high a grade." Such self-defeating behavior was not unusual twenty-five or so years ago. In a series of experiments conducted in the seventies, psychologist Matina Horner discovered that women characteristically underachieved when competing with men. She reasoned that women feared success because to win any contest against a man was actually to lose—to lose his love or goodwill, and to lose her feminine identity.

Then in 1981, Colette Dowling published *The Cinderella Complex*, a book that elaborated on Horner's thesis and struck a chord with thousands of women. Dowling postulated that because women commonly believed their happiness depended on marrying a competent and successful man who would take care of them completely, becoming competent and successful themselves posed a great threat. If marriageable princes were interested only in rescuing helpless damsels, then strong, smart, independent damsels would be left by the wayside. Even after marrying and having children, most women held themselves back. As my editor, Alexia Dorszynski, puts it: "I vividly remember the way my school friends' voices dropped to a whisper when they talked about a classmate whose mother 'had to work.' Lord knows what they'd have said if the woman had ever insisted that she *wanted* to work."

Not only did many of those from earlier generations hide their abilities, but they sometimes denied that they *had* them at all. Georgia State University researchers Pauline Clance and Suzanne Imes who, in the late seventies, studied women's self-concepts, found that exceptionally bright women were often "convinced they had fooled everyone"; they would attribute their high examination scores to sheer luck, or their admission to prestigious graduate schools to errors of one kind or another, or their promotions in the workplace to supervisors' nonobjective evaluations. Clance and Imes called this the "imposter phenomenon."[1]

The beware-of-achieving messages that I heard as a young woman caused me a great deal of confusion and self-doubt. When I applied to a doctoral program in 1978, my mother worriedly asked, "Has Bruce given you his permission to do such a thing?" and "Won't Leah and Jonathan suffer if you do this?" Her anxiety fed my own worst fears—that by pursuing my interests and passions I would penalize those closest to me. In a related vein, after telling me the good news that my application had been approved and I was now a doctoral candidate, my advisor laid on the bad news: I could expect my marriage to fall apart and my women friends to pull away from me. "Women with Ph.D.'s make men feel inferior and other women envious," he said in all sincerity. "Expect to be lonely."

My daughter and her friends cannot relate to such concepts. The idea that not long ago females of all ages were afraid of competing and succeeding is alien to them. Clearly, the women's liberation movement, which gathered tremendous force in the seventies, succeeded in raising consciousness and changing lives. The world of today's daughters is dramatically different from that of their mothers and grandmothers. For one thing, the majority of today's college students are female;

additionally, more women than men are pursuing advanced degrees.[2]

This is not to say that all internal and external barriers to achievement have been lifted. A well-publicized study recently conducted by the American Association of University Women concludes that present-day school systems do not adequately foster girls' intellectual development and that, compared with boys, girls are given fewer opportunities to succeed.[3] As a result, say some social analysts, girls do not develop the self-confidence needed to follow high-pressure, high-power career tracks. Indeed, women do remain underrepresented in politics, policy making, the sciences, engineering, and upper management, and those who enter these fields are likely to find their upward mobility impeded by the "glass ceiling."[4]

Mounting evidence supports the notion that during adolescence many girls in our culture lose their initiative, focus, and direction. To be sure, the transition from girlhood to womanhood is fraught with anxiety in a society obsessed with beauty, sex, and drugs. How is it possible for a girl to concentrate on math problems or compose a poem or practice the cello if she is preoccupied with her weight or a physical flaw of any sort? How can she look forward to going to classes if she is afraid of being sexually harassed in the hallways? How can she think clearly and creatively if she is "getting wasted" with her friends on the weekends?—a problem that also affects boys, of course.

Nurturing Our Daughters' Talents

In *Reviving Ophelia*, Mary Pipher postulates that our present culture is "girl poisoning" and implores us to replace it with one that is "less complicated and more nurturing, less violent and sexualized and more growth producing."[5] Such a change will require a relentless effort on our parts for many years to come. A more immediate solution would be to partially "immunize" our daughters against the culture's junk values by promoting from the start all that is most alive, vibrant, and individualistic in them. When a girl grows up knowing that her parents value not only her prettiness and pleasantness but also her capabilities, interests, accomplishments, and passions, she, in turn, will value these aspects of herself.

Fatima Mernissi, in *Dreams of Trespass*, tells how one wise mother-figure assures a young girl of her specialness and of her ability to cultivate it and thereby overcome her anxieties about the future:

> But Aunt Habiba said not to worry, that everyone had wonderful things hidden inside. The only difference was that some managed to share those wonderful things, and others did not. Those who did not explore and share the precious gifts within went through life feeling miserable, sad, awkward with others, and angry too. You had to develop a talent . . . so that you could give something, share, and shine. And you developed a talent by working very hard at becoming good at something. It could be anything— singing, dancing, cooking, embroidering, listening, looking, smiling, waiting, accepting, dreaming, rebelling, leaping. Anything you can do well can change your life.[6]

In becoming aware of our daughters' talents, we must be very careful not to appropriate them, to remember that these talents are theirs, not ours. I once counseled a young woman who had no idea what she wanted to do after graduating from college; she felt dull, uninspired, and unmotivated. As we went over her history, I learned that as a child Brenda had studied piano, performed at many concerts, and was thought to have exceptional talent. After entering high school, however, she gave up the piano for good, without knowing exactly why. In our later discussions, I discovered that her parents, excited and proud to have such a gifted child, had become overinvolved and overly invested in her musical career. They did not let Brenda develop her talents at her own pace or in her own way. Indeed, they were so consumed with her progress, so concerned that her piano teacher was doing everything right, so anxious about her public appearances that she could no longer feel that her music belonged to her. Had Brenda's parents supplied her with a piano, financed music lessons, let her know she had a special talent, *and then stepped back*, I suspect she would be joyously creating music today instead of experiencing listlessness. An anecdote about a different kind of parent from Brenda's comes to mind: When I asked a colleague, the mother of a thirteen-year-old who is a passionate musician, what *she* did to nurture her daughter's talent, she replied, "One thing and one thing only—I made sure that the car I bought had a trunk large enough to hold Heather's cello."

Whereas controlling our daughters' activities is almost always disempowering, providing opportunities for them to explore, experiment, and become more deeply involved is empowering. It was the Irish poet William Butler Yeats who said, "Education is not the filling of a pail, but the lighting of a fire." Psychologist Barbara Kerr, while studying the lives of eminent women, found that access to books was, without exception, paramount in their development. To be sure, educated parents generally make books available to their children; how children respond to books will vary from child to child. In my own home, the walls are lined with overpacked bookcases, and when my daughter lived with us it bothered me that, in spite of parental prodding, she did not read much. I see now that it was precisely because my husband and I put such emphasis on books that Leah stayed away from them. Only after she moved away from home and our *nudging* did she become a voracious reader. Now the walls of *her* apartment are lined with overpacked bookcases.

According to Mary Field Belenky, Blyth McVicker Clinchy, Nancy Rule Goldberger, and Jill Mattuck Tarule, the authors of *Women's Ways of Knowing*, boys have traditionally been encouraged to explore and take risks, while girls have been expected to be quiet, predictable, obedient, and conforming. Although such passive behaviors may enhance a girl's agreeableness, they do nothing to increase her mastery. Instead, parents wishing to enhance their daughters' competence would do well to start them out with games and other playthings that operate in response to their actions. (Watching TV—the most popular recreation for some children—requires no interaction on their part and therefore does not enliven the mind or foster a sense of accomplishment.)

As I noted earlier, parents should try to ensure that their daughters have ample unstructured time to themselves. However, they would also do well to point them to activities that build skills, such as team sports or classes in art, music, computer, karate, or cooking. Enrolling Leah in a drama class at the age of seven seemed to change her life. Exposed to the theater world, she began working fervently to hone her talents as an actress. For years, she was so focused on giving life to the characters she played that she managed to bypass the feelings of boredom, emptiness, and general discontent that plague countless girls. Having opportunities to be effective is a powerful antidote to anger or apathy. Indeed, the *will to be competent*—to confront a problem and find a solution—is innate in every child. Its emergence during the earliest months of life is splendidly described in the following passage by the American writer Tille Olsen from her autobiographical novel *Yonnondio from the Thirties*:

[Baby] Bess who has been fingering a fruit jar lid—absently, heedlessly drops it—aimlessly groping across the table, reclaims it again. Lightning in her brain. She releases, grabs, releases, grabs. I can do. Bang! I did that. I can do. I! A look of neanderthal concentration is on her face. That noise! In triumphant, astounded joy she clashes that lid down. Bang, slam, whack. Release, grab, slam, bang, bang. Centuries of human drive work in her; human ecstasy of achievement, satisfaction, deep and fundamental as sex:

I can do, I use my powers, I! I! Wilder, madder, happier the bangs.
The fetid fevered air rings with. . . . Bess's toothless, triumphant
crow. Heat misery, rash misery transcended.[7]

At every stage in our daughters' growth, their feelings of
joy are directly tied to their experiences of competence.
Whether they have just learned to walk, to tie their shoelaces,
to ride a two-wheeler, to shape a bowl out of clay, to solve a
frustrating algebra problem, or to drive a car, their chant is one
of personal victory: "I can do; I use my powers; I! I!"

The Guiding Mother

When a child trusts that she *can* be successful at something,
she probably *will* be successful, for confidence and mastery are
linked. According to research conducted by Martin E. P. Seligman, a University of Pennsylvania psychologist best known for
his studies on the prevention of depression, children seem to
absorb their mother's optimism—her belief that her children
have within them the power to cope with problems and overcome setbacks.[8]

How a mother's attitude affects her baby's behavior is
demonstrated in a series of now-famous "visual cliff" experiments conducted in the eighties by researchers Mary Klinnert,
Joseph Campos, and Robert Emde.[9] In one of these experiments, a baby is placed at the edge of a table that is covered
with a red-and-white checkered cloth topped with a sheet of
glass. Due to special lighting effects, the glass surface is invisi-
ble and the checkered pattern at this end of the table appears as
solid ground. The baby's mother stands at the opposite end of
the table next to a bright and beautiful toy Ferris wheel. Excitedly, the baby crawls toward the mother and the Ferris wheel,
but when she reaches the halfway point, she notices that she
no longer seems to be on solid ground. (The experimenters

designed the cloth so that it appears to drop precipitously, and the baby has the illusion of being on the edge of a high cliff.) Looking down, she becomes naturally scared and is tempted to stop her exploration and return to safe ground; at the same time, she wants to get to Mother and the enticing toy. Unable to resolve her ambivalence, she looks toward her mother to assess *her* emotional response to the situation. If Mother has followed instructions to show fear on her face, baby does not cross the imaginary cliff. If, on the other hand, mother is smiling and confident, conveying the message "Come on, darling, you're doing fine," baby masters the "cliff" and continues crawling forward. Time and again, I have observed that the optimism expressed by mothers inspires daughters of all ages to push forward. The trusting smile and calm demeanor that say, "Sure, you can; I have faith in your capabilities; you'll make it, if you try," have the power of a magic potion.

Of course, mothers cannot fake this display of confidence. It comes from within. Some women are naturally confident. Others, like myself, develop this quality only after overcoming anxieties, depression, or fears. At some point in elementary school I developed a severe case of performance anxiety, and my knocking knees, pounding heart, and cracking voice continued into adulthood each time I faced an audience. After publishing my first book about mothers and daughters, Oprah Winfrey's producer telephoned and asked me to appear on the show, a publicity opportunity that any new author would have coveted. Instead of jumping for joy, I was gripped with my old fear. Every instinct prompted me to decline the invitation, warned me not to risk making a fool of myself in the living rooms of millions of TV viewers. *Every instinct save one:* I knew that by saying no, I would be a poor role model for my teenage daughter. How would I be able to motivate Leah to overcome her fears if I gave in to mine without a fight? And so, clutching the telephone receiver so hard that my knuckles turned white, I accepted the producer's invitation to appear on the program, which turned out to be the first of many TV appearances. With the help of experts, including a media specialist who gave me tips and a psychiatrist who prescribed medication to control performance anxiety, I gradually overcame my stage fright and became an effective public speaker.

Many years ago I treated a beautiful and brilliant high school senior who, upon learning that she had been admitted to the college of her choice, suddenly stopped eating and dropped her weight to a dangerously low level. Hiroka explained that the opportunities facing her racked her with guilt because they contrasted so strongly with the bleak existence of her mother, Natsu. At Hiroka's request, I soon began meeting with Natsu as well. Having emigrated from Japan to the United States a few years before, she was deeply ashamed of her broken English and consequently avoided contacts with people outside the family. Most days, she sat in her cramped apartment, staring out the window or occupying herself with meaningless tasks. I soon discovered that Natsu had been both a watercolorist and a poet but had given up her crafts when she came to this country. It did not take much encouragement from me to persuade her to pick up her pen and brush once again. When she did, her depression began to lift. Buoyed by my admiration, she eventually became confident enough to introduce her work to some local artists, who also responded enthusiastically. And as Natsu, painting her gorgeous flowers, blossomed, Hiroka recovered from her illness. It is no secret that a mother's growing sense of confidence is the ground from which a daughter's confidence emerges.

The French writer Colette wrote extensively about her mother, whose zest for life inspired Colette to love and to work with passion. One of my favorite passages comes from her collection of short stores titled *My Mother's House and Sido*:

> It was not until one morning when I found the kitchen unwarmed and the blue enamel saucepan hanging on the wall,

that I felt my mother's end to be near. Her illness knew many respites, during which the fire flared up again on the hearth, and the smell of fresh bread and melting chocolate stole under the door together with the cat's impatient paw. These respites were periods of unexpected alarms. My mother and the big walnut cupboard were discovered together in a heap at the foot of the stairs, she having determined to transport it in secret from the upper landing to the ground floor. Whereupon my elder brother insisted that my mother should keep still and that an old servant should sleep in the little house. But how could an old servant prevail against a vital energy so youthful and mischievous that it contrived to tempt and lead astray a body already half fettered by death? My brother, returning before sunrise from attending a distant patient, one day caught my mother red-handed in the most wanton of crimes. Dressed in her nightgown, but wearing heavy gardening sabots, her little grey septuagenarian's plait of hair turning up like a scorpion's tail on the nape of her neck, one foot planted on the beech trestle, her back bent in the attitude of the expert jobber, my mother rejuvenated by an indescribable expression of guilty enjoyment, in defiance of all her promises and of the freezing morning dew, was sawing logs in her own yard.[10]

The Guiding Father

All daughters observe their mothers with passionate, sustained interest, and what they see affects who they become. Their fathers' influence is equally profound. His capacity to lead, solve problems, achieve goals, think linearly, and act decisively can help his daughter cultivate many behaviors that will serve her well in the classroom, workplace, and life itself. Marianne Neifert ("Dr. Mom") provides the following example of a father's guidance. As she and her husband were driving their daughter to the out-of-state college she would attend, Marianne thought of countless things to tell her and conjured up all sorts of traumas from which to shield her. Larry, her husband, provided a different kind of care: "Tricie," he began, "I'm going to give you only three words of formal advice. I have every confidence in your ability to apply this simple three-word formula to every new situation you will face at college." Marianne, sure that these three words were "Call me anytime"—for this is what she wanted to tell her daughter—almost blurted them out but restrained herself. As Larry continued, his daughter listened expectantly: "Figure it out. . . . Figure it out intellectually, figure it out socially, figure it out practically," he said. "Whatever the challenge, Tricie, know that you have within you the ability to 'figure it out' successfully."[11]

Mariah, a client in her early twenties, shared this memorable story about her single father. Soon after sixteen-year-old Mariah and her twin sister passed their driving tests, he took them for a ride in the snow-packed Colorado mountains, intentionally heading into a snowbank, where the car became good and stuck. "Okay, girls," he said, "there are shovels, chains, and sand in the truck, and I'm going to hang around for as long as it takes the two of you to get the car out of this mess and moving again." After about two hours of pushing and shoving, the girls were victorious. Now that Mariah is a working woman, she commutes long distances to and from her job each day. And she is an expert driver, undaunted by reports of hazardous weather conditions during Colorado's long, snowy winters.

Throughout adolescence, when girls are at risk for becoming overly absorbed with body image, fathers can be especially empowering by helping them reevaluate their priorities. My friend's twenty-year-old daughter brought this fact home to me. "One of the reasons I continued to be active and do well during my teen years was that my dad kept on valuing me for my accomplishments," Emily explained. "He didn't notice when I had a bad hair day or when I weighed five pounds more or less. He *did* notice when I said something particularly intelligent, or when I fielded especially well for my softball team. I guess I figured that if he was more turned on by my accomplishments than my looks, other guys would be too someday."

It is, of course, natural and healthy for a teenage girl to want to be attractive to the opposite sex. How fortunate she is when the first man in her life—her father—lets her know that by being smart and competent she is!

Support Versus Pressure

Sometimes a father's well-intentioned efforts to promote his daughter's strength and capability can excessively pressure her. This is true of a young executive I am counseling. Although it would be in her best interest to cut back on work, which has become so grueling that she now suffers from myriad stress-related health problems, she does not want to lose her father's favor. As Jackie explains:

> My father is my number-one fan. He bursts his buttons when I get a promotion at work. He assures me that working twelve-hour days is the way I'll get to the top. He also clips every article he comes across about young superwomen. The last one he sent me described a woman pilot who flies for a major airline, exhibits her paintings in major museums, sews her daughter's clothes, and ran for political office. My father is so intent on my being extraordinary that I am afraid to be ordinary.

When I ask Jackie to close her eyes and envision the kind of life *she* wants to create, she does not talk about becoming the president of her company. "Work is important," she says, "but so is having time with my husband and watching sunsets and smelling flowers." I suspect that Jackie speaks for many women driven, by others or by themselves, to achieve *too* much.

To be sure, it is not only fathers who may push their daughters overly hard. Mothers may fall into the same trap. I have observed that many women who have missed out on a good education or career fulfillment *impose* "opportunities" on their daughters, driving them to outperform themselves. In insisting that her daughter become *all she can be*, such a mother often forgets that it is simply best *to let her be.*

Psychologist Abraham Maslow, who studied the conditions leading to "self-actualization," had this advice: "If you want to learn about ducks, then you had better ask the ducks instead of telling them. So also for human children . . . it looks as if the best technique for finding out what is best for them is to develop techniques for getting *them* to tell us what is best for them."[12] He went on to say, "My finding is that, that which you love, you are prepared to leave alone."[13]

While growing up, and especially during her teen years, a girl will require time alone to discover and develop her unique gifts. In Barbara Kerr's analysis of thirty-one eminent women, Eleanor Roosevelt, Marie Curie, Georgia O'Keeffe, and Maya Angelou among them, she discovered that what they had in common was ample opportunity to be by themselves: a protected, private, quiet space in which to grow. As Kerr writes: "Georgia O'Keeffe seemed typically to prefer aloneness, and her parents allowed her to explore the world by herself. Eleanor Roosevelt was isolated by circumstances that left her in the homes of relatives who knew little about providing for the social needs of a child. Marie Curie's intellectual hunger was so insatiable that it drove her to withdraw into private concentration even in the midst of a busy family. Maya Angelou was isolated by violence and fear of others."[14] Regardless of circumstances, long periods of aloneness were a blessing for these women. When our own daughters seek privacy, when they retreat into their rooms and shut the doors behind them, when they close us out, we will be wise to avoid intruding on them and to respect the solitude that feeds the soul.

New Age, New Fears

Despite the advances American women have made in recent years, Freud's prescription for psychological wholeness—to love *and* to work—may still elude our daughters. For a growing number of young women, the *fear of loving* is replacing the *fear of achieving.* Now that satisfying, lasting relationships seem to be the exception rather than the rule, it is all too easy to be cynical about love. I recall a conversation with a nineteen-year-old whose parents split up during her first year in college. "I thought my parents had a pretty good marriage and that we would always be a united family," Michele explained, "but I guess I was deluding myself." She then assured me that she would never become involved in a serious relationship "because even if it seemed to be going well, it could only end badly." Paula Logan, a waitress at one of Boulder's hangouts for teens, tells me that Michele is not exceptional. "So many of the teenagers I talk to have lost all faith in love relationships," she says with a sigh. "They don't expect to live 'happily ever after' with anyone. They can't even imagine trying." Mary Pipher, reflecting on the messages conveyed in Hollywood movies, points out that in our current culture, sex, not love, is emphasized: "In the fifties people met, argued, fell in love, then kissed," she writes. "By the seventies, people met, argued, fell in love and then had sex. In the nineties people meet, have sex, argue and then, maybe, fall in love."[15]

I suspect that many young women not only anticipate bad endings in relationships but fear that in truly caring about another, they are in great danger of being exploited or, worse still, of losing their selfhood. One of my single male clients observes that "comfortable" relationships between men and women are becoming obsolete: "It's hard for couples to be at ease," he says, "when women are always on the lookout for ways they're being taken advantage of and men never know for sure if something they're saying or doing is offensive." The

Simon and Garfunkel song "I Am a Rock," written for a generation of flower children, rings true for many of their progeny—those who build their walls and fortresses so thick that no one can penetrate them and who, like rocks, are hard and devoid of feelings.

Influenced by a new brand of academic feminism that characterizes males as inherently violent, exploitative, and conspiring to keep women down, impressionable college women are also under increasing pressure to reject heterosexual love and wifely aspirations. Exposed to incessant male-bashing rhetoric, they may come to believe they are dependent and weak, if not warped, for desiring men as sexual partners.[16] And just as many reactionaries humiliate lesbian women for loving women, many radical feminists humiliate straight women for loving men. Scratched on a bathroom wall at the university where I taught are the cautionary lines:

> *Trust no man, not even your brother,*
> *If women must love, let them love one another.*

Campus *misandrism*—a newly coined word meaning hatred of men and the counterpart of misogyny or hatred of women—seems to be manifesting in alarming ways. Christina Hoff Sommers, a Clark University philosophy professor and author of *Who Stole Feminism?*, points out that in feminist classrooms and workshops, women are increasingly encouraged to see themselves as potential victims and men as potential victimizers. She describes an extreme example of this tendency: in 1993 a group of women at the University of Maryland plastered the campus with posters and fliers listing the names of dozens of male students under the heading "Notice: These Men Are Potential Rapists." The unlucky men, *chosen at random*, had not committed any acts of violence; for these misandrist women, being born male was a crime.[17]

Sommers also suggests that long before they get to college,

girls begin learning to devalue heterosexual relationships. She reports that in an extensive survey of new textbooks written for elementary and high school students, New York University psychologist Paul Vitz could find no positive portrayals of romance, marriage, or motherhood. "Though great literature, from Tristan and Isolde to Shakespeare to Jane Austen to Louisa May Alcott, is filled with romance and the desire to marry, one finds very little of that in these texts," he writes. "Hardly a story celebrates motherhood or marriage as a positive goal or as a rich and meaningful way of living."[18] In a similar vein, Sommers notes that although the writers of history and social science textbooks for the primary and secondary grades are making special efforts to provide role models for girls, they are one-sided: "Precollege texts usually have an abundance of pictures; these now typically show women working in factories or looking through microscopes. A 'stereotypical' picture of a woman with a baby is a frowned-on rarity. Instead, a kind of reverse stereotyping has become an informal requisite."[19] In the push to elevate the feminine capacity to achieve, it appears that young girls are being steered away not only from intimacy but also from caregiving roles. All the while, what they are not learning is that being a loving mother is a fine and noble calling.

But since time immemorial, heart and hearth have been essential to the female experience. As Carol Gilligan, a Harvard professor, writes, "Women not only define themselves in a context of relationship but also judge themselves in terms of their ability to care."[20] In our laudable efforts to increase girls' self-esteem by encouraging their intellectual and creative achievements, we are wise to remember that their self-esteem also depends on the richness of their relational life. Jeanne and Don Elium, co-authors of *Raising a Daughter*, remark that girls who renounce relationship become disconnected from their own feelings: "They become resentful, enraged, depressed, and lonely. They learn to be overbearing, insensitive, and controlling to get what they need."[21] The Eliums state—quite correctly, I believe—that to achieve healthy womanhood, a girl must not only realize her talents and ambitions but also stay tied to her feminine soul, "that which values caring, connection, relationship, nature, and all of life."[22]

The Art of Loving

I met Fawzia, an exchange student from Kuwait, at a peace rally. Interested in learning about her culture, I arranged an interview with her. Smart and disciplined, Fawzia ranks at the top of her university class and will have no difficulty getting admitted to a prestigious graduate school. She marvels at the achievement opportunities available to American girls and women, possibilities that her peers in the Third World would never dream of. At the same time, she notices the general lack of regard for such traditionally feminine values as strong emotions, displays of affection, relatedness, compassion, and concern for family members, which are of great importance in her culture. Indeed, in the Arabic language, there is a word for the most generous form of caring: *hanan.* Thought to be a divine gift, *hanan* is defined as the free-flowing, easygoing, unconditionally available kindness that "bubbles up like a fountain, splashing tenderness all around, regardless of whether or not its receiver is well behaved."[23]

Fawzia asks how a woman can have *real* power if her feminine identity—those natural inclinations to feel deeply for others—is suppressed. As busy as Fawzia is with her studies, she remains deeply connected to her parents and siblings, who live in Kuwait. Her strong family relationships, which bring her both pain and joy, are as vital to her being as is her intellectual drive; her self-worth derives as much from her acts of care and nurture as it does from her success at the university. And although she suffers from overwork, financial pressures, and worries about her family members, she does not suffer from the feelings of emptiness that plague many young American women who reject deep relationships.

The capacity for love—and its expressions of nurture, empathy, care, and altruism—resides in every child, male and female. Cared for by loving parents, a child, in turn, wants to be loving. Certainly, girls model themselves after their mothers. Observing their mothers in caregiving roles, they too become attuned to the needs of others and want to help them out. According to Yale Child Study Center psychiatrist Kyle Pruett, nurturing fathers also foster the development of this precious quality.[24] In fact, caregiving fathers have been found to produce the most compassionate adults; of all parent-related factors contributing to the development of empathy, early paternal involvement is the single strongest.[25]

We can further help our young daughters develop their generous natures by giving them opportunities to be nurturing, allowing them to assume age-appropriate care of a baby sibling or a family pet, a garden, or a potted plant, or encouraging them to give comfort and aid to an old person. When Leah was barely four years old, for example, the two of us would often visit my ninety-four-year-old grandmother, who, no longer able to take care of herself, was confined to a nursing home. Wanting to be helpful, Leah would take it upon herself to spoon-feed Grandma Grete, a task she carried out with great gentleness and competence.

Many years later, at the age of twenty-three, Leah had the opportunity to care for her newly widowed and ailing paternal grandfather, who lived near her. For weeks, she was at his beck and call, responding to medical emergencies day and night. All the while, Leah grew in compassion, strength, and self-confidence. When I asked if providing routine care for an old man created problems for her, she responded that although it was awkward in the beginning, she was now surprisingly at ease. Her grandfather's neediness, however, eventually began to wear her out, whereupon her father and I insisted that she set some limits. Aware that nurturing can degenerate into an unbounded giving that depletes women of their own vitality, we gave our daughter explicit instructions, which she readily accepted. "Tell Grandpa," we advised, "that instead of calling you at work or during the night, he *must* use his emergency alert system to contact a medic. Let him know that you have a life of your own and cannot always be there for him." We also assured her more than once that by setting boundaries of this sort she was not being disrespectful or unkind.

If a mother leads a balanced life, functioning not only in the service of others but in the service of herself *and* others, a daughter is likely to follow suit. In the past, Leah had seen me pull back from social and family obligations during periods when I had to concentrate on work, and I suspect this observation was in part responsible for the permission she gave herself to pull back from her grandfather.

Paradoxically, it becomes easier for a young woman to develop her loving relational side if she knows she can, when necessary, withdraw from other people and tend to her own needs and tasks. When a woman is always in service to others, she necessarily becomes resentful and hostile. She may express her anger directly or, more likely, indirectly by becoming manipulative, passive, or physically sick.

One of the stories I often share with clients who are struggling to find a balance between giving and taking is the ancient Greek myth of Psyche and Eros. Before Psyche and Eros can consummate their love and enjoy the fruits of marriage, Psyche must learn about setting limits and accept that there are times when she cannot be available to others. This is part of the meaning of the fourth, and most difficult, task set for her by her future mother-in-law, Aphrodite. Specifically, Aphrodite instructs Psyche to journey to the underworld, procure a small cask of beauty ointment from the goddess Persephone, who resides there, then return to the upper world with the cask. A helper, in the form of a tower, gives Psyche explicit instructions not to lose her focus, concentration, and direction during the arduous journey; difficult as it will be for her, she must learn to curb her feminine generosity by not being drawn into other people's lives at this time. Hence, when a lame man asks her help in collecting the sticks he has dropped and when a dying man reaches out to her, Psyche succeeds in refusing their appeals. Having learned to say no—what Jungian psychologist Robert Johnson calls the "creative no," as opposed to the "indifferent no"—she is psychologically ready to marry. As Johnson states, "There are only certain times when the creative no is required. Then one drops it and can be generous again."[26]

Love takes many forms, and a rich relational life, whether between spouses or lovers, men and women, women and women, or men and men, is always a good thing. In the most fortunate circumstances, a daughter will observe her parents' lasting and loving marriage and see it as a model for her future relationships. Children who know that their mothers and fathers are devoted to one another and bound by their marriage vows grow up trusting that love lasts, that promises are kept, that commitments are real. Children who observe their mothers and fathers working out problems in an atmosphere of mutual respect grow up believing that conflicts do not destroy relationships and can be resolved. Same-gendered couples can also provide their daughters with these gifts.

But what happens in less fortunate circumstances, when parents do not get along and marriages break up? A client of mine divorced his wife when their only child was three. Although he does not care for his ex-wife, he is always kind and respectful to her for his daughter's sake. "The way I treat my daughter's mother is the way she is someday going to expect her own husband to treat her," he explains. Similarly, a dear friend who left her alcoholic spouse a few years after their third child was born worried that the children, having lived through a bad marriage, would not know how to participate in lasting, loving relationships when they grew up. Although my friend could not undo her children's losses, she could mitigate them. Hence, she made sure that her children spent ample time with their paternal grandparents, whose married life served as a positive model for them and whose fundamental decency as human beings was evidence that marital partners can be trusted.

Another client with a grim history of sexual abuse perpetrated by her father and her ex-husband wants nothing more to do with men but does not want to impose her jaded views on her daughter. "My natural tendency is to warn my fourteen-year-old to stay away from boys and forget about ever marrying," she says, "but I hold my tongue. It's not my right to brainwash my daughter against the opposite sex. Although my own experiences were bad, it may be possible for her to thrive in a relationship with a man, and I don't want to stand in the way of that possibility."

The negative feelings that many women harbor against men, however, often are transmitted to our daughters, who are encouraged to mistrust boys and get back at them for wrongs they have not committed. The popular "Take Our Daughters to Work Day," launched in 1993, may be a case in point. According to Christina Hoff Sommers, the Ms. Foundation, which initiated this event, suggested that on the day mothers and fathers take their daughters to work, boys remain in the classroom doing exercises to help them become aware of the oppression of women—and to see their part in it. While "the girls are off for a fun day with their parents being 'visible, valued, and heard' . . . the boys are left behind to learn their lesson," Sommers writes. "Of course," she emphasizes, "boys must learn to be thoughtful and respectful of girls, but they are not culprits; they are not silencing girls or lowering their self-esteem, and no one should be sending the boys the message that they are doing any of these things."[27] No one should be sending girls this message, either.

From the time our daughters are able to carry on conversations, we can encourage them to treat *all* human beings—

young and old, male and female—with respect and kindness. And we can encourage them to understand differences between people rather than be fearful or contemptuous of these differences. Tom, a member of my parents group, explained that when his eleven-year-old daughter told him that the boys who paid attention to her were "jerks," he assured her that there were lots of nice boys, too—and that maybe the boys she knew were acting a little jerky not because they were mean or stupid but because they felt shy and nervous around her. Similarly, Charles, another group member, helped his preteen daughter develop empathy for the boy who was telephoning her every night by suggesting that instead of getting annoyed or feeling afraid of him, as was her tendency and her mother's, she try to imagine how he must be feeling calling her and risking her rejection.

I, too, have tried to help my daughter find gentle, noninjurious ways of turning away boys and young men who do not interest her. As the mother of a son, I know firsthand that even when he displays a tough veneer a boy is tender of heart and painfully vulnerable to rejections and insults, especially about his prowess and competence. Whenever my son is in a relationship with a young woman, I secretly hope that her parents have taught her to treat young men with sensitivity. For the truth is that, contrary to conventional wisdom, a boy's rejected heart heals less easily than a girl's.[28]

Many of us mistakenly think that love comes naturally, requiring no special skill or effort. In reality, however, love, like all great practices, calls for good teachers. The great German poet of the twentieth century Rainer Maria Rilke once wrote, "Young people, who are beginners in everything, cannot yet know love, they have to learn it. With their whole being, with all their forces, gathered close about their lonely, timid, upward-beating heart, they must learn to love."[29] But perhaps, as Robert Johnson wisely says, "we are all yet beginners in love."[30]

Whole Daughters, Whole Parents

In guiding our daughters toward the art of loving, we are wise to reconsider the ways in which *we* love—as parents, spouses, friends. Achieving wholeness means balancing "work" and "love," combining giving and receiving, being both other directed and inner directed. And so we must ask ourselves, are we overly involved in the lives of those we love, or less involved than we should be? Too generous or not generous enough? Do we allow ourselves to be exploited or use others for our purposes? Ought we to let go or hold on? Give advice or remain quiet?

Similarly, in encouraging our daughters to cultivate their interests and talents, we might take stock of the ways *we* are productive and contribute to humanity. Recalling the words of Aunt Habiba in *Dreams of Trespass*, everyone has wonderful things hidden inside, but we must explore, develop, and share these precious gifts within; we must work very hard at becoming good at *something*. Then, like our daughters, we will shine.

THE EIGHTH GIFT:

Courage

In the normal course of parenting our daughters, we will participate in many of their small and big hardships: not making the team, having to move, being rejected by a girlfriend or a boyfriend, getting turned down for a special school program or the college of their choice, experiencing the loss of a loved one, sustaining a serious injury or becoming ill. Without minimizing their disappointment, frustrations, and grief, we do well to assure them (and remind ourselves) that situations are never hopeless and that, hard as it is to believe that *anything* good can possibly come out of a misfortune, this is what often happens.

Of course, it hurts us to see our daughters in any kind of pain. Far, far worse than enduring our own suffering is being witness to theirs. Yet through personal hardship our daughters are often able to develop powers of resilience, endurance, ingenuity, insight, humanity, and fortitude. Pain, when faced squarely, can fuel their creativity (indeed, most art and literature are products of pain) and deepen their compassion for others. I am reminded of the development of a pearl. It begins as a grain of sand—an irritant—embedded within an oyster shell. Unable to rid itself of the painful grain of sand, the oyster encases it in layers of hard, silvery brilliance and transforms it into a precious jewel.

A dear friend shared this story: During her daughter's senior year in high school, her three closest girlfriends began excluding her from social activities. Their phone calls stopped, they no longer dropped by the house, and when Liz caught sight of them at school they averted their glances. For reasons they kept from her, Liz was no longer a member of "the club" that had been her support for years. Hurt and confused by her friends' unexplained rejection, she tried everything she knew to win them back—including taking a job after school to earn enough money to buy them expensive Christmas presents—and when all her attempts failed she fell into a dark mood. Listening to Liz cry herself to sleep each night, my friend's heart would break for her. There were many times that she wanted to approach the girls' parents, whom she had known for years, and urge them to "do something" about their daughters' hurtful behavior, but she held herself back, which turned out to be a good thing. Liz began to make positive changes on her own. No longer able to depend on her three childhood friends for support, she decided to look elsewhere for satisfaction and, as a result, expanded her interests. She became a more serious student; she took up drawing; she traveled around the country by herself to check out colleges and worked hard to be admitted to a very fine one; she became more self-assertive. And, despite having been rejected, when she started college she reached out, making several new friends who have remained loyal to this day.

In my practice, I have counseled many young people who have transformed what was troublesome or, indeed, painful (the unwelcome grain of sand) into something precious (the pearl). Those who come immediately to mind are a twenty-nine-year-old woman who as a child was badly injured in a house fire and is now preparing to study medicine with the intention of helping sick children; a graduate student who, having overcome a life-threatening condition of anorexia, counsels other people with eating disorders; a hearing-impaired girl who developed a passion for learning foreign languages; a college student who, having suffered a severe head injury, is forced to cultivate the qualities of patience and determination during her long rehabilitation. Coincidently, the day I began writing this chapter, I attended a community event at which a young woman paid tribute to her sister, explaining that during the months before she died from a brain tumor, her sister developed an exquisite appreciation for the "ordinary" wonders in the natural world and taught those closest to her to look at life—whether reflected in a small flower, a cloudless day, or a night sky—with awe. In the cherishing language of a lover, the poet W. H. Auden addressed his inner pain as a gift and thanked it for the insight it bestowed on him. "Knowing you," he said, "has made me understand."[1]

Reflecting on the stories of my clients, I wondered if I could find a common pattern. Was there a "formula" for transforming the painful grain of sand into the precious jewel? Although the circumstances and personalities of these women were different, it was clear that they all had courageous spirits. Faced with their injuries and disabilities, they learned about them and did whatever was necessary to live life purposefully. The word *courage* means *dealing* with anything deemed dangerous, difficult, or painful, instead of withdrawing from it; it comes from the Latin root *cor* or "heart." When my twenty-one-year-old son was dealing with a major emotional crisis, he would tap into his courage by closing his eyes, taking a deep breath, and putting both hands with fingers pointed upward on his heart. We parents cannot directly teach our children to be courageous in times of trouble, but we can gently instruct them to put their hands on their heart so that they may discover their own strong spirits.

The Right to Feel Bad

Among the many pressures we face in our perfectionistic culture is the pressure to be always "up." "Americans are very strange," a French acquaintance once told me. "You smile constantly." He had a point. We Americans are so insistent on being happy that we have made the "smiley face" our national logo. I am often taken aback by the falsely cheery messages some of my clients leave on their answering machine. For example, when I recently called to check on a new client who, after a year of many losses, was understandably depressed, I was greeted with the recorded message: "Hi! No one home . . . having a *great* day, hope you are too!" Similarly, when clients come in for a session and I ask, "Well, how have you been?" many respond automatically, "Oh just fine!". . . . and then, realizing that here in therapy they are safe to be themselves, burst into tears and disclose their true feelings. The pressure to be always in good spirits translates into the pressure to raise perennially cheerful children. Because we have been taught that it is unacceptable—even *shameful*—to experience mental pain for more than ten minutes, we may pass on the same message to our children. A more enhancing message would be that human life is not problem free and that it is quite normal to experience periods of great sadness, or as psychologist Lesley Hazelton writes "the pains and perils of being 'merely' human."[2]

Recently, a teenage girl confided that one of the worst aspects about going through a psychological crisis was believing that all her peers were having fun, that she was *supposed* to be happy, and that her tendency toward depression was a character flaw. During our early sessions, as she opened up and the tears began to flow profusely, she managed to keep on smiling. I told my client that her present unhappiness was neither a sign of weakness nor of being flawed but rather an indication of her growing humanity; I also assured her that smiling wasn't mandatory.

Certainly, being *chronically* unhappy is not desirable; and when children, adolescents, or adults are debilitated by depressions or anxieties from which they cannot shake themselves free after several weeks, they require treatment—usually psychotherapy and sometimes medications. However, all human beings ought to make some room in their lives for depression and suffering. During the Renaissance, people often created a bower in their gardens dedicated to Saturn, the Roman god associated with melancholy, to which they could retreat, undisturbed, to reflect on their sorrows. From time to time, we all need such shady lairs. Indeed, we will find that when we approach, rather than avoid, the difficulties, anxieties, and fears that torment us, they lose most of their abusive power. This bit of wisdom is revealed in a Tibetan parable that Dawna Markova includes in her book *No Enemies Within*. Here is my version, suitable to share with children:

Many years ago in a faraway country there lived a good man named Milarepa. One day when Milarepa was returning to the small hut that was his home, he found it filled with enemies— terrifying, horrifying demons that would make most people want to run far, far away. But Milarepa did not run away. Instead, he turned to the demons, looked them straight in the eye, bowed respectfully, and said, "You are here in my home now. I honor you and am interested in what you have to teach me." As soon as he uttered these words, all but five of the demons departed. Those that remained were ugly, grisly creatures. Once more Milarepa bowed before them and welcomed them. In his sweet voice he sang a song to them—a song about their suffering and *their* need for kindness. As he ended his song, four more demons evaporated into thin air, leaving only one. This last demon—nostrils flaring, fangs oozing bile, open jaws revealing a dark, gaping hole—seemed the scariest-looking of all. But Milarepa was not repulsed by him and whispered in his ear: "I would like to understand your pain and what it is you need from me in order to be healed." Then he put his head in the mouth of the demon. Instantly the demon disappeared, and the small hut that was Milarepa's home became a peaceful dwelling once more.[3]

Daphna, a nine-year-old, brought the parable of Milarepa down to earth when she told me: "If I keep my fears a secret they get bigger and bigger, but if my mother says, 'Daphna, let's take a good look at what's upsetting you and get to the bottom of it,' they get smaller and smaller."

The Ways Through Pain

Nature endows human beings with an amazingly effective mechanism for facing pain: this is the capacity to cry. Unfortunately, many of us have been trained to interpret crying as a sign of weakness and as an outlet appropriate only for babies; perhaps as children we were even taunted by our parents or peers when we cried in public. In therapy, adult clients will frequently apologize for crying, explaining that it makes them feel stupid and out of control. Some tell me that they are afraid if they begin to cry, they will never be able to stop. If we as parents can learn to appreciate the value of tears—as a *safe* release for every kind of pain, a way to express our most profound feelings and to connect with others who suffer—we are bound to help our daughters feel more free to cry, even as they grow into adulthood. My friend Ellen once told me, "The richest days of our lives are those when we have a good cry and a good laugh." And an Hassidic proverb reminds us that tears are for the soul what soup is for the body. Instead of soothing our tearful daughters of any age with words such as, "Now, now, stop the crying," we will help them more by saying something like, "Good for you, go ahead and cry. Just let it out."

We can also encourage our daughters to express their anger or sorrow creatively. From the time they are three or four, we might suggest that they make up a song or create a dance or draw a picture to describe their strong feelings. Or we might ask them to tell a story about their troubles and offer to record it; by taping their words or writing them down and then reading them back, we demonstrate our respect for our daughters' inner experiences. Of course, after they start elementary school, they will be able to write down their own thoughts and feelings. One of the finest material gifts parents can give their school-age daughters is a beautifully bound journal along with the assurance that its contents will not be read without their permission.

If our daughters feel free to talk openly to us about their travails, they will likely experience relief; as the saying goes, problems shared are problems halved. By maintaining an optimistic attitude during our communications, we will teach our daughters to do the same. Optimism does not mean denying reality or pretending everything is well and good or thinking only "positive thoughts." It is rather the conviction that we are not helpless in the face of a crisis and the confidence that through personal efforts (and with a little help from our friends) we will eventually find solutions (or at least partial solutions) to many of our problems and also learn to adapt to the unsolvable ones. Optimism is also the ongoing decision to see the cup as half-full rather than as half-empty, to focus on assets instead of liabilities. Even if we have become cynical, for our daughters' sake we might try to cultivate the attitude of optimism; in doing so, we will improve our own mental health immeasurably. Incidentally, the most optimistic person I have ever known—my mother-in-law, Sylvia Bassoff—was not someone blessed with an easy life. She was a woman who, at age two, was stricken with polio and moved through the world with wooden crutches and a heavy brace on one leg. Still, the day before Sylvia died, she said to me, "My life has been magic!"

In addition to conveying optimism, we can follow certain guidelines that will help us communicate with our daughters in a comforting manner. For instance, it is useful to keep in mind that all young children are afraid of being abandoned; hence, they require calm and frequent assurances that we will not leave them alone to deal with their troubles and that they can depend on our "being there" for necessary support. Even those children facing grave troubles such as chronic or terminal illness are soothed by the assuring parental words: "I am right here by your side. I won't go away." We might remember that in our children's favorite fairy tales, magical figures—angels or fairies or spirits—often appear to guide the child through the dark forest; these helping figures represent none other than us, the loving parents.

At the same time young children feel powerless and vulnerable, they also see themselves as the center of the world. Thus, it is only natural that they harbor grandiose fantasies of being responsible for all the events in their family's lives, including such heartrending ones as divorce, a family member's physical or mental illness, or a sibling's death. When we repeatedly say to our daughters, "What's happened is not your fault," we relieve them of scary intimations that they are wicked people who ought to be ashamed of themselves and are sure to be punished.

Intuitively, my grandmother understood the things that frightened a child, and whenever I brought up a problem to her she was able to quell my anxieties so that I would not feel helpless or hopeless. When I was five, my paternal grandfather, who lived with us, became very ill and was taken to a nursing home, where he died a few weeks later. My parents withheld the information about his death from me. Perhaps they didn't want to burden me by bringing up my grandfather's death. Perhaps they—especially my stoic father—were afraid of breaking down in front of me. Perhaps they didn't know how to explain death to a young child without being morbid. And perhaps they rationalized that with the passing of time I would forget about my grandfather in the nursing home. Of course, this would never have been the case. I loved *Opa* and missed him terribly.

As the weeks went by without a word from him and with only evasions from my mother and father—"Oh, he's still too sick for you to visit him. Next week maybe"—I figured out that he must be dead. I also came to believe that death must be so hideous, so fearsome that even grown people dared not speak about it. Not surprisingly, I began to obsess: I worried that my parents would be killed in a car accident and became frantic when they went out for the evening; I also worried that I had inadvertently done something to bring about my grandfather's death. Perhaps, I reasoned in child's way, my parents knew I was to blame all along and, too kindhearted to tell me what I had done, were keeping the details of his death a secret from me. As my gruesome fantasies occupied more and more of my mental life, I pretended to be happy so that no one would guess what I was thinking about.

However, the day I discovered my pet goldfish belly-up and could not, despite prodding, probing, and throwing more and more fish food into his bowl, bring him back to life, I panicked. No longer able to hold in my fears, I decided to turn to my maternal grandmother, who I knew would tell me the truth about my grandfather, about everything. And indeed, quite matter-of-factly, she confirmed the fact of his death, explaining that, as happens to very old, sick people, his body had worn out and now was part of the earth again, which was as Mother Nature intended. When I asked if I had caused his death, she looked me straight in the eye and said, "No, don't be silly. He died because he was old and sick. Ach, you poor little girl—thinking you were to blame must have frightened you ever so much." Then she held open her arms and let me nestle against her soft breasts where I cried and cried. To be sure, I had been quietly crying myself to sleep for many nights anyway, but to sob openly and not feel ashamed at my outpouring was a great relief.

A few days later, I asked my grandmother if she thought that since my grandfather was now part of the earth he might have turned into a flower, and she agreed that that was certainly a possibility. Imagining *Opa*, who had been an ornery old man, transformed into something as sweet and delicate as a violet or primrose made me less afraid of death. Grandma and I also began engaging in discussions about the soul. "No one who has died has ever come back to tell us about it," she explained, "but I have an idea that your grandfather's soul has found his dead wife's soul so that they aren't lonely anymore." I closed my eyes and saw *Opa* and *Oma*, my paternal grandmother, who had died when I was a baby, draped in gossamer robes, floating on a cloud, holding hands. Yes, I thought, Grandma's explanations all made sense, and my fears and obsessions began to fade. (Writer Ruth Goode remarks that "in an effort to give good and comforting answers to the young questioners whom we love, we very often arrive at good and comforting answers for ourslves."[4] I trust this happened for my grandmother.)

Self-Soothing

People try to avoid facing painful matters because to do so stirs anxiety, which often creates worse pain. If we are to encourage our daughters to put their heads in the mouths of demons as Milarepa does, we would be wise to help them find ways to do so *calmly*. As I noted in an earlier part of this book, early mothering behaviors such as nursing, stroking, rocking, holding, and carrying regulate the baby's nervous system and lower her level of stress; a baby seems to absorb into her own body a mother's soothing presence and gradually to learn to calm herself when distressed. For example, her discovery of the "suckable" thumb or finger(s), as well as her attachment to "transitional objects" such as the soft blanket, enable her to pacify herself. D. W. Winnicott includes this descriptive anecdote in his book *The Child, the Family, and the Outside World*:

> A baby girl used her mother's rather long hair for caressing while thumb-sucking. When her own hair was long enough she pulled it—instead of her mother's—across her face, and sniffed at it, when she was going to sleep. She did this regularly until she was old enough to have her hair cut so as to be like a boy. She was pleased with the result until bedtime when, of course, she became frantic. Fortunately, the parents had kept her hair, and a switch of it was given to her. Immediately she put it across her face in the ordinary way, sniffed at it, and went to sleep happily.[5]

As our daughters pass through babyhood and toddlerhood and give up the transitional objects that comforted them, we can help them develop a repertoire of behaviors (other than feeding on comfort foods, which can lead to compulsive eating) that will soothe them. Soaking in a warm bubble bath, listening to music, singing to themselves, lying on the grass watching the clouds make pictures in the sky, and closing their eyes and paying attention to their breathing are calming activities suitable even for very young children.

With our guidance, our daughters can learn to soothe themselves simply by sitting quietly with their feelings and taking a friendly interest in them. We might, for example, suggest that when they are upset for no ostensible reason they settle into a comfortable chair, close their eyes, breathe slowly, and direct their mind's energy to whatever they are experiencing at the moment . . . then to find a word, phrase, or image that fits with their inner experience and see what happens. The paradox is that as you pay attention to the disturbing thoughts, feelings, emotions, and sensations that stir within, they begin to evaporate, much as Milarepa's demons evaporated when he showed them respect.

During the course of normal conversation, we can pass on soothing words and instructions to our daughters that will become part of their healing self-talk. In times of trouble Leah often heard me say, "This too shall pass" or "Everything irons itself out" (one of my mother-in-law's oft-repeated sayings) or "Everybody makes mistakes, oh yes they do!" (which both of us learned from Big Bird on *Sesame Street*). In the midst of my son's emotional crisis, when he worried about lots of things, he took great comfort in Mark Twain's words: "I am an old man and have known many troubles, but most of them never happened." A colleague of mine once half joked that she had come up with a wonderful treatment for anxious, perfectionistic people, called the "so-what therapy." As she explained, thinking and saying "So what!" transformed problems from mountains to molehills. My maternal grandmother had her own version of the "so-what therapy." *"Nicht so gefahrlich,"* which translates from the German to "not so dangerous" or "nothing to get panicked about," she would mumble when I was upset.

Of course, when children hear their elders respond to trouble with alarm—"Oh, my God!" "You *didn't*!" or "That's terrible, *absolutely* terrible!"—they will internalize these responses too, which will have the effect of increasing rather than decreasing their anxiety during stressful times. Similarly, being shouted at or receiving an icy parental stare is unnerving and shocks the body as it chills the heart.

If we can help our daughters find even a single way to express themselves creatively—whether or not they have great natural talents—we will provide them an outlet for being soothed. A client of mine throws clay pots when she is worried or harried and in this way becomes centered again; another knits; another weaves; another quilts; another sews; another writes in a journal; another plays the guitar; another paints clouds and trees. Through creative activity human beings transform their inner turmoil into something coherent, often something beautiful. Or, as poet and novelist May Sarton explained, the creative energy lifts you out of suffering into joy.[6] As a child, I had a friend named Rachel. Rachel was a girl of many moods, and when she was in a dark one she went to her piano and played "Beautiful Dreamer" over and over and over. "Not that song again," I would mumble under my breath. On the other hand, I knew that after Rachel had finished playing she would be out of her dark mood and I could count on her being very nice to me for the rest of the day.

Recently I had a reunion with an old friend who used to be the guidance counselor at P.S. 28 in Manhattan, where I taught in the sixties. "Lee," I asked, "I never did figure out your secret powers. I would send you an absolutely distraught, out-of-control child, and a half hour later the child would return to my classroom calm and content. What did you do?" And Lee confided that her "magic" was nothing more than a ball of clay. " 'Here, take this in your hand,' I'd tell the children. 'Use it any way you want to express your feelings.' Some kids would pound the clay or throw it or tear it up into little pieces or shape it into something—a person, an animal, a weird creature. And as they worked the clay, the tension just seemed to ooze from their bodies."

Nature as Healer

In *Dreams of Trespass*, Fatima Mernissi writes about her maternal grandmother, Yasmina, who lived on a farm with cows and sheep and endless fields of flowers. Yasmina tells her granddaughter that the saddest thing for a woman is to be cut off from nature. "Nature," she says, "is woman's best friend . . . . If you're having troubles, you just swim in the water, stretch out in the field, or look up at the stars. That's how a woman cures her fears."[7] There are two words for emotional pain in Arabic: *mushkil* and *hem*. A female who has *mushkil* knows the reason for her pain and can usually do something about it; a female suffering from *hem*, akin to our clinical depression, does not know what causes her suffering.[8] The Muslim women in Mernissi's childhood world understood that only quiet and beauty could cure those afflicted by *hem*, and for this reason they would take the depressed women on retreats to sanctuaries high in the mountains.

The curative power of nature is evoked in a lovely vignette appearing in Mernissi's novel: Dark and frail, Yaya is one of many wives in the Moroccan harem of Mernissi's grandfather. Having been uprooted from the Sudan, she deeply longs for her homeland and is often terribly sad. To help her overcome her depression and feel comfortable in her new surroundings, the other co-wives decide to buy a banana tree—a tree indigenous to the Sudan—and plant it on the communal farm. Finding a banana tree in this windy part of Morocco proves extremely difficult, but at long last the determined co-wives succeed in buying one from a nomadic salesman. Mernissi writes:

> Yaya was so excited to see it that she took care of it as if it were a child, rushing to cover it with a large white sheet every time the cold wind blew. Years later, when the banana tree bore fruit, the co-wives organized a party and Yaya dressed in three layers of yellow caftans, put flowers around her turban, and danced away toward the river, giddy with happiness.[9]

By helping our daughters develop an interest in nature—taking walks in the woods, lying under a leafy tree, noticing flowers, exploring mountains and deserts, or watching the waves break along the shore—we will provide them beautiful places to go to, in reality or in imagination, when they are distressed. Of course, if we live in an urban setting, we are more limited in providing our daughters with these experiences, but perhaps it is possible for us to take them to the country or the seashore for vacations or to send them to summer camps outside the city. Failing this, we may be able to bring nature, in the form of living plants, flowers, or terrariums, into our homes. As a city child myself, I remember how excited I was to receive a packet of morning glory seeds in the third grade. Although the seeds, which I planted in a red window box, never did mature, my Jack and the Beanstalk fantasies of waking one morning to the sight of a profusion of blue blossoms provided pleasure enough.

A colleague who was physically abused as a child once told me that two things saved her from losing hope during her growing-up years: reading books, especially myths and fairy tales, and spending considerable time alone in the wild places that surrounded the family ranch in New Mexico where she lived.

For my client Irene, being in nature was also comforting and inspiring. During one of our sessions Irene presented me with the following poem, which she wrote when she was twelve and, as a result of family problems, quite forlorn:

> *I propped myself against the rough*
> *Gray bark of an old spruce tree,*
> *And closed my eyes for the world that day*
> *Had not been kind to me.*
> *I closed my eyes with a little sigh,*
> *As the weary often will,*
> *And thought how good to lean on one*
> *So straight and strong and still!*
> *High up above, her branches moved*
> *Against the spacious sky,*
> *And little wandering breezes*
> *Played a gentle lullaby.*
> *Her branches showed a simple strength*
> *And silent sympathy.*
> *Tolerance . . . endurance . . . acceptance*
> *Flowed quietly from her to me.*

In her benign moods, Mother Nature is a nurturant power, a healer. How can we explain this? Perhaps the harmony of color, texture, and form, which are inherent in natural environments, instills a harmony within us. Being in nature we may feel whole and at one with the universe, relieved of the conflict and fragmentation that otherwise tear at us.

Nature is also a great teacher, and through her cycles of growth and change we gain insight into our own. With my grandmother's help, I learned that like the trees that managed to grow wedged between apartment buildings or out of the cracks in the sidewalk, we human beings are capable of finding enough nourishment to live under less-than-ideal conditions; I learned that just as clouds suddenly burst into showers, there is nothing wrong with our having a good cry every so often; and I learned that the dark, bitterly cold days of winter are *always* followed by the warming, life-giving days of spring.

The Navajo refer to the processes of nature as Changing Woman. As art historian Merlin Stone writes:

> It is Changing Woman who teaches the flow of life, the restlessness of the sand as it flies in the wind, the wisdom of the ancient rocks that never leave their home, the pleasure of the sapling that had risen through them. . . . It is Changing Woman who teaches the cycles, the constant round of hot and cold, of birth and dying, of youth and aging, of seedling to corn, of corn to seedling kernel, of day to night, of night to day, of waxing moon to waning moon. . . . It is to Changing Woman that we look as we search for the meaning of life.[10]

Altruism

Although periods of suffering help us become more human, the chronic experience of emptiness, alienation, apathy, and hopelessness that afflict more and more people, especially young people, have no constructive value. The founding father of the Hassidic movement, the Baal Shem-Tov, is reputed to have said that the sin is not in *being* depressed but in *staying* depressed—immobilized and thus unable to do anything good or anything at all.[11] Martin E. P. Seligman attributes the sense of meaninglessness that pervades the modern world to "the waxing of the self and the waning of the commons":

> The society we live in exalts the self. It takes the pleasures and pains, the successes and failures of the individual with unprecedented seriousness. . . . If it happened in isolation, exalting the self might have had a positive effect, leading to more fully lived lives. But it was not to work out that way. The waxing of the self in our time coincided with a diminished sense of community and loss of higher purpose. These together proved rich soil for depression to grow in.
>
> The life committed to nothing larger than itself is a meager life indeed. Human beings require a context of meaning and hope . . . . I call the larger setting the commons. It consists of a belief in the nation, in God, in one's family, or in a purpose that transcends our lives.[12]

The current problems in our society need not leave us feeling helpless or hopeless. There *are* things we can do to counter the self-centeredness and isolation that feed chronic depression. For one, instead of encouraging our children to become overinvolved in the pursuit of their personal happiness—having fun all the time, satisfying every material whim, striving to be the most popular, the best dressed or looking—we can encourage them to become more involved in the welfare of others. Through our example, we can teach them to help people in need, to care about the environment, to become involved politically, to take social action—in short, to make the world a better place. "Many people my age don't understand how this can be," a fourteen-year-old friend, Chen Shuker, told me, "but what I love doing most of all is being a volunteer in a home for mentally retarded children; I feel happy when I am helping children learn new things or like themselves better." And in *Reviving Ophelia*, Mary Pipher tells this personal story: "When my daughter was in the seventh grade, we worked at a homeless shelter. It put her in contact with adults trying to do something good, it taught her that drug and alcohol use wasn't romantic or sophisticated, and it let her know that when you see problems, you get to work instead of getting angry."[13]

Among traditional Hindus, the person who gives alms to a beggar incurs a lifelong debt of gratitude to him, not the other way around. The Hindus see clearly what we Westerners may have lost sight of: acts of kindness benefit the giver even more than the receiver. By accepting alms, the beggar enables the benefactor to feel generous, virtuous, humane, and connected to another human being.

Rabbi Deborah Bronstein, of Boulder, Colorado, shared the following true story with her congregation: It is an extraordinary example of the life-affirming power of human kindness.[14]

There once was a famous rabbi who lived in Poland during the early part of the twentieth century. He was revered for his knowledge, wisdom, and for his skill as a teacher. When Hitler came to power the rabbi was taken to a concentration camp, where he perished. A few years ago a scholar, himself a rabbi, was visiting Tel Aviv. Walking along the beach, he fell into a conversation with a middle-aged man who was sweeping the sand from the boardwalk. The scholar could not help but notice that the sweeper spoke Hebrew with a Polish accent, and as they talked, he discovered that he had been one of the students who had been taken to the camp with the famous rabbi. The scholar wanted very much to know what the sweeper remembered about the rabbi's teachings, but the sweeper insisted that he remembered nothing. "So much pain, so much inhumanity, so much horror that I experienced under Hitler—I lost everyone I loved, I lost my childhood, I lost all," he explained and asked, "How do you expect me to remember what I was taught as a little boy? It has all been washed away, like the waves that wash over the sand."

"Please," the scholar persisted, "is there not anything you remember of the great rabbi's teachings? Not anything at all?" Then, hesitantly, the sweeper spoke: "Well, yes," he offered, "when we were in the rebbe's class, he told us that each day we must take it upon ourselves to do a mitzvot [a good deed] for someone. This is the teaching that I have taken with me. Do understand, please, that it was difficult for me, as a child, to follow the rabbi's instruction in the concentration camp. I struggled with my dilemma. What could a young boy possibly do for the starving, the bereaved, the tortured, the dying? There was no food to give to the hungry, no blankets to warm the freezing bodies, no words of hope in the face of certain death, no nothing. But then I thought of something. Each day I could take the hand of a suffering man and hold it in my own small one. This became my daily act of kindness. Oh, I know it wasn't much, but it was the only thing I had to give."

The scholar continued his conversation with the sweeper, and as they talked, it was obvious that with the passing of time the rabbi's lessons had not been lost. Fifty years after his liberation from the concentration camp, the sweeper on the beach in Tel Aviv still carried on his daily acts of small kindnesses. One day he might say a comforting word to a crying child or help a harried mother push her baby stroller across the sand or pick up a conversation with a lonely old person. And on the days when the sweeper was himself filled with sadness, when he thought about taking off his shoes, and walking, walking far into the ocean, putting an end to his scarred life, he remembered that he had a purpose—to do another small loving kindness—and this was reason enough to go on, reason enough to live, reason to believe in the meaningfulness of his life.

Like the wise rabbi who taught his young students to commit to a daily act of kindness, let us as parents teach our children the same. One small act of kindness each day. If we can do this, we will protect them, not from emotional pain—not from the bad things that inevitably happen to good people—but from the despair of futility.

PART FOUR

ROOTS AND WINGS

There are only two lasting bequests we can hope to give our children. One of these is roots; the other, wings.

—HODDING CARTER

THE NINTH GIFT:

Roots

The United States is largely a nation of immigrants who fled from poverty, war, persecution, or lack of opportunity to make a new life. Our uniquely American ethos is that we are not bound or defined by our history or traditions. We value autonomy, adaptability, and self-definition and believe that we can reinvent ourselves at will. Yet by shedding our pasts, we risk losing our rich and layered identities. Many years ago, the writer Isaac Bashevis Singer told me a story about an Orthodox Jew who left his shtetl (small village) in Poland for New York City. In his efforts to assimilate, he decided to go bareheaded, although this went against his religious custom; he also exchanged his long black overcoat for a stylish Western suit; then he shaved off his *peyes* (sidelocks); and finally he cut off his beard. One day as he was walking down the street, a mirror in a store window caught his reflection. Glancing at the mirror, he did not recognize himself and saw only a stranger peering back at him.

At the time I was told this particular story, I saw little value in honoring old ways (which is precisely why my wise acquaintance chose to tell it to me). Over the years, however, I have reversed my thinking. As a result of personal experiences and discussions with clients, I have come to believe that our roots nourish and ground us and that severed from them, we are likely to feel incomplete and disconnected from ourselves. Indeed, the isolation that feeds chronic depression seems directly related to the cutting away of roots. One of the ways we can protect our daughters from such isolation is by feeding and watering the roots that connect them to family, and to cultural, religious, and female traditions.

The stories clients share with me are often poignant reminders of the importance of having strong roots. Currently I am counseling a college senior who left Thailand four years ago to study science at the University of Colorado. Pearl's parents, who still live there, encourage her to forget Thai customs and to westernize herself so that she can get ahead in the world. However, Pearl remains emotionally attached to the traditions of her homeland. Indeed, she has discovered that an effective way to combat the feelings of depression and anxiety that plague her is to make visits to the waiting area of one of Boulder's Thai restaurants. On a student's budget, Pearl can hardly afford to eat out, yet simply getting whiffs of the dishes being served and hearing the restaurant owner call out orders to the kitchen employees in her mother tongue begin to nourish her.

Another young woman in my practice was adopted as an infant and knows nothing about her biological family and little about her adoptive parents, who were remote and withholding. Cara, a talented and prolific artist, paints one subject: human heads without faces. When I first asked her about her work, she smiled sadly and explained that the paintings are self-portraits, reflecting her missing identity. In therapy we are now trying to piece together from old photographs and yellowing letters the life stories of Cara's adoptive parents. Eventually Cara would like to search for her birth mother. Perhaps then she will be free to paint faces with noses, mouths, and eyes.

My Search for Roots

Some members of oppressed minorities are eager to let go of their traditions and identify with the majority culture. This was the case for my own parents, and as a result, I grew up without being conscious of my past, which led to feelings of alienation and confusion.

Both my parents were born in Austria. Until Hitler came to power, my mother's Jewish heritage had not presented problems for her. With her blond hair and blue eyes, she was probably not thought of as Jewish by most people. Then, too, her parents were secular Jews who did not stand out from the Christian townsfolk of Wimsbach, the hamlet where they lived and operated a button factory. To be sure, my rebellious grandmother, who identified herself alternately as a freethinker and a pantheist, was tactful enough not to divulge any of her unconventional beliefs to her neighbors.

My father's circumstances were less benign. The child of working-class parents, he grew up in the Jewish ghetto of Vienna at a time when anti-Semitism was rampant. Although my father rarely revealed anything about his childhood, he once told me that after getting the highest grade in class on an important mathematics examination, his teacher accused him of being a cheater. "How could a Jew-boy outdo his classmates if *not* by cheating?" the teacher asked him.

My mother and father met in Vienna and married in 1938, just as the Third Reich was taking over Austria. Soon afterward, life became progressively harder for the young newlyweds. They were fired from their jobs; their valuables were confiscated; my father was arrested, tortured, and imprisoned by the Gestapo; my pregnant mother (the baby didn't live) barricaded herself in their apartment; members of the extended family fled to Cyprus, Palestine, Argentina, and England or simply "disappeared." Only through a combination of good luck and cunning did my parents survive the Nazi occupation. After a few weeks of captivity, my father was released from prison and ordered to leave the country within seventy-two hours; many of his fellow inmates, however, were sent off to the concentration camps. My father found refuge in England at an internment camp for displaced persons, where my mother was eventually reunited with him. Then, a year later, through the sponsorship of a benevolent American uncle who owned a bakery and could guarantee them jobs, they were granted visas to the United States and settled in New York City.

I was born just about the time my parents became citizens. Their first act as proud, new Americans was to drop the family name, "Sprinzeles," which, in Austria had marked them as Jews, and to assume the more generic surname "Silten" that my father had come up with. Not wanting to "burden" me with a Jewish-sounding first name, my parents went against the custom of naming a baby after a deceased ancestor. By naming me Evelyn Silten, my father believed that, unlike him, I would never know the humiliation of listening to Jew-haters snicker during a roll call, of being discriminated against at a job interview, or of being falsely told by an innkeeper, "No, we have no rooms to let."

The truth of the matter is that as I grew up, I came to dislike both my first name and my last; they were empty of meaning for me and hid my true identity. Unknown to my parents, I envied classmates who had ethnic names, like Peggy O'Keefe, Elana Rosenblatt, Lee Chang, Jesus Rodriguez, that connected them to other people in their culture, to faraway places, and to times past. Most of all, I was intrigued by the hyphenated name of one of my classmates—Judy Goldman-Hosokawa—which, like a mini–United Nations, linked two disparate cultures, generating all sorts of imaginative possibilities.

To further the happiness of their daughter, my mother and

father encouraged me to take up the habits of a "real" American girl. My mother urged me to drink Coca-Cola, which I detested (to this day I gag on carbonated drinks), and each Christmas we put up a tree in our living room. However, their efforts to Americanize me were inconsistent, undoubtedly because they felt confused about their allegiances. In my earliest years, I heard much more German (sprinkled with Yiddish words and phrases) than English, and family friends were, with few exceptions, Jewish refugees like my parents. Indeed, it was evident that my parents felt awkward around American gentiles. Nevertheless, in our home, Jewish traditions and rituals were not practiced, Jewish holidays were not celebrated, and the past—stories of loved ones lost at Hitler's hands, of shame, of fear, and of *courage* in the face of great danger—lay buried in silence.

As a child, I often felt that my parents and I—especially I—were misfits, although I could not say why this was so. One time when I was ten, I acted out these feelings in a most bizarre way. I am told that on Christmas Eve I walked into the living room in my sleep and, while my parents watched in stunned silence, headed with outstretched arms toward the Christmas tree, removed a glass ball suspended from a waist-high branch, crushed it in my hand, and then, still in my somnabulistic trance, returned to my bed. I now believe with this symbolic act I was trying to tell my parents what I had not been able to say to them in words: it was disturbing to celebrate a holiday that did not hold personal meaning while ignoring the holidays that did.

For me, the most intriguing place in our home was my father's top dresser drawer. I had discovered that in this "secret" place, hidden behind his rolled-up socks and pressed handkerchiefs, was a bundle of old letters and photographs. Sometimes when I was home alone, I would spread out these photographs on the floor and study the faces of the people in them. Intuitively, I knew that these were snapshots of relatives who had perished at the hands of the Nazis and were never spoken of in my household. Here, in my father's secret drawer, I discovered ties to a forbidden past, to familiar faces with smiling eyes, like those of my father. And here, squeezed into the corner of the drawer, I also found my father's yarmulke, the skullcap he must have worn while praying in the Viennese synagogue.

My determination to explore my parents' past waned when I left home at age twenty to marry. Undoubtedly, I absorbed their discomfort about being different from the majority, and like them, I tried to mask my Jewishness. It is only within the last few years that I have felt compelled to reconnect with both my cultural and religious roots, just as I had tried to do as a child. From a second cousin, I recently learned that among my relatives who did not survive the Holocaust was a maternal great-aunt named Marianne (Mitzi) Felsenburg-Frank, who arranged transports of Jewish children from Austria to Holland, where they were placed with Christian families. Eventually, the Nazis uncovered her activities, located her, and in full view of her fourteen-year-old daughter, shot her to death. I carry Tante Mitzi in my heart these days—and am a better person because of it. Now, when I am called on to do something gutsy and I get "cold feet," thoughts of her magnificent strength and goodness inspire my small acts of courage.

I think about the baby son my parents lost and the other young children in our extended family who died at Hitler's hands. Of course, I cannot undo their gruesome fates. However, I suspect that the spiritual connection I feel with these unlived lives partly accounts for my calling, which is to promote the care of living children. My friend Ellen tells me, "Our roots keep us growing upright. Without roots we'd all be on our bellies like lizards."

My parents associated the practice of their religion with only fear and suffering, and understandably so. Even their marriage ceremony, which should have been a happy event, had to be "celebrated" in secret because Jews were not allowed to congregate in groups of three or more during the Nazi occupation. In fact, my mother was late for her wedding because some S.S. men were loitering in front of her apartment house, and afraid of being interrogated or followed to the synagogue, she stayed inside and out of sight till they finally ambled away.

Unlike my parents, I am able to celebrate religious traditions and holidays in a spirit of joy and fearlessness. These celebrations have come to mean a great deal to me, and to have been able to share them with my children when they lived at home was a special gift indeed. (Leah, who is very happy living two thousand miles away from us, has confided that the only times she gets homesick are on the Jewish holidays.) Beautiful sacred rituals feed the soul and temporarily transport us from our mundane world to a mysterious and profound one, which is probably why human beings in all societies, everywhere and in every age, have practiced them. For the eight nights of Hanukah, my husband, children (when they are with us), and I light candles, recite a prayer together, give each other hugs, and share small gifts; on the Days of Awe we pray with other Jews in the synagogue; on Sukkoth we build a hut with a roof of leafy branches from which we hang pomegranates and grapes to celebrate the harvest; on Purim we bake hamantaschen— small, three-cornered pastries stuffed with prunes or poppy seeds—at the home of longtime Boulder friends. And on Passover I prepare a traditional dish of sweet-and-sour pot roast to share with many old and new friends.

Curiously, after recovering my cultural roots, interesting things began to happen. Because as a girl I never took part in the preparations for a Passover Seder, I was at first especially careful not to deviate from the recipe for pot roast included in the Jewish cookbook I had bought; after all, I wanted to "do it right." About five years ago, as I was preparing this dish, I realized that I was out of ketchup, a critical ingredient. In the refrigerator, much to my relief, I had a jar of very hot Mexican salsa—a staple item in my adolescent son's diet—and I decided to substitute the hot salsa for the ketchup. The result was sensational. Everyone at the Seder raved. Living in Colorado, a state with a rich Mexican heritage, I felt a particular delight knowing that my spicy pot roast represented the joining of Jewish and Mexican culinary traditions, a "melting pot" of the highest order.

The Life-Giving Power of Roots

Hanging in the Boston Museum of Fine Arts is a stunning painting by the French impressionist Paul Gauguin titled *Where Do We Come From? What Are We? Where Are We Going?* The central figure, a luminous Tahitian Eve, stretches her arms high over her head to pluck a fruit from the mythical Tree of Knowledge. For me, the painting portrays the human longing for self-understanding. If we are to know ourselves, we need to know our origins; to know where we are headed, we need to know where we came from.

When we are encouraged to be ourselves—fully connected to our past as well as our present—we also come alive. Similarly, when those of us who are in the minority become confident that our practices, traditions, and history are as glorious as those of the majority culture, we develop true self-esteem; we are no longer ashamed of ourselves. During the sixties, while I was teaching school in Harlem, the chants "I'm black and I'm proud" and "Black is beautiful" took hold of many people in the community. For many of us civil rights activists, the sixties were full of hope, aglow with the sense our country was getting ready to embrace us all, despite our differences.

Even school meetings came to life. Many African-American parents, having discarded their conventional clothes, came dressed in colorful dashikis emblazoned with bold patterns; others came bedecked with strings of painted African beads; hair that had been straightened and made limp was now liberated, and big, glorious Afros filled the room. Not surprisingly, as parental pride rose, the children also seemed happier. One day in class, a spirited third grader named Angie Boom jumped on top of her desk and belted out "Respect," the Otis Redding song that Aretha Franklin had made famous.

Thirty years later, it is Generation X-ers who ask, "Where do I come from?" and insist—sometimes with shrill voices—on finding answers. At the University of Colorado, for instance, where I was an adjunct associate professor until recently, students are protesting against the dearth of multicultural studies on campus and the underhiring of minority teachers. Here also a group of young Japanese-Americans are piecing together the silenced stories of their parents and grandparents who were imprisoned in American "relocation" camps between 1942 and 1945. "When I look at my grandparents and what they've gone through," says Kashina Kessler, who is learning about their internment from her great-aunts, "it gives me a lot of strength . . . a drive to go on and make the best of my life—just like they did."[1] Kashina's comment is a reminder that connections with family members who have weathered life's storms with integrity inspire confidence and resiliency in the younger generation. On the contrary, the failure to learn about the life experiences of one's elders—and all the wisdom and insights they hold—is a terrible waste of human resources.

Even when parents deny their ethnic roots, their children may dig them up anyway. I have a young friend Elizabeth whose Puerto Rican mother moved from San Juan to the Bronx in her teens. Aside from the coconut liquor she concocted each Christmas, this émigré shared no Hispanic traditions with her daughter. Indeed, she made it very clear to all her children that their identity was only with the USA. Nevertheless, Elizabeth confided that whenever she hears a Latin beat, she goes wild: "I can't sit still. I have to get up and dance. I put my hand on my belly, roll my shoulders, close my eyes, and sway. The music is in my blood and soul; it is a part of me."

Ancestral Roots

The tenacity of human roots has also become evident in my work with adopted daughters of all ages, who often go to great pains to find blood relatives and discover their heritage. Several years ago, for example, I counseled a middle-aged woman who had been adopted as an infant. Although Cassandra enjoyed warm relationships with her adoptive parents and a host of adoptive aunts, uncles, and cousins, she felt a hole in the middle of her heart that could be filled only by knowing about her birth parents. After some wild goose chases and many, many frustrating encounters with adoption agencies and government offices, Cassandra finally secured a copy of her birth certificate. As she explained to me one afternoon, just by seeing the names of her first mother and father on this commonplace document, she felt special—as though she were a "somebody"—and that she belonged to a long line of people who probably looked like her. As is true of some adoptees, Cassandra had no desire to meet her birth parents; affirming their existence was enough to affirm her own.

Although it is not unusual for adoptive parents to feel rejected when their daughters reach out to their birth parents, many are able to overcome these fears and actively support their daughters' biological ties. From the time her adopted daughter was very young, Rosalind told her stories about the courageous fifteen-year-old girl who lovingly carried her within her womb for nine months and then unselfishly gave her up for adoption so that she would have a mother and father financially capable of taking care of her. As a result, Rosalind's daughter grew up believing in the goodness of her biological mother, which helped her to think well of herself. Interestingly, Rosalind confided to me that the adoption agency had given her very little personal information about the child's birth mother. Believing that it was in everyone's best interest to assume she was a wonderful person—someone with whom her daughter could gladly identify—Rosalind took the sparse details she had about the young woman and fleshed her out to make her into a real person.

Jeannette, a colleague who adopted an abandoned Vietnamese baby eighteen years ago, created a scrapbook with color photos of Vietnam and of beautiful Vietnamese women for her daughter. For Marcy, this scrapbook—a tribute to the birth mother—became a prized possession, one that she proudly displayed to her schoolmates during show-and-tell. Jeannette has honored Marcy's ancestry in other ways as well. She has often arranged for her daughter to meet other Vietnamese youngsters and their families, with whom she might feel a special kind of communion, familiarity, and coziness. And her high school graduation present to Marcy was a trip to her homeland.

Certainly, adopted children, like tender transplanted shoots, also need to throw out roots in their new soil so that they can flower and thrive. For Jeannette and Marcy, birthday celebrations, Fourth of July picnics, family meals, and afternoons spent together at the ballpark are just a few of the ways that have helped Marcy feel at home in her adopted family and adopted country.

Gender Roots

In addition to a yearning for connection with cultural or family roots, girls and women hunger for connections to their own femaleness. When, in 1984, Jean Shinoda Bolen published *Goddesses in Everywoman*, my female counseling students at the University of Colorado quickly purchased all the available copies from our local bookstore. These young women were used to reading books almost always written by and about men. However, in the Greek goddesses that Bolen described, they discovered *themselves* and could identify with the uniquely female qualities that are as old and valuable as human life itself.

In a similar vein, one of my clients shared with me that as a sexually abused child she found inner peace by worshipping the Virgin Mary, who symbolized a feminine healing spirit.

In Western society, we have had no sacred traditions and rituals that initiate girls into womanhood and join them to their foremothers in a positive way, which probably accounts in part for our derision of women's bodies and womanly functions such as menstruation. Indeed, Christiane Northrup, a gynecologist in Yarmouth, Maine, traces a host of female troubles, from ovarian cysts to uterine fibroids, back to shame at menarche— the time of a young woman's first period.[2] Many non-Western cultures do, however, celebrate the female cycle.

Among the Navajo, for example, the menstruating girl becomes Changing Woman, the creation goddess associated with the cycling seasons. An older woman in the tribe ritually washes the girl's hair and jewelery while chanting; she also gently massages her to soften and dissolve the child's body into the shape of a woman. For four days, during which time the girl wears ceremonial clothing and runs in special races, she is believed to renew the creative power of her community by blessing everyone and everything with which she comes into contact.

In an ancient Panamanian rite, the older women of the tribe escorted the menstruating girl to a sacred hut, which stood amid a grove of saptur trees. Instructing the young one to lie on the earth near the shrine, the women gathered about her in a ring of protection, tossed sacred soil upon her, and through prayer evoked the spirit of their goddess Mu, the Blue Butterfly Lady. Then the women painted the red juice of the saptur, which symbolized menstrual blood, on the young girl's face, chanted their blessings and honored her with a dance of new womanhood. After this, they led her into the shrine, where they cut her hair, letting the black strands fall to the earth as her childhood fell from her. When the girl emerged from the shrine as a grown woman, the older women presented her with

a felled saptur and a name that belonged only to her and was
not to be revealed to others.[3]

Such rites of female passage are inspiring some Western
women to create their own rituals to honor a girl's coming-of-
age. Tamara Slayton, director of the Menstrual Health Foundation, in Sebastopol, California, is one of a group of activists,
authors, and psychologists working toward this end. At a retreat for girls on the threshold of womanhood, she brings
preadolescents and middle-aged women together on a beach
where they sculpt a huge fertility goddess and honor "her im-
mutable laws by arranging around her, like spokes of a halo,
twenty-eight pieces of driftwood, one for each day of the menstrual cycle."[4]

For most of us parents, elaborate rituals such as the ones
Slayton proposes are not feasible. However, family members
may be able to recognize their daughters' passage into womanhood with modest celebrations. Taking one's daughter out to a
special restaurant or presenting her with a little gift, such as a
vial of perfume or a bouquet of flowers or a book of poems
written by a woman, are perfectly fine ways of honoring her
new status. Indeed, most of the enhancing things we do as parents are not big, impressive, or lavish. We promote our daughters' feelings of well-being mainly through the modest acts that
we perform with care, love, and attention.

Parents as Bearers of Traditions

In many religious traditions, the father is seen as the link
between the past and future, the transmitter of the laws and
principles that bind together a community. Reverend Dick
Thomas, a minister at the Rancho Community Presbyterian
Church, suggests that father-absence itself may be part of the
spiritual uprootedness, disorientation, and disconnection that
are common among today's youth.[5] This viewpoint is shared by

Rabbi Martin Levin of Congregation Beth-El in San Diego, who describes his commitment to his own children:

> It is important for me to transmit to my children their identity through our history. My wife will talk with them about grandparents and their aunts and uncles; I'll talk with them about their ancestors. My wife will talk with them about when they grow up and have children, and I'll talk with them about three generations from now.
>
> This is where my life crosses the boundaries of both spirituality and religiosity, because my role as a father is attached to a sense of eternity. I am not just a person who's going to live a human life span, but I'm a link in a very long and hopefully eternal chain. In the Jewish tradition, religious identity is transmitted through the mother, but tribal identity is transmitted through the father.[6]

Mothers as well as fathers can help their daughters feel a sense of belonging to the past and a feeling of pride in their heritage. In *A Leak in the Heart; Tales from a Woman's Life*, a collection of autobiographical essays, *New York Times* contributor Faye Moskowitz describes her mother's unflagging insistence that she be herself, although, as a Jewish youngster growing up in small-town America, Faye wanted more than anything to be like everyone else ("I would have sold my soul in exchange for being 'Piscopalian' like my friend Eileen"):

> Even though she was having her own crisis of faith, [my mother] doggedly insisted that I be proud of my religion. . . . The year I was in sixth grade, one of my teachers decided to put together a school program on the concept of "America as the Melting Pot." She pounced on me eagerly, of course. "Won't you contribute something to the program?" she asked. My stomach lurched in misery. I didn't want to be different, no matter what my mother believed.
>
> I received no sympathy at home. My mother stared at me in-

credulously when I told her of my reluctance to be singled out. "For five thousand years the Jews have been persecuted because of their faith, and you want to hide your heritage," she scolded. "Go to school and sing them Hatikvoh and be proud of what you are."

"Mama," I said. "What if I sing off-key? You know what happens when I get nervous."

She looked at me for a long moment and then she laughed. "How many people in your school know the Hebrew National Anthem?"

"No one," I said.

Triumphantly she pushed the bangs off my worried forehead. "Then who will know if you sing off-key?"

Amateur psychology it certainly was, but it worked. Some weeks later, fortified by my mother's advice, I stood in the little assembly room of the T. A. Wilson School while my heart stopped thumping long enough for me to hear the stirring anthem—absolutely on key—ring out over the heads of my schoolmates sitting cross-legged on the floor to their mothers sitting behind them on wooden folding chairs. But my mother, hands clasped in her lap, eyes shining, was the only person I saw.[7]

Calendar Holidays

Some of the most nourishing roots sprout from the rituals that mothers, fathers, and children create around holiday time. As Evan Imber-Black and Janine Roberts write in their book *Rituals for our Times*, the holidays on the "outside calendar" can "provide opportunities for us to come together with our families and friends, and to be linked to the outside world with community and cultural fellowship."[8] Of course, the bombardment from the media to celebrate calendar holidays, especially Christmas, in lavish ways can turn these occasions into pressured, unpleasant ones. In order for holiday celebrations to nourish the soul, they need to be personally meaningful. Every Christmas, for example, one of my friends takes out a painted wooden box filled with tree ornaments handed down through generations of children. She and her daughter carefully unwrap the protective tissue paper from the metallic stars, gossamer angels, and painted figurines and retell the stories associated with each ornament—who crafted it and how, what special meaning it might have had. Not surprisingly, these stories lead to reminiscences about family members and to shared memories of Christmases past.

Nontraditional rituals can also provide children with strong roots to their families. A young friend, whose mother came from a Roman Catholic home and whose father came from a Jewish one, explained that while her family is agnostic and does not affiliate with any religion, they celebrate two holidays of their own invention, which are always great fun. On "Hanumas" they sing seasonal songs, light menorah candles, and decorate a Christmas tree, and on "Eastover" they have an egg and matzoh hunt.

Kwanza, which in Swahili means "first fruits," is an example of a holiday ritual that is evolving as a result of a whole community's previously unmet needs to celebrate its heritage meaningfully. This seven-day celebration was created in 1966 by Mulan Karenga, a professor at the University of California in Los Angeles, to honor the links of African-Americans to Africa and has its roots in African harvest festivities. Each day of Kwanza honors a different principle of a fruitful harvest: unity on the first day, then self-determination; collective work and responsibility; cooperative economics; purpose; creativity; and, finally, faith.

Stories of Belongingness

Children love to hear all sorts of stories from their mothers and fathers—made-up fairy tales, parables about birds and flowers and friendly animals, adventure tales, anecdotes about relatives and ancestors. And they love to hear stories about themselves, for these affirm their unique identity and foster the self-confidence that grows from knowing who they are. In his account of the Mbuti people of Zaire, Colin Turnbull, one of the world's foremost anthropologists, describes how in the last few months of pregnancy, Mbuti women find a favorite spot in the forest and introduce their unborn children to biographical stories. The first story is always a lullaby:

> The lullaby that she sings is special in several ways. . . . It is composed by the mother for that particular child within her womb. It is sung for no other; it is sung by no other. The young mother sings it quietly, reassuringly, rocking herself, sometimes with her hands on her belly, or gently splashing her hands or feet in the water of her favorite stream or river, or rustling them through leaves, or warming herself at a fire. In a similar way she talks to the child, according it the intelligence, though not the knowledge of an adult. . . . What she says to the child is clear, informative, reassuring, and comforting: "The forest is good, the forest is kind; mother forest, father forest."[9]

Turnbull goes on to say that some mothers describe in detail the place where their children will be born, the playmates they will have, and perhaps the wife or husband they will marry someday. Mbuti children hear these stories over and over again and thus carry with them a detailed account of their earliest beginnings, which, in turn, provides self-definition. Whether the stories told by mothers are exact or even verifiable does not really matter. What matters is that the children *have* stories— lovely ones—that are their own.

In cultures that have not replaced human interactions with TV, storytellers are highly esteemed for their ability to transform lives. The Islamic mythical heroine Scheherazade, for example, is the princess of storytelling. The clever Scheherazade prevents her husband, the woman-hating King Schahriahr, whose habit is to take a bride for one night and then have her executed, from murdering her by enchanting him with stories night after night, for a thousand and one nights. Humanized by Scheherazade's tales, he falls in love with her, can no longer imagine living without her, and turns into a "sensitive guy."

Leslie Marmon Silko's novel *Ceremony* begins with this sage advice:

> *I will tell you something about stories. . . .*
> *They are all we have, you see,*
>   *all we have to fight off*
>   *illness and death.*
> *You don't have anything*
> *If you don't have stories.*[10]

When my daughter was very young, I felt awkward making up stories for her and preferred reading from children's books. My husband, gifted with a flair for theatrics, was the natural raconteur, not I. I soon discovered, however, that to capture Leah's interest, I did not need the expertise of a Scheherazade. Both my daughter and my son loved (and, as young adults, *still* love) to hear stories about their early years—how, for instance, baby Leah had fearlessly toddled over to a Great Dane and giggled when he gave her a full-body lick that knocked her over feet first, or how five-year-old Jonathan had deduced that his grandpa, who wore dentures, had become rich solely through the benevolence of the tooth fairy.

In addition to stories, my children valued the family picture albums we put together over the years. When they were little, we would spend hours looking through them. Jonathan would count the mounted photographs on each page to make sure there were as many shots of him as of his sister. (Fortunately, we had not slighted him.) These days when the grown-up Leah and Jonathan come to visit us, they routinely do two things: check out the refrigerator for the foods associated with "home" and take out the photograph albums. The hundreds of photographs of them, meticulously mounted and labeled, help them know who they are by affirming their experiences from babyhood through young adulthood. Just as children yearn for connectedness to their ancestry and the natural world, they also want to be rooted to their personal histories. I have always believed that if there were a fire in our house, the possessions I would try to salvage would not be legal papers or jewelery but the photograph albums and scrapbooks that serve as repositories for my children's histories.

In *Rituals for Our Times*, Imber-Black and Roberts include a description of a high school graduation celebration for Imber-Black's nineteen-year-old stepdaughter, a young woman with severe cognitive impairments. Here is a beautiful example of the way parents promote a child's feelings of belonging to her past and of being valued and loved:

> Jennifer wanted a party at a Chinese restaurant—her favorite festive food. Her mother and stepfather chose a restaurant and made a list of people to invite who were important to Jennifer, including extended family who lived far away, friends who had supported her from her young childhood on [and more]. . . . Unbeknownst to Jennifer, the invitation included a secret that read, "We are making a special 'becoming an adult woman' album for Jenni. If you would like, please bring anything you want to add to this album, including poems, letters, photos, stories, drawings, etc." During the weeks before the party, her mom worked secretly to construct an album that began when Jennifer joined the family as an adopted infant, and marked it with significant sections of her development, such as toddlerhood, starting school, and adolescence. Since her handicaps sometimes made it difficult for both Jennifer and those around her to notice her growth and changes, this album recorded them for all to see. After we ate Jenni's favorite foods, people were invited to give their presentations to Jennifer. A very moving and unexpected ceremony unfolded as person after person spoke about who Jenni was to them,

what she meant to them, how they experienced her, and gave her their own special brand of advice about living.[11]

The Ties That Do Not Bind

The other night at a potluck with close friends, my husband, our friends, and I engaged in a lively conversation about family traditions, rituals, and religious practices. Most of our friends indicated that children who grow up in families that practice a religion are at an advantage. Two people vehemently disagreed. Ed and Ian, having grown up in very religious families, felt bound and shackled by them. As youngsters, they were expected to embrace their parents' values and beliefs and were forbidden from defining their own. Moreover, they were strongly discouraged from associating with people outside their religion because their parents were convinced that only their beliefs were right. Ed's and Ian's justifiable resentment toward their authoritarian parents started in adolescence and built as the years went on. Now fathers themselves, they avoid involving their children in organized religious activities. In Ed's word, "I'm not about to bind my kids to religious dogma and to rigid belief systems. And I'm not going to turn them into copies of me by insisting that they believe what I believe."

After the dinner party, I could not sleep well. Tossing and turning in bed, I wondered if, in response to my childhood feelings of rootlessness, I had become too insistent on mooring my children to their cultural and religious heritage. "Had I exposed them to the pageantry of the past for their good or for my own?" I wondered. "Whose need was I *really* fulfilling?" I also wrestled with the question, How can a parent help her child establish roots to old ways yet avoid being strangled by them?

The morning after my restless night, I remembered a

favorite folktale, which inspired the beginnings of answers for me.

Many, many thousands of years ago, when the earth began, there lived a husband and wife named Smoke and Wild Pony. Walking across the young earth, they were joined by a magical creature, what the Jicarilla Apache people called a *hatsin*, which taught Wild Pony the art of making clay into bowls.

Years passed. Wild Pony bore children, who in turn bore their children. She made many clay bowls, which held the corn and water that the Indian people needed to survive. When Wild Pony became a very old woman, realizing her time on earth would shortly come to an end, she decided to pass on the art of making clay bowls to her daughter's daughter. Just as the *hatsin* had taught her, Wild Pony tried to instruct the girl to mold the red earth into the shape of a bowl, to dry the bowl in the sun, then to wrap it in the bark of a pine tree, and finally to place it in a smoldering fire. But despite her detailed instructions, each time the girl tried to form the clay into a bowl, it cracked and fell apart in her hands. That night, Wild Pony, full of sadness that she could not pass on her art to her granddaughter, fell into a deep sleep. In a dream, the *hatsin*, which had not visited her all these many years, appeared once more. This time, it reminded Wild Pony that when it had instructed her to make clay bowls, it had kneeled with her on the ground, scooped up handfuls of red earth, and rubbed it into Wild Pony's hands, saying, "This clay is yours to use." The apparition of the *hatsin* advised Wild Pony to do with the young one what it had done with her; then it evaporated from the dream.

When morning came, Wild Pony took her granddaughter to the place of the red clay. Taking a handful of the clay and rubbing it into the child's hands, she said, "Now the clay is yours to use." As the grandmother knelt beside her daughter's daughter, the girl began to work the clay and it did not crack. But she did not turn it into a bowl, as her grandmother had first instructed. Instead she formed the first peace pipe on Earth.[12]

Yes, I decided we can and should pass on our traditions to our children, for these are often life-giving gifts. At the same time, we must hope that our children will shape them in their own unique, surprising, and wonderful ways.

Wings

Raising children lovingly is full of paradoxes. We give our daughters the gift of roots in order that they may have a sense of their heritage and feel connected to home. We also give them the gift of wings, which enables them to grow into full adults and leave home. In other words, we hold close while we let go; we embrace with open arms.

The loving process of letting go begins from the first days of parenthood and never stops: weaning from breast or bottle to cup; releasing our supporting hand to let her walk unassisted; hiring a sitter to take our place for a few hours; taking her to her first classroom; packing her bags for an overnight at camp or a visit with the grandparents; teaching her to drive; sending her off to college; accompanying her down the aisle on her wedding day; accepting that her first allegiance is to *her* spouse and children, not to us.

Our daughters' leave-takings, however, evoke in us feelings of being abandoned; their growing up reminds us that we are growing old. At a subconscious level, we may try to freeze time, to preserve eternally their childhood and our youthfulness. In *Einstein's Dreams*, writer and scientist Alan Lightman imagines a metaphysical realm where we would not have to let go. Here time, "fixed and frozen, like a butterfly mounted in a case," stands still:

> As a traveler approaches this place from any direction, he moves more and more slowly. His heartbeats grow farther apart, his breathing slackens, his thoughts diminish, until he reaches dead center and stops. For this is the center of time.
>
> And who would make pilgrimage to the center of time? Parents with children, and lovers.
>
> And so, at the place where time stands still, one sees parents clutching their children, in a frozen embrace that will never let go. The beautiful young daughter with blue eyes and blond hair will never stop smiling the smile she smiles now, will never lose this soft pink glow on her cheeks, will never grow wrinkled or tired, will never get injured, will never unlearn what her parents have taught her, will never think thoughts that her parents don't know, will never know evil, will never tell her parents that she does not love them, will never leave her room with the view of the ocean, will never stop touching her parents as she does now.[1]

In our own realm, however, time does not stand still. Our children change rapidly, learn ways of their own, lose their innocence, get hurt and hurt others, see our flaws, grow wings, and fly away.

To be sure, the passing of time gives meaning to our existence by pressuring us to treasure the present moment. An acquaintance who had children when he was over forty and, like most middle-aged people, is painfully aware of time flying told me that he consciously values each hour spent with them and marvels at every facet of their development. "Knowing that my kids will be all grown up in an eye blink," he says, "makes me determined not to take the magic of their childhood for granted. The simplest activities we share—making silly noises or watching cartoons together—take on special meaning because maybe by tomorrow they will have outgrown them."

Yet the ticking of the clock also heightens our awareness of loss. Once while my husband was cuddling with Leah, then about two years old, I noticed that he looked sad. Later, when I asked Bruce if anything had been wrong, he remarked that while stroking and kissing the soles of Leah's bare feet he noticed they were no longer the heavenly soft, sweetly perfumed baby feet she used to have; a little calloused and a little smelly, they were becoming "normal" human feet. That subtle physical change made him realize his "baby girl" was no longer a baby.

Feelings of loss sometimes take us by surprise. After Leah graduated from college, my husband decided to have our old home movies, which had been stored away in canisters and half-forgotten, transferred to a single video cassette. The project completed, Bruce and I snuggled in front of the TV, slipped the cassette into the VCR, and readied ourselves for an evening of sweet memories. In less than an hour, we saw our children grow from infancy to adulthood: There she was, baby Leah in her high chair transforming herself, like a quick-change artist, into a toddler licking an ice cream cone, a giggling schoolgirl with braces on her teeth, a leggy teenager mouthing show tunes with her girlfriends, and a young woman in cap and gown receiving a college diploma; and there he was, newborn Jonathan sleeping in my arms, suddenly appearing in the form of a bright-eyed little boy climbing a jungle gym, a scrappy center fielder wearing a yellow and black Little League uniform, and a soulful young man in a tux on his way to the prom. We did not anticipate that seeing a movie of our children's growing-up years would disturb us, and yet this is exactly what happened. For days after the viewing, we sniped at each other without understanding the reason for our anxiety. Only after Bruce and I sat down to talk and acknowledged how much we missed our young children, how much we missed being young ourselves, and how short life really is, did we regain our equilibrium.

As the years go by and our babies become toddlers, youths, teens, and, alas, adults, we will both celebrate and mourn their growing up. Approaching fifty, her nest now empty, the German artist Käthe Kollwitz wrote: "Last night I dreamed once more that I had a baby. There was much in the dream that was painful, but I recall one sensation distinctly. I was holding the tiny infant in my arms and I had a feeling of great bliss as I thought that I could go on always holding it in my arms. It would be one year old and then only two, and I would not have to give it away."[2] As was true for Kollwitz, I too have dreamed that my grown children are still my babies and that I am embracing them. After waking from these dreams, I feel utterly bereft. It is as if a pure and lovely part of myself were now severed.

The Passage from Childhood to Adulthood

A mysterious force within compels every child to grow up; if held back by her parents from this development, she will do everything in her power to wrench herself free. We can see this mysterious force at work in the two-year-old who insists on dressing herself, however long it takes; in the six-year-old who clunks around the house in her mother's high heels and smears lipstick on her mouth; and in the ten-year-old who resents the fact that you've hired a *baby*-sitter to take care of her while you're out. The lamentation, "Stop treating me like a little kid; you can trust me; I can take care of myself" gets louder over the years, becoming especially shrill when our daughters enter adolescence. Nonetheless, the passage from childhood to adulthood is rife with loss for the child as well as for the parent.

Judith Viorst writes in *Necessary Losses* that as adolescents grow out of childhood, they experience an intensity of grief unknown in previous stages of life. And this grief can take many forms. Thus, some adolescent girls defend against the pain of separating from home and family by masking their sad feelings with mad feelings: rebelling, finding fault, provoking fights with their parents. Other girls, while clamoring for more freedom, behave so irresponsibly that their parents are forced to take away adult privileges such as driving a car or staying out late at night. Still others prolong childhood dependency by having emotional breakdowns, their helplessness drawing caretaking adults to their side. To dull the hurt of separating, some girls comfort themselves by indulging in eating, drinking, or spending binges; or they may become promiscuous, not so much because they enjoy the sex act but because they desperately want to be held close and cuddled—to feel as warm and safe as they used to feel in mommy's and daddy's arms.

To be sure, not all defenses against growing up are necessarily destructive. Leah, for one, discovered that a sense of humor goes a long way in lightening life's burdens, even the onerous chore of becoming an adult. After settling into her first apartment during her junior year in Paris, she wrote this note to her father and me:

> Yesterday the weight of adulthood came crashing down on my shoulders. How did this happen? It was Saturday night. The corner grocery store was closed. My roommates and I had invited a bunch of Parisians over for what we hoped would be an elegant party. To my embarrassment, I noticed there was no toilet paper in the bathroom dispenser, no extra rolls under the sink. Yes, it was sad but true—after all these many years, the toilet-paper fairy had abandoned me! Mom and Dad, I can handle paying the rent on time and fixing meals—but to have to remember to buy toilet paper surely marks the end of my childhood.

Growing up always entails relinquishing the all-knowing, all-giving, all-available parents of childhood. Reflecting on the experience of late adolescence, Viorst writes:

> [The separation from our parents]—this loss of the closest attachments of our life—is often frightening and always sad. The gates of Eden are clanging shut for good, and to this add the loss of our self-as-child and the loss of our former familiar body and the loss of our fuzzy innocence as we tune into the truths on the evening news. . . . And so we feel nostalgia for a past, a Golden Age, that never will return to us again.[3]

To Jungian scholar M. Esther Harding, the biblical account of Adam and Eve's expulsion from Paradise is in one way a parable of the child's separation from the parents. By eating from the Tree of Knowledge (coming into their own consciousness), Adam and Eve, the first children on earth, defy God (father's absolute rule), lose their innocence, and are evicted from the Garden (mother's sheltering habitat). "Man gained his freedom," Harding writes, "and by the same act he cut himself off from the very source of his life. From that time on he was burdened with the necessity of making an adaptation in the world, of supporting himself. . . ."[4]

I once counseled a young girl who felt extremely sad upon graduating from high school. While Heidi's friends celebrated their new freedom by partying, she moped about at home for weeks. After a particularly dreary morning, without quite understanding her motivation, Heidi packed her favorite storybooks and stuffed animals into a tote bag, slung it over her shoulder, and climbed to the top of an old crab apple tree in her backyard. There, cradled between two sturdy limbs, she spent the afternoon cuddling a teddy bear and reading the stories her parents had read to her when she was a young child. For Heidi, revisiting childhood was necessary before she could begin to move on to adulthood.

Who's in Charge?

Charles Spezzano, psychotherapist and founder of the Colorado Center for Psychoanalytic Studies, writes that if children are to grow into full adults, they need to learn to parent themselves, to cross from childhood dependency into adult self-management. The difficulty in this transition is that it feels safer to let someone who knows how to run a life—one of the "big people"—be in charge of yours. Crossing over into adulthood means not only taking care of yourself physically but giving up the idea that someone else will figure out the right things for you to do. It means relying on the "vague urges and ambitions we experience inside ourselves," which is a risky business. The first key principle of adulthood, Spezzano maintains, is that you forgo certainty—"you make it up":

> You make up your adulthood. The only clues are those images and urges and "maybes" that float in front of your mind's eye. No one can be of any help in sorting it out. You do what you want and then you see what happens. The talking it over with friends—with its implication of "What do you think about what I want to do, where I want to live, who I want to marry, how I want to work"—is just a last-ditch attempt to avoid that moment when you say, "I'm doing. . . ." Any predesigned scheme is someone else's game plan, to which, if you take the advice too seriously, you voluntarily submit.[5]

Virginia Woolf, in her novel *To the Lighthouse*, provides a wonderful example of the growth from childish dependency to adult self-sufficiency in the character of Lily Briscoe, a struggling young artist. Lily idealizes the formidably maternal Mrs. Ramsay, but as long as Lily remains under her influence, she is unable to sustain even a "miserable remnant of her vision." She can see the world only through the eyes of the older woman: "What did the hedge mean to her, what did the garden mean to

her, what did it mean to her when a wave broke?"[6] It is only after recognizing Mrs. Ramsay's human flaws—her failures of
understanding and her shortsightedness—that Lily begins to
trust her own clear-sightedness and to see what she *herself* sees.
Years after Mrs. Ramsay's death, Lily, now in her middle years,
returns to the Ramsay residence and discovers the painting she
had worked on there, the painting she could never get quite
right and finish:

> There it was—her picture. Yes, with all its greens and blues, its
> lines running up and across, its attempt at something. It would be
> hung in the attics, she thought; it would be destroyed. But what
> did it matter? . . . With a sudden intensity, as if she saw it clear
> for a second, she drew a line there, in the centre. It was done; it
> was finished. Yes, she thought, laying down her brush in extreme
> fatigue, I have had my vision.[7]

Although there are plenty of exceptions, girls more than
boys may find it difficult to rely on their internal guides—the
"images and urges and 'maybes' that float in front of your
mind's eye"—and turn to external sources of direction instead.
One reason for this is that while a boy's self-esteem is usually
connected to his prowess, leadership, and competence, a girl's
self-esteem often derives from the congenial relationships she
forges. Hence, many girls strive to please others, and pleasing others often entails doing as others say, agreeing with what
others think. Both men and women may expect girls to be compliant and get annoyed with them when they are not. I remember our family physician angrily ejecting me from his office as
an adolescent, because I had disagreed with his diagnosis. I recall as well that my father often put me in my place for challenging authority figures and doing things my own way. "Do
you have to be such a *wise guy*?" he would admonish each time
I "rocked the boat." After my father's scolding, I would try to

behave myself, although, sooner or later, Ms. Wise Guy would pop out of my mouth and get me in trouble again.

As I poured a cup of herbal tea for myself this morning, I noticed a quote from Anna Freud on the tea box that described in simple words the transition from dependence to maturity: "I was always looking outside myself for strength and confidence, but it comes from within. It is there all the time." If one as extraordinary as Anna Freud struggled hard to become a full adult, is it any wonder that ordinary young women find this transition fraught with difficulty?

The Diminishing Power of Parents

As parents we can help our daughters become adults in the fullest sense by encouraging them to develop, trust, and follow *their* convictions—even when these are contrary to our own, even when they rock the boat. A loving parental message is "You need not do as I do, see as I see, think as I think!"

We also empower our daughters by *gradually* discouraging them from depending on us as managers of their lives. We do this by allowing the toddler to decide whether she would prefer a peanut butter sandwich for lunch to an apple with cheese, letting the preschooler select the outfit she wants to wear today, assuming the fourth grader is responsible for doing her homework, and expecting the preteenager to take care of her laundry, and the teenager to pay the fine for her overdue library books. It is not always easy to refrain from taking charge of our daughters' lives, especially when they are running into trouble. As the following two stories from clients illustrate, however, as long as we persist in fixing, rescuing, deciding, caretaking, or coming up with good solutions for them, we inhibit their growing up.

Anton was used to bailing out his only child, Lauren. For example, he recently "took care of" the parking tickets she had accumulated and not bothered to pay, and he downplayed the seriousness of her running up a sizable bill on his credit card. When Lauren did not complete her college application until the day before it was due, despite the fact that she was very bright and had had plenty of time to attend to it, Anton finally lost his patience with her. Nonetheless, he did not want her to suffer any consequences as a result of her dallying. To ensure that Lauren would not miss the deadline and be unable to apply to the college of her choice, Anton raced the completed application over to Federal Express, just before closing time, for an overnight delivery. To his relief, Lauren's application did get to the school on time, and she was accepted there. It turned out, however, that midway into the semester, Lauren, unable to handle the pressures of academia, dropped out and came home. Without father to take care of things, she was—and, three years later, remains—quite lost. Only now is Anton coming to understand that from his having overfunctioned on her behalf, his daughter had learned to underfunction.

Years ago, I treated a young woman who, as a freshman in college, became manic-depressive. During her manic episodes, as if driven by dark, untamable forces within her, she would lose all reason and go on wild rampages, only to become deeply depressed afterward. With medications, psychotherapy, and hard work, Diana could learn to manage this disease and lead a productive life. However, Diana's mother, Helene, understandably distressed by the news of her daughter's illness, could not bear the fact that life had dealt Diana such a heavy blow. Wanting to soften her child's suffering, Helene began to indulge her whims and to make excuses for her "helplessness," which had the effect of further incapacitating Diana. Although Diana would have to struggle harder than most of her peers to create a meaningful life, her task to become a responsible, autonomous adult was no different from theirs. And although Helene's concerns for her adolescent daughter were more serious than those of parents with healthy children, her task was also no different from theirs: to foster her daughter's autonomy and independence. A friend of mine who began to hover over her twenty-year-old daughter after she became diabetic told me that she was jolted back to reality when a relative remarked, "I guess you'd like to wrap Tanya in wads of cotton and set her on the mantelpiece so that nothing else can happen to her, but is that where *she* wants to be?"

Supercompetent parents who are used to jumping in with both feet whenever a problem needs to be solved have to commit themselves to keeping their hands off and letting their daughters tend to their own affairs. One such parent told me about a note she had written to her daughter, who was home during winter break from college, that underwent two revisions. The original note read: "Kitty, I'll be back by 5. Also, don't forget your appointment with Dr. Cleeve at noon today. He's at 1634 Walnut Street." Realizing that Kitty could look up his address herself, she rewrote the note: "Kitty, I'll be back by 5. Also, don't forget your appointment with Dr. Cleeve at noon today." Then, reminding herself that Kitty should be responsible for her own appointments, she wrote the note a third and final time: "Kitty, I'll be back by 5."

I recently asked Brian, a psychologist friend who is the single parent of an independent, vivacious, twenty-one-year-old woman, what he had done to help her become that way, and he replied, "When Alma asked me questions like 'Dad, do you think I should major in English or engineering?' or 'Dad, should I take a full load of classes or go to school part-time so that I can also get a job?' I'd say 'I don't know, Alma. What do *you* think?' and she would come up with her own solutions. The 'I don't know's' are what helped Alma grow up."

Especially for parents who have been very involved with their children, assuming a less active role with them during their adolescence and early adulthood can feel unnatural and unkind. We want the best for our children; we don't want them to make unnecessary mistakes; we don't want them to fall flat on their faces; we don't even want them to stumble. Which is one reason it is so hard to say, "I don't know; I can't figure it out for you; I can no longer be there for you the way I once was." Deciding to back off—to take a less central position in our children's lives—is a task that has challenged parents of past generations as well as our own. "I long to put the experience of fifty years at once into your young lives," Harriet Beecher Stowe wrote to her twin daughters in 1861, "to give you at once the key of that treasure chamber every gem of which cost me tears and struggles and prayers, but you must work for these inward treasures yourself."[8]

By relinquishing our caretaking roles and our authority over our daughters, we necessarily strip away our own power, which can be a blow to our egos. Wearing and demanding as the early years of parenting are, during these years our children flatter us with their dependency and adoration. To our young children, we are the cleverest, wisest, and strongest in all the world. Helpless, little, and vulnerable themselves, they trust that we will keep them safe—and, for the most part, we do just that. Our jobs as guardian angels naturally make us feel very special.

Recently, I came upon a short story in *The New Yorker* that illustrates the seemingly magical, surely extrasensory powers with which the parent of the young child is endowed. Novelist and screenwriter Paul Auster tells of the accident that would have befallen his high-spirited toddler had he not been there to save her. The child caught the toe of her sneaker on the second-floor landing of a steep and narrow staircase, which sent her sailing through the air heading straight for an open window situated a yard from the bottom step:

> What did I do? I don't know what I did. I was on the wrong side of the bannister when I saw her trip. By the time she was midway between the landing and the window I was standing on the bottom step of the staircase. How did I get there? It was no more than a question of several feet, but it hardly seems possible to cover that distance in that amount of time—which is next to no

time at all. Nevertheless, I was there, and the moment I got there I looked up, opened my arms, and caught her.[9]

Reading this account, I became acutely aware of the fact that I am no longer there to break my daughter's falls when she loses her footing. And because I am not, she is learning to do this for herself, which is as it should be. Recently, after returning from her solo jaunt to Latin America, Leah described climbing to the crater of a volcano in Guatemala. The route was steep and extremely slippery, so slippery that she was forced to dismount her horse and continue on the trail by foot. Still, she tripped and fell many times, but whenever this happened she grabbed hold of a strong vine and pulled herself up again.

Tales of Letting Go

In discussions with middle-aged friends who, like me, have children who are young adults, we sometimes talk about our new tasks as parents. "And now what?" we ask ourselves. "What more must we do to grow and to foster our daughters' growth? What changes in behavior and attitude are required of us?"

I, for one, am convinced that my task is to learn to worry less. When I begin to fantasize about the many dangers awaiting my fiercely independent and adventurous daughter—dangers that may never materialize and that, even if they did, I could not prevent—I try to substitute positive images. I close my eyes and imagine a triumphant Leah smiling as she stands, encircled by blue skies and silver-lined clouds, near the crater of a volcano, for instance. When this strategy fails me, I throw myself into my writing with great fervor and am distracted from my worries. And when I cannot concentrate sufficiently to do creative work, I balance my checkbook or tidy my desk or, best of all, make a pot of chicken soup.

My friend Julie sees her midlife parental task as doing less talking and advising, more listening and learning. "My grown-up daughter is vastly different from the little daughter I mothered," she tells me over a cup of cardamom tea. "Over the last years, Rebecca has branched out into new areas—spiritual healing, bodywork, dance—about which I knew very little. Now I am student to her teacher, not the other way around." And Julie goes on to say, "After I left home, my mother stopped making any efforts to *know* me, to respect the person I was becoming. She just kept up her old habits of assuming that she knows what's best for me and giving me unsolicited advice. For this reason our relationship degenerated. Our conversations are stilted and empty. I am determined not to repeat the same pattern with Rebecca."

For Veronica, letting go means accepting that her adult daughter, Anne-Marie, is less than Veronica had hoped she would be. Her task is especially difficult, first because it is natural to personalize your child's unhappiness, seeing it as indicative of your failure; second, because it is excruciatingly painful to see someone you love falter. Bright, talented, and pretty, little Anne-Marie skipped through childhood with barely a stumble. But then in her senior year in high school, for reasons hard to discern, she began to make bad choices: falling in with a fast crowd, regularly cutting classes, drinking heavily, and experimenting with street drugs. Now at twenty-three, having flitted from one disastrous relationship to another and without prospects for a meaningful vocation, Anne-Marie also struggles with a substance-abuse problem; she tells Veronica that she goes to AA meetings, but Veronica doubts that her daughter's attendance is consistent and her commitment to rehabilitate sincere. Veronica is in therapy herself, learning to live with her real disappointment and to be supportive but not overly invested in her daughter's life. "Every mother wants her daughter to be the happy ending to her own life, but, unless Anne-Marie makes dramatic changes, it may not turn out this way for me," she confides. "I am learning important lessons in therapy. One is that the only life you can direct is your own; my 'good advice' to Anne-Marie only falls on deaf ears. Unless my daughter musters the courage to make changes, I cannot do anything more for her. And so, over and over again, I say to myself, I am not responsible for the way Anne-Marie chooses to live. Another is that you love your child forever not because she is happy or successful or makes you proud but because she is your child."

And for my friend Ray, letting go means letting in:

> Joanie is engaged to be married. That means that I'm not the number one man in her life anymore. I have to give way to another man, a younger man. Men tend to be competitive, as you know. We try so hard to be the strongest, the smartest, the most powerful. I have friends who are in competition with their sons-in-law. They manage to put them down so they can remain top dog in their daughters' eyes. But I'm determined not to do this. I think the finest way I can show Joanie that I love her, now that she is all grown up, is by respecting and, when it's fitting, deferring to the man who will be her husband.

As Ray relinquishes the role of the father who knows best, he undoubtedly will experience some loss of self-importance, and yet this loss may lead to gain. A reknowned psychoanalyst, Frieda Fromm-Reichmann, describing the changes inherent in growing older, said that "A door is closing behind us and we turn sorrowfully to watch it close and do not discover, until we are wrenched away, the one opening ahead." For Ray, and for all parents (and surrogate parents) who relinquish their positions of authority, the opening door may lead to refreshing and surprising relationships with the younger generation. This is surely the case for my husband. After asking a few of his college students to teach him about *their* music (a request to which they responded enthusiastically) Bruce became a great fan of

Johnny Rotten and The Sex Pistols. Our children and I now call him the "happening guy."

The growth pains accompanying each stage of a child's life revive in the parent-related developmental issues. Hence, as our daughters navigate the stormy waters of adolescence or young adulthood, we may find that long-buried emotions and unresolved issues from our own youth resurface. In fact, we may experience an identity crisis in which we seriously question the meaning of the way we choose to live and the quality of our closest relationships. Having to reexperience the conflicts of youth during one's middle years may seem like undue punishment; however, it provides a second chance to work things through. My friend Ramona explained that she began to fall apart as her adolescent daughter was separating from her. Ramona's emotional crisis led her to therapy and, consequently, to an awareness that her own separation from her parents was yet incomplete. For Ramona, a critical word from her mother or father inevitably triggered such negative and irrational thoughts as, I'm always messing up; I'm stupid and inept; my parents still disapprove of me, which plunged her into depression. Now in middle age, with her therapist's guidance, Ramona is learning what her eighteen-year-old daughter is also learning: parent and child need not be of the same mind, that conflict between them is natural, and there is no shame in making mistakes, which is what happens to each of us as we "make up" our adult lives.

In Germany, the advice offered to parents of grown children is summed up in three words: *staunen, schweigen,* and *schenken. Staunen* is to marvel at from a respectful distance. It means you take in, delight in, and praise whatever is admirable in your grown children while, simultaneously, honoring the boundaries that separate you from them. *Schweigen* refers to a disciplined silence. Hence, you relinquish the right to give unsolicited advice, criticize, lecture, interrogate, and impose your ideas on your grown children. *Schenken* refers to the giving of gifts. You give gifts that empower your grown children— material gifts such as tuition money, but also emotional gifts such as compassion, affirmation, support, encouragement, and praise. I would add a word of caution, however. The one who always gives assumes a position of superiority that reduces the one who always receives to a position of inferiority, which is why in countries such as India and Israel, the giver of alms remains indebted to the beggar, not vice versa. Parents empower their children by graciously accepting gifts from them and also by refraining from giving *too* much to them. This is what my friend Julie does so well in being learner to her daughter's teacher. And what my husband and I do by giving our daughter material gifts for special occasions that are not excessively generous.

Strong Wings, Delicate Wings, Injured Wings

A Chinese proverb tells us that "When birds and children grow wings, they fly away." What I have learned from my own experiences as a parent and from the stories told to me by clients and friends is that the flights and destinations of grown children are as various as the children themselves.

Some of our daughters take nonstop flights; they get where they want to go without undue difficulty. For other daughters, their passage is not so smooth. At eighteen or twenty-one (the arbitrary ages our culture sets for becoming adult), they have not yet taken off; or—perhaps after being in the air for a while—they have a crash landing in the form of a mental or physical breakdown, or a crisis of lost confidence. In these cases, we are called on to help our daughters heal their injured wings so that they will be able to fly again. Healing may require their being in psychotherapy, taking time off from college or graduate school to reassess future plans, or confronting family problems that had been swept under the rug. Whatever their treatment may be, our daughters will likely heal more quickly and fully if we are there to encourage and support them, but not pull them back into a dependency on us.

Althea, a young friend who is a first-year graduate student at Princeton, shared this anecdote:

> I have always been independent, but, as a result of all the demands at school, I was absolutely overwhelmed. I worried about failing my classes and felt, overall, very, very needy. And so, during the first weeks of the semester, I called home—every day. When my mother picked up the phone, I usually couldn't even speak. I just sobbed and sobbed, and she stayed on the line, patiently and lovingly, never making me feel foolish for my weakness. Just listening. And then I felt a little better. Thanks to the daily "home visits" with my mom, by midterm I had regained my confidence and knew I'd make it.

Some of our daughters sprout strong wings that carry them far from us—to out-of-state colleges and universities or jobs halfway across the country or Peace Corps assignments in Third World nations. Other daughters sprout delicate wings that do not take them far away; these young women may study at local schools or look for jobs in their hometown, for instance. The young woman who itches for novel experiences is not necessarily superior to the one who chooses to stay put, and the converse is also true. Becoming an adult has to do with *how* you choose to be—your will to be self-directive—not with *where* you choose to be.

I counseled a young woman in her senior year at the University of Colorado who, as graduation approached, became increasingly anxious. Jodi believed that after getting her business degree she should move to a big city, find a job there, and establish an independent life. To this end, she sent copies of her résumé to major corporations in New York, Boston, and San

Francisco and, in return, was invited for several interviews. As we talked, however, it became clear that what Jodi really wanted to do was settle in the small town in Tennessee where she had grown up and where her family still lived. "And what is wrong with this choice?" I asked her, to which Jodi replied that her friends and professors would probably think her returning to her hometown was a sign of immaturity and dependence. When I asked what her reasons for returning to Tennessee were, she answered that she did not want to go back home in order to be taken care of—in fact, she had every intention of supporting herself and living in her own place—but she did have a strong desire to be physically near the people she knew and loved best. "When I picture myself being happiest, I am having Sunday dinner in the company of my siblings, my parents, and grandparents. I can also imagine that one day I'll be bringing a beau along to these family gatherings, and that makes me smile," Jodi confided.

My role as Jodi's therapist was clear to me. During our sessions, I would repeatedly say, "Try to be less concerned about the opinions of your friends, your professors. Trust what your heart tells you. That, after all, is the true sign of being a mature and independent woman." And this is what Jodi did by moving back to her hometown in Tennessee.

No Place Like Home

Of the thousands of words in our language, few seem to evoke as much emotion as the word *home*. Home is associated with hearth, the conjunction of the male principle (fire) and the female principle (receptacle) that signifies love. Home is also where we are rooted, where we come from. Indeed, in many cultures around the world, the umbilical cord, placenta, or fetal membranes of infants are buried near the ground where they were born. Wherever the adult child may eventually live, she remains connected to this burial spot—the home originally shared with her parents.

In a radio interview, Holocaust survivor Gerta Weissman looked back to her experience as an inmate of Nazi concentration camps and reflects on the sustenance that images of the childhood home provide, even after one has grown up, and the extraordinary influence of ordinary family togetherness:

> You know, when people ask me, "Why did you go on?" there is only one picture that comes to mind. That moment was when I stood at the window of the first camp I was in and asked myself probably the most important question of my life. I asked if, by some miraculous power, one wish could be granted me, what would it be? . . . And then, with almost crystal clarity, the picture came to my mind. And what I saw was a picture at home—my father smoking his pipe, my mother working at her needlepoint, my brother and I doing our homework. And I remember thinking, my God, it was just a boring evening at home. I had known countless evenings like that. And I knew that this picture would be, if I could help it, the driving force to my survival.[10]

To be at home means to be safe, in one's element, to be unembarrassed, unconstrained, known, accepted, and acceptable. "I'll be home for Christmas," Peggy Lee sings, tapping into our own longing. "Going home, going home," ET squeaks in his little voice, and we in the movie audience, identifying with him, choke back our tears. "Oh, Aunt Em, I'm so glad to be home again!" Dorothy Gale calls out after returning from the Land of Oz, and our hearts fill up with joy.

After our children have grown wings and flown away, they will come home again, for weekly Sunday dinners, perhaps, or for yearly Christmas vacations. They will come home to water their roots, and then they will take their leave again. We invest homecomings with high expectations. Reuniting with our grown children, we anticipate only joy. The fact is, however, that all too commonly family gatherings are disappointing. Instead of meaningful conversations, our exchanges feel empty; instead of affection, we encounter distance. What goes wrong for so many families? Why do the rich connections we long for elude us?

Spezzano writes that the two ingredients necessary for cross-generational friendships are "adult children who are willing to turn off the TV at their parents' house and say something about their lives and who they have become and parents who can tolerate the truth."[11] Put another way, in order for our attachments to become rich and gratifying, we cannot hide from each other under a cover of evasions, small talk, or silences.

In many cases, our adult children harbor old hurts and resentments. They may want to "have it out with us" at last but are cowed into silence, perhaps by their fear of hurting our feelings or making us angry, or perhaps by their anticipation that we won't understand what they are trying to say. For our parts, we may not want to be told that we were unkind, insensitive, or unfair to them, that we sometimes abused our parental power or betrayed their trust in us; after all, we cannot undo what was done, and maybe we are ashamed of past wrongs. Thus, we collude with their silences and in so doing miss the opportunity to initiate the healing dialogues that would bring us closer together.

Some adult daughters have bad experiences when they come home because we treat them like the children they once were—or they are seduced or goaded into acting like the children they once were. A thirty-year-old client, herself the mother of a daughter, cringes when she tells me that her parents have maintained her old bedroom just as it was when she left home as an adolescent; each time she visits them, she has the eerie feeling of stepping back into time and into childhood. A graduate student complains that when she stays at her parents' house, they "micromanage" her life, scrutinizing what she eats, what she wears, and what company she keeps. Our daughters, we ought to remind ourselves, have fought valiantly for their independence, autonomy, and maturity; to be pulled back to being considered little girls feels degrading to them. What they ask for is to be recognized as competent and responsible women; we provide this by relinquishing our control over their lives.

Going "home" can also become uncomfortable if it becomes associated with guilty feelings. "It is painful for me to visit my mother," a client in her late twenties recently confided, "because as soon as I get to her apartment, she tells me how unhappy she'll be when I leave and berates me for not visiting her more often." Even if we are lonely for our daughters, even if we could be happier with them close by, for their sake we cannot hold on to them too tightly or too long; loving them generously and unselfishly means letting them go. This is Margaret Mead's sentiment in a poem she wrote to her daughter, Catherine Bateson:

That I not be a restless ghost
Who haunts your footsteps as they pass
Beyond the point where you have left
Me standing in the newsprung grass.

You must be free to take a path
Whose end I feel no need to know,
Nor irking fever to be sure
You went where I would have you go. . . .

So you can go without regret
Away from this familiar land,
Leaving your kiss upon my hair
And all the future in your hands.[12]

Alan Lightman's fantastic world of timeless perfection where beautiful children never leave their parents is not our world. In our world, time does not stand still. Our daughters change and grow. As long as we remain flexible and open, we change and grow too. What we may have been less capable of during our early years of being parents—truthfulness, wisdom, forgiveness, humility, stepping back, backing off, accepting our flaws, and our children's flaws—we may become more capable of during our later years.

While we lovingly stroke the wings of our daughters, allowing them to fly and soar, we may notice something tickling, pushing, and prodding between our shoulder blades: it is, of course, our own fine set of wings, and these wings are capable of carrying us to ever-greater heights of understanding and love. For by allowing our daughters the gift of freedom, we achieve greater humanity.

PART FIVE

A DAUGHTER'S GIFTS

A child strips away our illusions that we are perfect, that we have it all figured out, that we are all grown up. In fact, we grow up with our children if we are willing to remain open to their innate goodness as well as our own.

—PEGGY O'MARA

From Daughter to Father: Bruce's Memoir

W hen my wife was pregnant with our first child, I expected a son. It wasn't that I *wanted* a son rather than a daughter, it was that circumstances assumed a collective weight that seemed to make the birth of a son inevitable.

In my wife's seventh month, her father died. I had admired my father-in-law, a man of great decency and intelligence who had never been blessed with the opportunities I took for granted but who had never complained about life's unfairness. Evi and I agreed that if our child was a boy, we would name him after the man we were mourning and whose grace as a person our child would inherit.

In addition, though my mother and my mother-in-law were neutral in the matter, my father and my four grandparents strongly wanted a boy, as they had wanted a boy when I—the firstborn of my parents and the first grandchild of my grandparents—was born. In the Jewish religion, when the first child is a boy, the family celebrates a *pidyon haben*, in which it symbolically ransoms the boy from the high priest (or *Koin*) of the tribe. In my case, ten pieces of silver had been paid to a family friend who had played the role of the *Koin*, and the celebration had begun. My mother's father, who had hosted the celebration, had invited not only family from both sides but also cronies from the old country. He had provided herring, pickled watermelon, sturgeon, Nova Scotia lox, pickles, sauerkraut, schnapps, and wine in abundance; and toward evening, when no one wanted to leave the party, he had returned to the Lower East Side to replenish the table.

The *pidyon haben* I anticipated for my firstborn had more than ritual significance for me. In buying my son back from the *Koin*, I imagined I would be redeeming him from those forces that had held me back as a child. Though both my parents were wonderful people whom I loved and respected, they had handicaps that had made my childhood fraught with conflict and guilt. Both of them had contracted polio when young children, and my mother's crutches and my father's atrophied leg had made me feel like a child of Holocaust survivors—unable to believe that he would or should escape from the disaster that had overtaken his parents. Surely the fate that had "struck them down," as I thought about it, would strike me down also—if not with polio, then with some other disaster. Besides this anxiety, I was inhibited by the fact that my parents' handicaps made them less able to "handle" me if I wanted to defy them in the normal way. If I ran away, for example, they could not catch me; and I felt as if I were taking unfair advantage of my wholeness and my mobility. Later, as I contemplated having a son, I imagined the ways I would help him cultivate and enjoy his physical abilities and his natural desire to roam.

I would also do something else that my father could not or would not do: I would let him see me as the strong male who blazed the trail for his equally strong son. My father had overcome poverty, his parents' bitter marriage, and polio to go to college and to work his way through law school, but he could not overcome his own insecurity as a father and my mother's proprietary attitude toward her children. In the home she was the expert, she was the decision maker, and he was the secondary parent. Where I needed him to lead the way as a man, he let my mother lead; where I needed him to intervene, to tell my mother sometimes to let me alone to fend for myself, he deferred to her; where I needed to see him at his most powerful and most competent—in the courtroom, for example—he never let me see him in action. With my own son, I would not allow myself to become the secondary parent. I would be involved in his day-to-day rearing, I would let him see me at my most competent, and I would step between him and my wife when I felt that she was being too controlling.

When our obstetrician came into the waiting room of the hospital and told me that my wife and baby daughter were doing fine, the stage set I had composed around my child's birth seemed to reorganize itself. Stage center was a baby *girl*, not a baby son; and there would be no *pidyon haben*. In the perfunctory Judaism we practiced at the time, in fact, there was no ritual to welcome Leah into the world and to establish our roles as parents. Far from being disappointed, however, I found I was relieved. I no longer felt that I had to be vigilant on behalf of a child with whom I identified; I no longer felt that I had to protect that child against my wife; and I no longer felt that I had to undo my own travails as a child through this new child. Leah was a girl, and as I looked at her that first day, I felt wonder at her difference—her otherness. Having no set agenda for her, I could relax and enjoy the unanticipated ways she would develop.

And relax I did, though, wired for hypervigilance, I do not relax easily. Holding Leah for the first time, I felt a warmth and a peace pervade my whole being, so that I fell asleep with her in my arms. Whereas earlier, in seeing her, I had experienced her otherness, now, in holding her, I experienced a oneness with her. Then, and many times afterward, I felt an ease and a comfort, a perfect stillness and letting be, that I hadn't experienced before. One night, I remember, Leah cried and cried as she struggled with colic. I picked her up, placed her over my right shoulder, and paced back and forth, back and forth while she cried. After a while, I turned on the television, volume off, and glanced at a Knicks game while I walked, and eventually forgot about Leah, who stopped crying. When the game ended, I looked at her, sound asleep and melded to my shoulder. It was as if she had flowed over the shoulder and then congealed—a perfect fit.

Though I was much less burdened with the past than I was when I anticipated having a son, I was still determined to be as much Leah's primary parent as my wife was. I liked doing all the little things one did in nurturing a baby: feeding her, changing her, comforting her, bathing her, dressing her. The only thing I wouldn't do was manipulate her feet, which turned in and had to be manipulated outward. It wasn't only that I didn't want to cause her pain—my wife had difficulties with that also—but also that the problem with her feet reminded me of my parents' handicaps. Otherwise, I did everything and also felt closer to Evi in feeling so close to our daughter. Only once, as I remember, was my old susceptibility to feeling excluded aroused. One New Year's Eve, I stormed out of my parents' apartment, where we were staying on a visit, because I felt that Evi and Leah were nesting together and excluding me; but that exception proved the rule. For the most part, Evi respected my need to be involved.

From the very beginning Leah seemed to enjoy her world. As a baby, she giggled in her crib while looking at her decals. As a toddler, she confronted the biggest dog I've ever seen and stuck her face into his. When the big dog licked her face with a mile-long tongue, she plopped onto the sidewalk and looked up at the dog with amazement rather than fear. She seemed so confident and happy in her world that she gave me confidence in mine. She was like a talisman that helped me overcome the anxiety I felt in difficult situations. When she was two, for example, I was applying for a university position in a very bad job market. I remember going to a convention in Chicago to be interviewed by committees from several English departments, and the tension was so great that I struggled with migraine headaches all the way through. When I was subsequently invited for a day's worth of interviews, presentations, and other get-togethers at Wesleyan University, I drove from New York to Connecticut with Evi and Leah—dressed in her little white shoes and in her OshKosh B'Gosh overalls. Despite the stress of competing for a job I really wanted, I didn't feel as tense as I had in Chicago. With Leah around, I felt nothing could go that wrong. So much was right with the way she was—with the way *we* all were together—that I knew that if I did not get this job, I would get another.

One might ask, of course, how much of what I perceived in Leah was really there and how much was my own projection, my own imagination. I had always had a mixture of anxiety for and confidence in my mother, who seemed both fragile and strong and capable. Her crutches, made of wood, might crack, I used to think; or the strap that held her brace might break; or an icy patch on the street might make her slip. But she was also my anchor—the person who would listen to me, help me solve my problems, and protect me (even as I sometimes thought I had to protect her). She had been, I knew, an activist all her life, who refused to accept all but the most necessary limitations imposed by her handicap. As a young woman, for example, she had led other handicapped people on a march on Washington in a demand for jobs for the handicapped. As a grandmother, I could see, she identified with Leah—with the wide-eyed little girl and the determined and adventurous young woman she became—and perhaps I identified Leah with my mother. But Leah had no crutches. Leah had my mother's spirit, but not her encumbered body.

Whatever I projected onto her, Leah still seemed very much her own person. And she dealt with me in ways that I found liberating. For example, though I had always been averse to sharing my food, Leah treated this neurotic quality with comical irreverence. She took what she wanted from me. She also counteracted the exaggerated sense of empathy and concern I had developed as a child. One story in particular illustrates her healthy disregard. Being an earlier riser than Evi, I used to get up with Leah. I put her in her high chair, fixed her juice and cereal, and then, being in a health-food phase, prepared my own health-food drink. While Leah chatted away and I tried to listen and respond, I mixed together papaya juice, nutritional yeast, and several other ingredients. One morning, as I turned to listen to something she was saying, I knocked over the drink, which spilled all over the floor. As I watched it spread and contemplated cleaning up the viscous mess, Leah cackled. It was the funniest thing she'd ever seen. At this point, I decided to teach her some of the empathy that I had in abundance. I said to her, "Leah, do you think that's funny?" She replied, giggling, "Very funny." I said, "I want you to imagine something. You and Daddy are walking into town to get some ice cream." Leah's eyes widened: She loved ice cream as much as I did. "We go into the store and I get butter pecan for me and pistachio for you." "I *love* pistachio," Leah said. "I know," I said. "But as we walk home, you trip and your ice cream falls on the sidewalk. Is that funny or sad?" "That's very sad," she said, her face clouding over. "Now," I said, thinking I had her, "Daddy was making his drink this morning. He put his juice and his yeast and his banana and his nuts and his honey into the blender and mixed them up, and then the whole drink spilled on the floor. Was that funny or sad?" Leah thought for a moment before her face brightened with a smile. "Sad for you, funny for me," she replied. Clearly, Leah was her own person.

If later I was to share the rough-and-tumble of sports with my son, Jonathan, with Leah I shared imagination. I would take walks with her, tell her stories, and make the world come alive in fantastic ways. The berries, for example, would talk in individual voices to her, ask her how she was, and tell her their secrets. She developed a correspondence with leprechauns that required that little notes and poems be left for her each night, as well as little presents (which my wife was very ingenious in concocting).

When Leah was not yet three, I began taking her to movies, ballets, plays, even opera, and she was never restless, never talkative. She sat attentively, always absorbed by what she was seeing and hearing. One of my favorite memories is of taking her, when she was six, to the Metropolitan Opera to see *Der Rosenkavalier*, the very long but very gorgeous (both visually and musically) opera by Richard Strauss. Leah looked adorable in her special dress, but the middle-aged couple who shared a box with us darted hateful glances in her direction. She would, they knew, get restless, move about, talk, ruin the opera for them. Leah, however, listened attentively as I told her the romantic story of the opera. She watched wide-eyed as the chandeliers ascended and dimmed and as the conductor emerged and took his bows to our applause. She watched and listened attentively for four hours as comedy mixed with drama and romance and as Strauss's music moved from comic and romantic waltzes to the soaring music of love lost and triumphant. And when it was over, the couple in the box could not be effusive enough to the little girl who had not fidgeted, who had not said a word.

What was this quality of hers? This ability to be so attentive? This ability to take things in? She had the same imagination I did, the same imagination my wife did (Evi had been absorbed by drawing and painting throughout her childhood and adolescence), but it did not, as far as I could see, compensate for things she wasn't getting out of life. Leah, it seemed, could get from life what she wanted, and she did not have to pay a price for it. Loyal to my parents, I had always assumed that any gratification I got in life had to be paid for one way or another. So I anticipated illness or other misfortunes as "payment" for the good things that happened to me. Leah never did; she accepted gratification as a matter of course, and she rejected utterly my overconcern with health. Her attitude, in a way, encouraged me, enlivened my own sense of hope. I can still picture her, in the orchards of Athens, Ohio, where I taught at the university, reaching out for apples as I held her up. That was Leah, and she was a lesson to me.

To what degree was Leah shaped by my expectations, by my projections, by my attitude toward her? To what degree was my way of looking at her determined by who she was—even as a child? Whatever the answers, Leah became an eternal volunteer. When she was six or seven, for example, Boulder, Colorado, built its downtown mall. On weekends during the summer, musicians, jugglers, rope walkers, magicians, and other assorted performers could be found all along it. Evi and I would take Leah and her little brother to the mall in the evening, buy ice cream, and stroll from one attraction to another. In a flash Leah would be gone, only to reappear a moment or two later as a volunteer for a juggler or a magician. One evening, in fact, I saw her reappear with a magician who had placed her little neck in a miniature guillotine. While Evi and I gulped, Leah waited with a smile of excited anticipation as the magician prepared to chop off her head. Years later, in fact, when Leah was already an adolescent, I ran into one of the mall's magicians who remembered her. "I remember Leah," he said. "She was always ready."

Later on this same daring was expressed in an activity that was to prove enormously important to her development: acting. When she was little, she loved the sagas I made up for her, which often had her as the heroine; she also loved storytelling records, which she often listened to with a faraway look that betokened the fantasies she was living. When, as good middle-class parents always on the lookout for enrichment for their children, we enrolled her in a young people's acting school called The Boulder Act, we did not know what Leah and we were getting into.

The woman who ran The Act was a professional actress who had no intention of making it anything cute or dilettantish. She and the other actors on the school's staff taught classes in which children ranging from elementary school through high school learned to get in touch with their feelings and perceptions, to express them in voice and movement, and to improvise. Though Evi and I had been quite self-conscious as children and adolescents, Leah, as she got older, seemed quite eager to tackle roles in which she very easily could have looked foolish. As a young adolescent, for example, she chose as an audition piece the role of Maggie the Cat in Tennessee Williams's *Cat on a Hot Tin Roof*. And when she performed her scene, I was stunned by her willingness to get into that part—to explore its longing, its frustration, and its sensuality. In a million years I could never have attempted what actors call a "stretch" of that magnitude. How, I wondered, could such a skinny little thing throw herself into such a part with so little self-consciousness?

Throughout her adolescence (and into her adulthood), I never worried about the problems that seemed to beset so many of her peers: the emotional turmoil, the sex, the alcohol or other drugs, the eating disorders. Though she rolled her eyes and expressed incredulity ("I don't believe it!") whenever we limited her or prevented her from doing something, she seemed so focused, so committed both in school and in The Boulder Act that I did not worry about her going astray. Though she seemed confident about exploring her sexuality in the plays she did (culminating in her Juliet in *Romeo and Juliet*), she did not have a boyfriend in high school and did not seem interested in dating. Her life was her group of friends, most of whom were also in The Act. When she did develop relations with men in college, they seemed to work out well. She was so confident and had such a good self-image that she was not susceptible to manipulation or exploitation. She entered relationships, as she seemed to enter everything else, from a position of strength rather than neediness.

I knew that Leah had derived some of her qualities from me: her interest in theater and in music, her wacky sense of humor, and her interest in improvisation. Mine was essentially a histrionic personality, constructed, in part, to save myself from the depression that was never very far from the surface of my life. Leah again took what she needed and rejected what she didn't need. Whereas I had expressed my loyalty to my parents by making some of their problems my own, Leah knew how to be benignly disloyal, refusing what she needed to refuse. For that reason I often referred to her—only half humorously—as my role model. She was, I thought, living out that liberating disloyalty of which I had wanted to be capable, the disloyalty that said, "I can love you, learn from you, without taking on your suffering." Perhaps I had, in some way, encouraged this quality in her, even though I had not cultivated it sufficiently in myself.

I continued to learn, however, and Leah was part of the project that for me was one of the great breakthroughs. A professor of English literature, I had wanted for some time to do some creative writing but had felt stymied. Feeling duty-bound to produce scholarly work, I could not allow myself the creative playfulness I wanted and needed. But as I watched Leah grow as an actress and as I shared the work my wife was doing in her first book, which was on mother-daughter relationships, I had my breakthrough. I began writing a play about a weekend that four mothers spend with their teenage daughters in the Rocky Mountains. The writing was wonderfully pleasurable, and the play won a contest that resulted in its being produced by a Colorado theater company. More than that, Leah auditioned successfully for one of the roles, which she infused with her own extraordinary intensity.

As I think about the amazing role Leah has played in my

life—it's hard to imagine what I would be without her—I realize how mysterious the human spirit is. As a child, I escaped the small, constricting world of braces and crutches by entering the greater world of imagination. I listened to music, fantasized great adventures, read books, and fantasized through them. As a young man, and still today with my wife at my side, I escaped into travel. Leah also loves to travel, but her sense of adventure pervades everything she does. When I allowed myself to write creatively, I was, in a way, following her example, even as her dramatic work suggested the form for my first creative endeavor. That give-and-take between us has been one of the glories of our relationship.

Leah, I believe, has a gift for life. And she has made me more aware of my own gift. If she took from me, I also received from her. Though she did not have the *pidyon haben* that a first son would have had, she helped me further my own ransoming from the forces of the past.

From Daughter to Mother: Evelyn's Memoir

As I began this chapter, I planned to describe the ways Leah is a generous daughter; I thought I would write about her acts of kindness and care. I did not get very far into my writing, however, when I realized that Leah's most precious gift to me is not the love she bestows—although this is sweet indeed—but the love she engenders. From the time I was pregnant with Leah, the love I have felt for her has transformed and empowered me. It has fostered empathy, selflessness, compassion, and courage; it has infused me with a sense of meaning and purposefulness. Gifted with love for Leah, I have been able to accomplish tasks, have feelings, and grow in ways I never dreamed were possible.

Bruce and I were living in Paris when I became pregnant. Our baby-to-be was planned and much wanted. Nevertheless, separated from my mother and from other older female friends who would have told me what to expect from my "condition," I was not prepared to feel so sick, and I wondered if my symptoms were normal. I was nauseated all day. But wasn't "morning sickness" a morning phenomenon? Too thin to begin with, I could tolerate only melons and a field green called mâche and was losing weight. Didn't pregnant women gain weight?

Despite my physical discomforts, I was very happy. More than very happy, I was supremely grateful. The truth was that I had never thought I could become pregnant. As a thirteen-year-old, I overheard an aunt discuss with her doctor-husband her concern that medications I had taken as a child might make me infertile. When at fourteen I still had not gotten my period or developed breasts (I had the unenviable distinction of being the only girl in tenth grade who wore an undershirt) I thought for sure that something was wrong with my body, although I kept my fear a secret. Even after I matured physically, the fear lingered. Getting pregnant was an unanticipated blessing, and at times the prospect of becoming a mother filled me with so much joy that I thought I would burst. I remember meandering along a lovely tree-lined Parisian boulevard one drizzly spring afternoon musing about this blessing. Unable to contain my excitement, I needed to tell someone right then and there that I was *enceinte*, "with child." Of course, how could I expect the strangers who hurried past me to take an interest in my story? I looked at the treetops swelling with leaf buds and told *them* my secret.

It is still a mystery to me how a mother-to-be can feel so much love for the little creature she is carrying within her. From the first time that I felt my baby moving inside me, I knew I would cherish her (or "him," as my husband predicted) for the rest of my life. And, unconditional commitment, mind you, was new to me. Up until then, I had flitted from one enthusiasm to another. Although I had always been a conscientious student, I lacked drive and tenacity. Roger, a boy I had been in love with, who was endowed with uncanny insight, compared me to a bubble floating in the air—pretty and colorful, but without substance; he said I reflected his light, but did not have an inner light to guide me. Peter, my first serious boyfriend and trusted confidant, told me I was "fickle" by nature; when I ended our relationship, he prophesied that I would not stay married to one man. Bruce had more faith in me, though he too was dismayed by my lack of discipline, especially when I'd begin reading a celebrated novel with zeal only to lose interest midway through. (To this day, he has not let me live down the fact that I did not finish *Moby Dick*.) Whatever my shortcomings may have been, I was confident that I would never lose interest in my child. The new life I was harboring became my passion; fostering her well-being became my purpose.

In my third month of pregnancy, Bruce's parents came to visit us in Paris, and from there we set out to tour southern France together. Unfortunately, the Renault we rented had poor shock absorbers, or maybe none at all, and the ride along the unpaved country roads was bumpy. As Bruce drove, I began to worry that all this jostling would be bad for my baby. To cushion her against the jarring movements, I decided to sit on my hands, which after a while became tingly and numb. My mother-in-law, explaining that a fetus is well protected in the watery womb, implored me to resume a normal sitting position, but I was resolute. For two weeks, four or five hours a day, I sat on my hands as our car bumped its way past the Loire Valley, across the Pont d'Avignon, down to Marseilles, and back to Paris. Even before Leah was born, she was teaching me to love and care as I had never done before.

As it happened, my pregnancy did not follow a smooth course. I was exposed to German measles, which plunged me into a state of panic. Only months later did I learn that I had a natural immunity and that my exposure had not jeopardized my baby's health. In my seventh month my father died unexpectedly; overcome by shock and grief, I became diabetic. By then we had returned to the United States, where I had found an obstetrician I could trust. He immediately put me on a strict diet. Having a strong oppositional streak, I had never before been able to stick to any medical regimen, but for the duration of my pregnancy, I dared not eat one bite of the forbidden foods on my list or exceed the limited number of calories I was allowed. To quell my constant craving for food, I nibbled on raw cranberries—the only "eat as much as you like" item on my diet—while daydreaming about bagels piled high with cream cheese and strawberry jam. There was no question about it: If going hungry for a few months would ensure our baby's well-being, this was what I would do. Although my doctor informed me that the diabetes most likely would become chronic after childbirth (in fact, it did not), I never worried about this prognosis—which was out of character for me, as I had always been a hypochondriac. The love for my child-to-be had forced a transformation: I was focusing on *her* well-being, not my own.

Leah, perfectly formed and healthy, was born by cesarean section at Mount Sinai Hospital in New York City on January 21, 1971. After the delivery I was taken to the recovery room, where a nurse offered me pain medication. I told her the truth: I felt no pain. Indeed, I felt only joy and awe and glory. "Try to sleep now," she said ever so gently. "You've just been through major surgery." But I did not want to sleep and resisted the urge to close my eyes. A miracle had just occurred. Dozing off seemed like a sacrilege to me.

That week in the hospital was the happiest time I had ever known. Bruce visited Leah and me every day, and I was flooded with new feelings of love for him. What a sweet father he was! What a kind and nurturing husband! I took great satisfaction in concluding that my old boyfriend Peter was wrong about me after all. I did have it in me to stay married to one man, to this man, "till death do us part."

The day after Leah's birth, my doctor put in a special dietary order: I was to have not one sweet, gooey dessert, but two! When he came to see me, he told me that throughout the last months of pregnancy and during the long unsuccessful labor that had preceded surgery, I had been "very tough." Me, tough? Aside from my compulsion to speak my mind, I saw myself as fearful, cautious, and fragile. Yet, my doctor—whom I idealized and believed absolutely—said I had been very tough. His assessment changed my self-image. I began to think of myself as unbreakable, resilient, and strong.

After we brought Leah home from the hospital and the real work of being a mother began, I had many opportunities to demonstrate my toughness. During my last month of pregnancy, having fractured my coccyx while backing into a chair, I was in pain each time I sat on a hard surface. The unpadded wooden rocking chair, however, could not be abandoned. One of my maternal aunts, a self-proclaimed expert in child rearing, told me that it was imperative for mothers to nurse their babies on a rocker. Enduring considerable pain, I followed her directive; no cushy chair for me. If babies required rockers in order to be content, I would not deprive my Leah.

Before motherhood, I had been convinced that without eight hours of uninterrupted sleep every night, I would fall apart. With an infant who needed to nurse about every two hours around the clock, I now discovered that I could function (more or less) with little sleep. I also discovered other hidden capabilities: I could cook or vacuum or put groceries away with one hand while holding baby Leah with the other. And I found that when anyone threatened my child, I became ferocious. Once, to my husband's embarrassment, I barred a nice young man from attending a political meeting in our Manhattan apartment because he was coughing. "Sorry," I told him, "you can't stay. I have a baby, and I don't want her catching what you have." On another occasion, while Bruce looked on stunned, I pounded a man with my umbrella because he shoved into little Leah during a rush-hour subway ride.

Handless Maidens

One of my favorite folktales is "The Handless Maiden," which is about the empowering and transforming effect of maternal love. A Russian peasant without hands wanders exhausted and thirsty through the countryside carrying her baby under her arm. She comes to a spring and leans forward to drink from it, whereupon the child slips from her arm into the water. In a panic, she searches for help and soon encounters an old man who says, "Well, take the child out of the water." "But I can't; I have no hands," she wails. "Do it anyway," the old man insists. Which is what she does. When the maiden puts her arm stumps in the water, living hands grow on them, and with these she saves her child.

Leah was about one and a half years old when we moved from Manhattan to Athens, Ohio, where Bruce had a teaching job at Ohio University. Homesick for our city life, we returned to New York to spend a week with his parents before fall classes began. One afternoon, Bruce and his parents decided to take in a double feature; I was quite content to stay behind with Leah. When it came time for her nap, I put her in the Portacrib in the back bedroom of the apartment and decided to read on the balcony—a rare luxury. As I stepped outside, however, a great gust of wind shut the heavy door behind me, and, hard as I tried, I could not pry it open.

I was on the sixteenth floor, cut off from the neighboring apartments by concrete walls and from the people milling on the streets below by what seemed like infinite empty space; if I screamed for help, surely no one would hear me. Soon Leah would wake from her nap, call out for me, and become frantic when I did not come. *Somehow I had to get into the apartment.* In addition to the locked balcony door, there was one other route of entry to the apartment: a kitchen window, open but barred by a wrought-iron grate to keep out intruders. In the middle of the grate was a circular opening the size of a dinner plate, which my mother-in-law had designed so that she could pass food from the kitchen to the balcony when the family wanted to picnic outside. I studied the small opening. Could I possibly squirm through it? Not a chance; it was too small. "Do it anyway," an inner voice told me. "But I can't!" I argued back through hot tears. "Just climb in," the voice persisted. Which is what I did.

A few minutes after I landed on the kitchen counter, Leah woke up from her nap and cried out, "Mommy, Mommy." I rushed to the back bedroom calling, "Hi, honey, I'm right here." Then I lifted my baby out of the crib into my arms and held her close to my heart for a very long time.

And the Heart Grows

Over the years my ever-enlarging love for Leah enabled me to do more than squeeze through tight places. It inspired me to make the world a safer and kinder place for her—and, in small ways, for other children too. While living in Athens, I campaigned to have "Drive Slowly—Children at Play" street signs placed intermittently along our busy road. After moving to Boulder, Colorado, I worked hard to create playgrounds in our housing complex. When Leah entered elementary school, I got involved with the American Civil Liberties Union to ensure that the ideals of separation of church and state would be upheld during the Christmas season so that non-Christian children need never feel like outsiders in the classroom. Not surprisingly, my civic activities brought me in contact with many other conscientious parents, some of whom became good friends.

My growing heart also led me, along with my husband, to sponsor a young Muslim child in The Gambia—to furnish him and the other children in his village with some of the material gifts that would make their lives better. Perhaps writing books such as this one is the most significant outgrowth of my devotion as a mother. Convinced that the constancy of parental love and care can help cultivate creative and humane young people, strong enough to weather most any crisis, I want to reach out to other parents and affirm the importance of their involvement with their children.

From Darkness into Light

Fred Rogers, alias "Mr. Rogers," once said that in becoming a parent we have our biggest chance to change. While we nurture our children's growth, we can also nurture our own; parenthood gives us another crack at ourselves. As the child of parents who lived through the Holocaust, I grew up with the anticipation that my loved ones and I could never really be safe because something catastrophic might happen at any time. Of course, I tried to keep these dark thoughts to myself. The last thing I wanted to do was infect my children with fears of impending danger. But children are exquisitely aware of their parents' moods and sensibilities, however hard we may try to hide them. And at some point, it dawned on me that the best way to help Leah and Jonathan face the world bravely was for me to learn to become less afraid of it myself. Like the courageous Tibetan monk Milarepa, I resolved to put my head in the mouth of the monsters to free myself of them: I went into therapy; I visited the Yad Vashem Holocaust memorial in Jerusalem with Jonathan and the Holocaust Museum in Washington, D.C., with Leah; I sat through the film *Schindler's List* twice, once with my husband and friends and again with my mother. For my most recent birthday, Leah sent me the book *Holocaust Project: From Darkness into Light*, the artist Judy Chicago's study of concentration camps in her quest "to imagine the unimaginable." I, too, am trying to understand what I had always been afraid to know, to confront the horrors of my ancestral history instead of recoiling from them, to move from darkness into light.

David Luce, a Boulder-based holistic physician, tells me that people who live "out of their wounds" have difficulty healing; they continue in their victimhood. We human beings, he remarks, have the choice to dwell in fear or to dwell in joy. Being a mother, I want to pass on to my children a legacy of hope: the habit of seeing miracles everywhere and of living with a sense of wonderment. Toward this end, I am learning to cultivate the vision of miracles in myself.

I have always associated Leah with light. She is fair skinned, fair-haired; her eyes are golden brown. On her recent trip to Guatemala, Leah purchased a pewter fairy for me. The tiny fairy, which I fastened to a west-facing window, is encircled by a wreath of flowers that holds a hanging crystal. Catching the afternoon sunlight, the crystal makes rainbows that bounce off the walls, the carpet, my desk and chair. Sometimes I hold out my hand and let one of the rainbows nestle in it. Then I imagine my daughter. I see her smiling. I smile back. I feel the energy of my great love for her surge through my body. I am aglow with my own inner light.

Notes

The First Gift: Mother's Devotion

1. Paddy O'Brien, cited in *Around the Circle Gently: A Book of Birth, Families, and Life*, Lynn Moen and Judy Laik, eds. (Berkeley: Celestial Arts, 1995), p. 28.
2. "Moms with Tots at Risk in On-the-Job Injuries," *Denver Post*, February 28, 1995.
3. Cited in Moen and Laik, *Around the Circle Gently*, p. 59.
4. In research done in collaboration with Gene Glass, we found a strong, positive correlation between masculinity and mental health. Although androgyny (the combination of masculine and feminine traits) was also associated with higher levels of mental health than was femininity, it was the masculine component of androgyny, rather than the integration of femininity and masculinity, that accounted for this. We interpreted our findings to mean that in a society such as ours, which is partial to its masculine members, men and women with higher levels of masculinity will value themselves highly and demonstrate high self-esteem and psychological adjustment; however, men and

women with high levels of femininity, unrecognized by a society that favors ambition and achievement, may come to devalue themselves. See Evelyn Silten Bassoff and Gene Glass, "The Relationship Between Sex Roles and Mental Health: A Meta-Analysis of Twenty-Six Studies," *The Counseling Psychologist*, vol. 10, no. 4 (1982), pp. 105–112.

5. Robert A. Johnson, *Femininity Lost and Regained* (New York: Harper Perennial, 1990), p. 77.

6. Jessie Bernard, *The Future of Motherhood* (New York: Penguin, 1974), p. 115.

7. Naomi Ruth Lowinsky, *The Motherline: Every Woman's Journey to Find Her Roots* (New York: Jeremy P. Tarcher/Perigee, 1992), p. 26.

8. Cited in Alexandra Towle, ed., *Mothers* (New York: Simon & Schuster, 1988), p. 20.

9. D. W. Winnicott, *The Child, the Family, and the Outside World* (Reading, Mass.: Addison-Wesley, 1987), p. 11.

10. Cited in Moen and Laik, *Around the Circle Gently*, p. 30.

11. See Diane Eyer, *Mother-Infant Bonding: A Scientific Fiction* (New Haven: Yale University Press, 1992).

12. Hope Edelman, *Motherless Daughters: The Legacy of Loss* (Reading, Mass.: Addison-Wesley, 1994), p. 23.

13. "During the nineteenth century more than half the infants in their first year of life regularly died from a disease called 'marasmus,' a Greek word meaning 'wasting away'. . . . As late as the second decade of the twentieth century the death rate for infants under one year of age in various foundling institutions throughout the United States was nearly 100 percent! . . . It was not until after World War II, when studies were undertaken to discover the cause of marasmus, that it was found to occur quite often among babies in the 'best' homes, hospitals, and institutions. . . . What was wanting in the sterilized environment of the babies [in these institutions] was mother love. . . . What the child requires if it is to prosper, it was found, is to be handled, and carried, and caressed, and cuddled, and cooed to, even if it isn't breast-fed." From Ashley

Montagu, *Touching: The Significance of the Human Skin* (New York: Harper & Row, 1971), pp. 93–95.

14. Colette, *My Mother's House and Sido* (New York: Farrar, Straus, and Giroux, 1953), p. 29.

15. Sigmund Freud, 1938, cited in Robert Karen, *Becoming Attached* (New York: Warner Books, 1994), p. 95.

16. Carl G. Jung, "Analytic Psychology and 'veltanschaung': The Structure and Dynamics of the Psyche," *Collected Works*, vol. 8 (New York: Pantheon [Bollingen Series XX], 1960), pp. 373–74.

17. Colette, *My Mother's House and Sido*, p. 5.

18. Kathie Carlson, *In Her Image: The Unhealed Daughter's Search for Mother* (Boston: Shambala, 1989), p. 48.

19. Cited in Marshall Klaus and Phyllis Klaus, *The Amazing Newborn* (Reading, Mass.: Addison-Wesley, 1985), p. 52.

20. Anthony DeCasper and W. P. Fifer, "Of Human Bonding: Newborns Prefer Their Mother's Voices," *Science*, vol. 208 (1980), pp. 1174–76.

21. Martin E. P. Seligman, *Learned Optimism* (New York: Alfred A. Knopf, 1991), p. 128.

22. Fatima Mernissi, *Dreams of Trespass: Tales of a Harem Girlhood* (Reading, Mass.: Addison-Wesley, 1994), pp. 214–15.

23. D. W. Winnicott, *The Child, the Family, and the Outside World*, p. 24.

24. Heinrich Zimmer, *The King and the Corpse*, Joseph Campbell, ed. (New York: Pantheon, 1948), pp. 203–35. This story also appears in my book *Mothering Ourselves: Help and Healing for Adult Daughters* (New York: Dutton, 1991), pp. 52–53.

25. Cited in Moen and Laik, *Around the Circle Gently*, p. 52.

The Second Gift: Father's Care

1. See Victoria Secunda, *Women and their Fathers: The Sexual and Romantic Impact of the First Man in Your Life* (New York: Delta, 1992); Margo Maine, *Father Hunger: Fathers, Daughters, and Food* (Carlsbad, Calif.: Gurze Books, 1992).

2. Arthur Colman and Libby Colman, *The Father, Mythology, and Changing Roles* (Wilmette, Ill.: Chiron Press, 1988), pp. 149–50.

3. Richard Louv, *Father Love* (New York: Pocket Books, 1993), p. 3.

4. Jerrold Lee Shapiro "Letting Dads Be Dads," *Parents*, vol. 69, no. 6, June (1994), p. 165.

5. Louv, *Father Love*, p. 201.

6. Ibid.

7. Michael Yogman, "Observations on the Father-Infant Relationship," in *Father and Child*, S. Cath et al., eds. (Boston: Little Brown, 1982), pp. 101–22.

8. E. Abelin, "The Role of the Father in the Separation-Individuation Process," in *Separation-Individuation: Essays in Honor of Margaret S. Mahler*, J. McDevitt and C. Settlage, eds. (New York: International Universities Press, 1971), pp. 229–52.

9. Jeanne Elium and Don Elium, *Raising a Son: Parents and the Making of a Healthy Man* (Hillsboro, Ore.: Beyond Words Publishing, 1992), p. 77.

10. Cited in Maine, *Father Hunger*, p. 36.

11. Secunda, *Women and Their Fathers*, p. 107.

12. Karen Hill Anton, "Remembering a Father Who Mothered," in *Being a Father: Family, Work, and Self*, Anne Pederson and Peggy O'Mara, eds. (Santa Fe: John Muir, 1990), p. 129.

13. Louv, *Father Love*, p. 90.

14. Richard Koestner, Carol Franz, and Joel Weinberger, "The Family Origins of Empathic Concern: A 26-Year Longitudinal Study," *Journal of Personality and Social Psychology*, vol. 58 (1990), pp. 709–17.

15. Karen Hill Anton, "Remembering a Father Who Mothered," p. 131.

16. Vivian Gornick, *Fierce Attachments* (New York: Simon & Schuster, 1987), pp. 74–75.

17. See Maine, *Father Hunger*, p. 71.

18. Cited in Louv, *Father Love*, p. 95.

19. See Henry Biller, "The Father and Personality Development:

Paternal Deprivation and Sex-Role Development" in *The Role of the Father in Child Development*, Michael Lamb, ed. (New York: John Wiley & Sons, 1976), pp. 89–157.

20. Cited in Louv, *Father Love*, p. 116.

The Third Gift: Loving and Letting In

1. Carol Dunham, *Mamatoto: A Celebration of Birth* (New York: Penguin, 1991), p. 160.
2. Lucy Rose Fischer, *Linked Lives: Adult Daughters and Their Mothers* (New York: Harper & Row, 1986), p. 127.
3. Moen and Laik, *Around the Circle Gently*, p. 119.
4. Ibid.
5. Arthur Kornhaber, *Grandparent Power!* (New York: Crown Trade Paperbacks, 1994), p. 119.
6. Ibid., p. 69.
7. Cited in Moen and Laik, *Around the Circle Gently*, p. 116.

The Fourth Gift: Protectiveness

1. Sara Ruddick, *Maternal Thinking: Towards a Politics of Peace* (New York: Ballantine, 1989), p. 71.
2. Ibid., p. 72.
3. Cited in Towle, *Mothers*, p. 132.
4. Judith Viorst, *Necessary Losses: The Loves, Illusions, Dependencies, and Impossible Expectations That All of Us Have to Give Up in Order to Grow* (New York: Fawcett Gold Medal, 1986), p. 229.
5. See Ruddick on preservative love, *Maternal Thinking*, pp. 65–81.
6. Ellen Goodman, "There Are Risks in Teaching Children to Fear Strangers," *Daily Camera*, July 14, 1996, p. 2C.
7. Cited by Mary Sykes Wilie in "Swallowed Alive," *The Family Networker*, vol. 18, no. 5 (September–October 1994), p. 31.
8. Barbara Dafoe Whitehead, "The Failure of Sex Education," *The Atlantic Monthly*, October 1994, pp. 55–80; quote is on p. 68.

9. Joy Overbeck, "Sex Too Soon," *Parents*, September 1994, p. 42.

10. Social critic Barbara Dafoe Whitehead ("The Failure of Sex Education") notes that, by and large, sex-education programs in the schools have had little effect on teenagers' decisions to have sex or not; knowledge alone, in other words, does not seem to affect sexual behaviors. She points out that, as a rule, today's children are having sex considerably earlier than their parents did, with the greatest rise in sexual activity among younger teenagers.

11. Whitehead ("The Failure of Sex Education") reports that parent-child communication is far less important in influencing sexual behavior than parental discipline and supervision. Moreover, there is a strong relationship between diminished parental supervision and early sexual activity.

12. Mary Pipher, *Reviving Ophelia: Saving the Selves of Adolescent Girls* (New York: Ballantine, 1994), p. 208.

13. Brothers Grimm, "Briar Rose," in *Grimm's Fairy Tales*, translated by E. V. Lucas, Lucy Crane, and Marian Edwards (New York: Grosset & Dunlap, 1945).

14. It is not by fluke that Briar Rose pricks herself on a distaff. A distaff symbolizes femaleness. Although the word commonly refers to the rod on which flax or wool is wound, it also means women's work or women's concerns: the term "distaff side of the family," for instance, signifies maternal lineage.

15. Bruno Bettelheim, *The Uses of Enchantment: The Meaning and Importance of Fairy Tales* (New York: Vintage, 1977), p. 233, notes that the German name of the girl and the tale, "*Dornroschen*," emphasizes both the hedge of thorns and the hedge rose. In German, *Dornroschen—Roschen* is the diminutive form of Rose—stresses the girl's immaturity, which must be protected by the wall of thorns.

16. Ibid., p. 235.

The Fifth Gift: Limits and Boundaries

1. In *Between Mothers and Sons: The Making of Vital and Loving Men* (New York: Dutton, 1994) I describe in detail the development of boys, especially their psychological separation from the mother.
2. Bruno Bettelheim provides a detailed analysis of "The Fisherman and the Jinny" in *The Uses of Enchantment: The Meaning and Importance of Fairy Tales*, pp. 28–34.
3. Cited in Beth Mende Conny, *The Quotable Family* (unpublished manuscript), p. 42.
4. Cited in Pipher, *Reviving Ophelia*, p. 83.
5. In the poor families followed through the Minnesota Mother-Child Interaction Project, 70 percent of mothers who reported being abused in childhood were maltreating their children in some way. (Maltreatment is defined broadly in this study to include subtle forms of neglect and verbal abuse.) However, 30 percent of mothers had apparently broken the cycle of abuse and were taking good care of their children. The statistics tend to be more encouraging in samples of more privileged populations. Erickson cites a recent review in which only 30 percent of abused children went on to become abusive parents. From Martha Farrell Erickson, "How Often Do Abused Children Become Child Abusers?" *The Harvard Mental Health Letter*, vol. 8, no. 1 (July 1991) p. 8.

The Sixth Gift: Respect

1. Heinz Kohut, *How Does Analysis Cure?* (New York: International Universities Press, 1971), p. 143.
2. Cited in Carl Rogers, *On Becoming a Person* (Boston: Houghton Mifflin, 1961), p. 63.
3. Cited in Moen and Laik, *Around the Circle Gently*, p. 63.
4. Irene Claremont de Castillejo, *Knowing Woman: A Feminine Psychology* (New York: Harper Colophon Books, 1973), p. 29.

5. Deepak Chopra, *The Seven Spiritual Laws of Success* (San Raphael, Calif.: Amber-Allen/New World Library, 1994), pp. 95–97.
6. Daniel Stern, *The Interpersonal World of the Infant* (New York: Basic Books, 1985), p. 196.
7. Richard Geist, "Therapeutic Dilemmas in the Treatment of Anorexia Nervosa: A Self-Psychological Perspective," in *Theory and Treatment of Anorexia and Bulimia*, S. W. Emmett, ed. (New York: Bruner/Mazel, 1985), p. 272.
8. Cited in Rogers, *On Becoming a Person*, p. 110.
9. Ruddick, *Maternal Thinking*, p. 120.
10. Rogers, *On Becoming a Person*, p. 18.
11. Ibid., p. 63.
12. Nel Noddings, *Caring: A Feminine Approach to Ethics and Moral Education* (Berkeley: University of California Press, 1984), p. 59.
13. Isak Dinesen, *Letters from Africa, 1914–1931* (Chicago: University of Chicago Press, 1984), pp. 426–28.
14. *Starting Points: The Report of the Carnegie Task Force on Meeting the Needs of Young Children* (New York: Carnegie Corp., 1994), p. 8.
15. Cited in Moen and Laik, *Around the Circle Gently*, p. 58.

The Seventh Gift: Wholeness

1. Pauline Clance and Suzanne Imes, "The Imposter Phenomenon in High Achieving Women: Dynamics and Therapeutic Intervention," *Psychotherapy: Theory, Research, and Practice*, vol. 15 (1978), pp. 241–45.
2. Christina Hoff Sommers, a Clark University professor and author of *Who Stole Feminism?: How Women Have Betrayed Women* (New York: Simon & Schuster, 1994), documents the enormous progress girls and young women have made in recent years in the educational arena: in primary and secondary schools girls outnumber boys in all extracurricular activities except sports and hobby clubs. Almost twice as many girls as boys participate in student government, band, orchestra, drama,

and service clubs. More girls work on school newspapers and are members of honor and service societies. Although boys far outnumber girls in sports, that gap is narrowing each year: in 1972, only 4 percent of girls were in high school programs, whereas by 1987 the figure was up to 26 percent, more than a sixfold increase. On the 1990 National Assessment of Education Progress tests administered to seventeen-year-olds, males outperformed females by 3 points in math and 11 points in science; however, females outperformed males by 13 points in reading and 24 points in writing.

At the level of higher education, women are also making outstanding progress. Today 55 percent of college students are female. Additionally, the UCLA Higher Education Research Institute's annual survey of college freshmen shows a tripling in less than twenty-five years in the percentage of women aiming for higher degrees with more women (66 percent) than men (63 percent) planning to pursue advanced degrees. Although women are still behind men in earning doctorates, the U.S. Department of Education indicated that the number of doctorates awarded to women has increased by 185 percent since 1971. These statistics are truly remarkable indicators of social change.

3. *The AAUW Report: How Schools Shortchange Girls* reviewed over a thousand existing studies on the education of girls. In her book *Who Stole Feminism?*, Christina Hoff Sommers challenges the methodology of the report and a previous survey conducted by the AAUW (*Shortchanging Girls, Shortchanging America* [Washington, D. C.: American Association of University Women, 1990]). Hence, although the findings of the AAUW are provocative, they remain controversial.

4. It is particularly significant that women are underrepresented in these fields, since they are the "power" fields in which one is rewarded with high salaries and prestige.

5. Pipher, *Reviving Ophelia*, pp. 12–13.

6. Mernissi, *Dreams of Trespass: Tales of a Harem Girlhood*, p. 127.

7. Tillie Olsen, *Yonnondio, from the Thirties* (New York: Delta/ Seymour Lawrence, 1989).
8. Seligman, *Learned Optimism*, p. 128.
9. Mary Klinnert, Joseph Campos, and Robert Emde, "The Role of Maternal Facial Signaling on the Visual Cliff," *Developmental Psychology*, vol. 21 (1985), pp. 195–200.
10. Colette, *Sido*, p. 13.
11. Marianne Neifert, *Dr. Mom's Parenting Guide: Commonsense Guidance for the Life of Your Child* (New York: Dutton, 1991), p. 7.
12. Abraham Maslow, *The Farther Reaches of Human Nature* (New York: Penguin, 1971), p. 14.
13. Ibid., p. 15.
14. Barbara Kerr, *Smart Girls, Gifted Women* (Dayton: Ohio Psychology Press, 1985), p. 64.
15. Pipher, *Reviving Ophelia*, p. 244.
16. Sommers, *Who Stole Feminism?*, p. 102.
17. Ibid., p. 44.
18. Cited in Sommers, *Who Stole Feminism?*, p. 61.
19. Ibid., p. 59
20. Carol Gilligan, "Women's Place in Man's Life Cycle," *Harvard Educational Review*, vol. 49 (1979), p. 440.
21. Jeanne Elium and Don Elium, *Raising a Daughter: Parents and the Awakening of a Healthy Woman* (Berkeley: Celestial Arts, 1994), p. 7.
22. Ibid., p. 26.
23. Mernissi, *Dreams of Trespass*, p. 159.
24. Kyle Pruett, *The Nurturing Father* (New York: Warner Books, 1987).
25. Richard Koestner, Carol Franz, and Joel Weinberger, "The Family Origins of Empathic Concern: A 26-Year Longitudinal Study." *Journal of Personality and Social Psychology*, vol. 58 (1990), pp. 709–17.
26. Robert A. Johnson, *She: Understanding Feminine Psychology* (New York: Harper & Row, 1976), pp. 62–63.
27. Sommers, *Who Stole Feminism?*, pp. 155–56.

28. See Evelyn S. Bassoff, *Between Mothers and Sons: The Making of Vital and Loving Men* (New York: Dutton, 1994), p. 58.
29. Rainer Maria Rilke, *Letters to a Young Poet* (New York: W. W. Norton, 1934), p. 54.
30. Johnson, *Femininity Lost and Regained*, p. 97.

The Eighth Gift: Courage

1. Cited in Emanuel Hammer, "Artistic Creativity: Giftedness or Sickness," *The Arts in Psychotherapy*, vol. 2 (1975), p. 175.
2. Lesley Hazleton, *The Right to Feel Bad: Coping with Normal Depression* (New York: Ballantine, 1984), p. 240.
3. Dawna Markova, *No Enemies Within* (Berkeley: Conari Press, 1994), p. 3.
4. Cited in Moen and Laik, *Around the Circle Gently*, p. 51.
5. Winnicott, *The Child, the Family, and the Outside World*, p. 169.
6. May Sarton, *Writings on Writing* (Orono, Maine: Puckerbrush, 1980), p. 11.
7. Mernissi, *Dreams of Trespass*, p. 55.
8. Ibid., p. 147.
9. Ibid., p. 55.
10. Merlin Stone, *Ancient Mirrors of Womanhood: A Treasury of Goddess and Heroine Lore from Around the World* (Boston: Beacon Press, 1984), p. 292.
11. Hazleton, *The Right to Feel Bad*, p. 229.
12. Seligman, *Learned Optimism*, pp. 282–84.
13. Ellen Uzelac, "In a Daughter's Voice," *Common Boundary*, September–October (1995), p. 53.
14. In the course of passing stories orally, the stories necessarily change somewhat. I hope that my version of the story of the sweeper retains its original meaning despite the fact that certain details may have been altered.

The Ninth Gift: Roots

1. Julie Stafford, "Families Endured in Internment Camps," *Daily Camera*, February 19, 1995, p. 1C.
2. Susan C. Roberts, "Blood Sisters," *New Age Journal*, May–June 1994, p. 89.
3. Stone, *Ancient Mirrors of Womanhood*, pp. 78–79.
4. Ibid., p. 87.
5. Cited in Louv, *Father Love*, p. 202.
6. Ibid.
7. From Faye Moskowitz, *A Leak in the Heart: Tales from a Woman's Life* (Boston: David R. Godine, 1985); included in *Mothers: Memories, Dreams, and Reflections of Literary Daughters*, Susan Cahill, ed. (New York: New American Library, 1988), pp. 253–55.
8. Evan Imber-Black and Janine Roberts, *Rituals for Our Times: Celebrating, Healing, and Changing Our Lives and Our Relationships* (New York: HarperPerennial, 1993), p. 18.
9. Colin Turnbull, *The Human Cycle* (New York: Touchstone, 1983), pp. 33–34.
10. Leslie Marmon Silko, *Ceremony* (New York: Penguin, 1977), p. 2.
11. Imber-Black and Roberts, *Rituals for Our Times*, p. 26.
12. I discovered this story in Merlin Stone, *Ancient Mirrors of Womanhood*, pp. 309–12, and included a version of it in my book *Mothers and Daughters: Loving and Letting Go* (New York: New American Library, 1988), pp. 251–52.

The Tenth Gift: Wings

1. Alan Lightman, *Einstein's Dreams* (New York: Warner Books, 1993), pp. 71–72.
2. Cited in Mary Jane Moffat and Charlotte Painter, eds., *Revelations: Diaries of Women* (New York: Vintage Books, 1975), p. 239.

3. Judith Viorst, *Necessary Losses* (New York: Fawcett Gold Medal, 1986), p. 167.

4. M. Esther Harding, *The Parental Image: Its Injury and Reconstruction* (Boston: Sigo Press, 1993), pp. 22–23.

5. Charles Spezzano, *What to Do Between Birth and Death: The Art of Growing Up* (New York: William Morrow, 1992), p. 17.

6. Virginia Woolf, *To the Lighthouse* (New York: Harcourt Brace, 1927), p. 294.

7. Ibid., pp. 309–10.

8. Cited in *Mother to Daughter, Daughter to Mother*, Tillie Olsen, ed. (London: Virago Press, 1984), p. 11.

9. Paul Auster, "Why Write?" *The New Yorker*, December 25, 1995–January 1, 1996, p. 86.

10. Cited in Julius Segal, *Winning Life's Toughest Battles: Roots of Human Resilience* (New York: McGraw-Hill, 1986), p. 57.

11. Spezzano, *What to Do Between Birth and Death*, p. 89.

12. Excerpt from "That I not be a restless ghost" in Margaret Mead's *Blackberry Winter, My Early Years* (New York: William Morrow, 1972).

Bibliography

Auster, Paul. "Why Write?" *The New Yorker*, December 25, 1995–January 1, 1996, p. 86.

Bassoff, Evelyn. *Between Mothers and Sons: The Making of Vital and Loving Men.* New York: Dutton, 1994.

———. *Mothering Ourselves: Help and Healing for Adult Daughters.* New York: Dutton, 1991.

———. *Mothers and Daughters: Loving and Letting Go.* New York: New American Library, 1988.

Bassoff, Evelyn Silten, and Gene Glass. "The Relationship Between Sex Roles and Mental Health: A Meta-Analysis of Twenty-Six Studies," *The Counseling Psychologist*, vol. 10, no. 4 (1982), pp. 105–112.

Bernard, Jessie. *The Future of Motherhood.* New York: Penguin, 1974.

Bettelheim, Bruno. *The Uses of Enchantment: The Meaning and Importance of Fairy Tales.* New York: Vintage, 1977.

Bolen, Jean Shinoda. *Goddesses in Every Woman: A New Psychology of Women.* San Francisco: Harper & Row, 1984.

Cahill, Susan, ed. *Mothers: Memories, Dreams, and Reflections of Literary Daughters.* New York: New American Library, 1988.

Carlson, Kathie. *In Her Image: The Unhealed Daughter's Search for Mother.* Boston: Shambala, 1989.

Castellijo, Irene Claremont de. *Knowing Woman: A Feminine Psychology.* New York: Harper Colophon Books, 1973.

Cath, S., Gurwitt, A. and J. Ross, eds. *Father and Child: Developmental and Clinical Perspectives.* Boston: Little, Brown, 1982.

Chopra, Deepak. *The Seven Spiritual Laws of Success.* San Raphael, Calif.: Amber-Allen/New World Library, 1994.

Clance, Pauline, and Suzanne Imes. "The Imposter Phenomenon in High Achieving Women: Dynamics and Therapeutic Intervention," *Psychotherapy: Theory, Research, and Practice,* vol. 15 (1978), pp. 241–45.

Colette, *My Mother's House and Sido.* New York: Farrar, Straus and Giroux, 1953.

Colman, Arthur, and Libby Colman. *The Father, Mythology, and Changing Roles.* Wilmette, Ill.: Chiron Press, 1988.

DeCasper, Anthony, and W. P. Fifer. "Of Human Bonding: Newborns Prefer Their Mother's Voices," *Science,* vol. 208 (1980), pp. 1174–176.

Dinesen, Isak. *Letters from Africa, 1914–1931.* Chicago: University of Chicago Press, 1984.

Dowling, Colette. *The Cinderella Complex: Women's Hidden Fear of Independence.* New York: Pocket Books, 1981.

Dunham, Carol. *Mamatoto: A Celebration of Birth.* New York: Penguin, 1991.

Edelman, Hope. *Motherless Daughters: The Legacy of Loss.* Reading, Mass.: Addison-Wesley, 1994.

Elium, Jeanne, and Don Elium. *Raising a Daughter: Parents and the Awakening of a Healthy Woman.* Berkeley: Celestial Arts, 1994.

———. *Raising a Son: Parents and the Making of a Healthy Man.* Hillsboro, Ore.: Beyond Words Publishing, 1992.

Erickson, Martha Farrell. "How Often Do Abused Children Become Child Abusers?" *The Harvard Mental Health Letter,* vol. 8, no. 1 (July 1991) p. 8.

Eyer, Diane. *Mother-Infant Bonding: A Scientific Fiction.* New Haven: Yale University Press, 1992.

Fischer, Lucy Rose. *Linked Lives: Adult Daughters and Their Mothers.* New York: Harper & Row, 1986.

Geist, Richard. "Therapeutic Dilemmas in the Treatment of Anorexia Nervosa: A Self-Psychological Perspective," in *Theory and Treatment of Anorexia and Bulimia*, S. W. Emmett, ed. New York: Bruner/Mazel, 1985.

Gilligan, Carol. "Women's Place in Man's Life Cycle," *Harvard Educational Review*, vol. 49 (1979), p. 440.

Goodman, Ellen. "There Are Risks in Teaching Children to Fear Strangers," *Daily Camera*, July 14, 1996, p. 2C.

Gornick, Vivian. *Fierce Attachments.* New York: Simon & Schuster, 1987.

Grimm, Brothers. *Grimms' Fairy Tales.* Translated by E. V. Lucas, Lucy Crane, and Marian Edwards. New York: Grosset & Dunlap, 1945.

Hammer, Emanuel. "Artistic Creativity: Giftedness or Sickness," *The Arts in Psychotherapy.* vol. 2 (1975), p. 175.

Harding, M. Esther. *The Parental Image: Its Injury and Reconstruction.* Boston: Sigo Press, 1993.

Hazleton, Lesley. *The Right to Feel Bad: Coping with Normal Depression.* New York: Ballantine, 1984.

Imber-Black, Evan, and Janine Roberts. *Rituals for Our Times: Celebrating, Healing, and Changing Our Lives and Our Relationships.* New York: HarperPerennial, 1993.

Johnson, Robert A. *Femininity Lost and Regained.* New York: HarperPerennial, 1990.

———. *She: Understanding Feminine Psychology.* New York: Harper & Row, 1976.

Jung, Carl G. "Analytic Psychology and 'Veltanschaung': The Structure and Dynamics of the Psyche." *Collected Works*, vol. 8. New York: Pantheon, Bollingen Series XX, 1960.

Karen, Robert. *Becoming Attached.* New York: Warner Books, 1994.

Kerr, Barbara. *Smart Girls, Gifted Women.* Dayton: Ohio Psychology Press, 1985.

Klaus, Marshall, and Phyllis Klaus. *The Amazing Newborn.* Reading, Mass.: Addison-Wesley, 1985.

Klinnert, Mary, Joseph Campos, and Robert Emde. "The Role of Maternal Facial Signaling on the Visual Cliff," *Developmental Psychology*, vol. 21 (1985), pp. 195–200.

Koestner, Richard, Carol Franz, and Joel Weinberger. "The Family Origins of Empathic Concern: A 26-Year Longitudinal Study," *Journal of Personality and Social Psychology*, vol. 58 (1990), pp. 709–17.

Kohut, Heinz. *How Does Analysis Cure?* New York: International Universities Press, 1971.

Kornhaber, Arthur. *Grandparent Power!* New York: Crown Trade Paperbacks, 1994.

Lamb, Michael, ed. *The Role of the Father in Child Development.* New York: John Wiley & Sons, 1976.

Lightman, Alan. *Einstein's Dreams.* New York: Warner Books, 1993.

Louv, Richard. *Father Love.* New York: Pocket Books, 1993.

Lowinsky, Naomi Ruth. *The Motherline: Every Woman's Journey to Find Her Roots.* New York: Jeremy P. Tarcher/Perigee, 1992.

Maine, Margo. *Father Hunger: Fathers, Daughters, and Food.* Carlsbad, Calif.: Gurze Books, 1992.

Markova, Dawna. *No Enemies Within.* Berkeley: Conari Press, 1994.

Maslow, Abraham. *The Farther Reaches of Human Nature.* New York: Penguin, 1971.

McDevitt, J., and C. Settlage, eds. *Separation-Individuation: Essays in Honor of Margaret S. Mahler.* New York: International Universities Press, 1971.

Mead, Margaret. *Blackberry Winter, My Early Years.* New York: William Morrow, 1972.

Mernissi, Fatima. *Dreams of Trespass: Tales of a Harem Girlhood.* Reading, Mass.: Addison-Wesley, 1994.

Moen, Lynn, and Judy Laik, eds. *Around the Circle Gently: A Book of Birth, Families, and Life.* Berkeley: Celestial Arts, 1995.

Moffat, Mary Jane, and Charlotte Painter, eds. *Revelations: Diaries of Women.* New York: Vintage Books, 1975.

Montagu, Ashley. *Touching: The Significance of the Human Skin.* New York: Harper & Row, 1971.

Moskowitz, Faye. *A Leak in the Heart: Tales from a Woman's Life.* Boston: David R. Godine, 1985.

Neifert, Marianne. *Dr. Mom's Parenting Guide: Commonsense Guidance for the Life of Your Child.* New York: Dutton, 1991.

Noddings, Nel. *Caring: A Feminine Approach to Ethics and Moral Education.* Berkeley: University of California, 1984.

Olsen, Tillie, ed. *Mother to Daughter, Daughter to Mother.* London: Virago Press, 1984.

———. *Yonnondio, from the Thirties.* New York: Delta/Seymour Lawrence, 1989.

Overbeck, Joy. "Sex Too Soon," *Parents,* September 1994, p. 42.

Pederson, Anne, and Peggy O'Mara, eds. *Being a Father: Family, Work, and Self.* Santa Fe: John Muir, 1990.

Perrine, Laurence, ed. *Sound and Sense.* New York: Harcourt Brace Jovanovich, 1977.

Pipher, Mary. *Reviving Ophelia: Saving the Selves of Adolescent Girls.* New York: Ballantine, 1994.

Pruett, Kyle. *The Nurturing Father.* New York: Warner Books, 1987.

Rilke, Rainer Maria. *Letters to a Young Poet.* New York: W. W. Norton, 1934.

Roberts, Susan C. "Blood Sisters," *New Age Journal,* May–June 1994, p. 89.

Rogers, Carl. *On Becoming a Person.* Boston: Houghton Mifflin, 1961.

Ruddick, Sara. *Maternal Thinking: Towards a Politics of Peace.* New York: Ballantine, 1989.

Sarton, May. *Writings on Writing.* Orono, Maine: Puckerbrush, 1980.

Secunda, Victoria. *Women and their Fathers: The Sexual and Romantic Impact of the First Man in Your Life.* New York: Delta, 1992.

Segal, Julius. *Winning Life's Toughest Battles: Roots of Human Resilience.* New York: McGraw-Hill, 1986.

Seligman, Martin E. P. *Learned Optimism.* New York: Alfred A. Knopf, 1991.

Shapiro, Jerrold Lee. "Letting Dads Be Dads," *Parents,* vol. 69, no. 6, June (1994), p. 165.

Shortchanging Girls, Shortchanging America. Washington, D. C.: American Association of University Women, 1990.

Silko, Leslie Marmon. *Ceremony.* New York: Penguin, 1977.

Sommers, Cristina Hoff. *Who Stole Feminism?: How Women Have Betrayed Women.* New York: Simon & Schuster, 1994.

Spezzano, Charles. *What to Do Between Birth and Death: The Art of Growing Up.* New York: William Morrow, 1992.

Stafford, Julie. "Families Endured in Internment Camps," *Daily Camera,* February 19, 1995, p. 1C.

Stern, Daniel. *The Interpersonal World of the Infant.* New York: Basic Books, 1985.

Stone, Merlin. *Ancient Mirrors of Womanhood: A Treasury of Goddess and Heroine Lore from Around the World.* Boston: Beacon Press, 1984.

Towle, Alexandra, ed. *Mothers.* New York: Simon & Schuster, 1988.

Turnball, Colin. *The Human Cycle.* New York: Touchstone, 1983.

Uzelac, Ellen. "In a Daughter's Voice," *Common Boundary,* September–October (1995), p. 53.

Viorst, Judith. *Necessary Losses: The Loves, Illusions, Dependencies, and Impossible Expectations That All of Us Have to Give Up in Order to Grow.* New York: Fawcett Gold Medal, 1986.

Whitehead, Barbara Dafoe. "The Failure of Sex Education," *The Atlantic Monthly,* October (1994), pp. 55–80.

Wilie, Mary Sykes. "Swallowed Alive," *The Family Networker,* vol. 18, no. 5, September–October (1994), p. 31.

Winnicott, D. W. *The Child, the Family, and the Outside World.* Reading, Mass.: Addison-Wesley, 1987.

Woolf, Virginia. *To the Lighthouse.* New York: Harcourt Brace, 1927.

Zimmer, Heinrich. *The King and the Corpse.* Joseph Campbell, ed. New York: Pantheon, 1948.

Index